MARY BERRY'S
BAKING BIBLE

MARY BERRY'S

BAKING BIBLE

FULLY UPDATED WITH OVER 250
NEW AND CLASSIC RECIPES

BOOKS

CONTENTS

INTRODUCTION
AND
TECHNIQUES

INTRODUCTION

When I published my first major baking book, *Ultimate Cake Book*, in 1994, it was with the hope that it would encourage more people to take up homebaking, and show inexperienced cooks that cake making isn't as complicated as it might first appear. The success of that book has been tremendous and I have been touched by how many people still rely on it even now, nearly thirty years later!

In 2003, as I wrote the introduction for the revised edition of the *Ultimate Cake Book*, I remember marvelling at the continuing demand for cake-making instruction. Now, it seems, people are turning to homebaking even more since the success of *The Great British Bake Off!*

In light of this increased interest in homebaking, I felt it was time to create a new complete book of baking – my Baking Bible. This is a new edition of *The Baking Bible* to include right up-to-date favourites – such as a glorious **Red Velvet Cake**, **Rainbow Cake**, **Quick Sourdough Loaf** and **Flatbreads**. I hope this book will inspire a new generation of cooks as well as prove useful to seasoned bakers.

The aim was to produce an easy-to-use baking collection to satisfy all your baking needs. I have included a bread section, containing my new bread recipes. There are some unusual cakes to try, like **Courgette Loaves**, and recipes for favourites, such as **Cupcakes**. But as this is a 'baking bible' I have tried to include as many classic recipes as possible. There are lots of traditional celebration cakes for occasions such as Easter, Christmas and christenings, birthdays and weddings, and some well-known favourites like **Victoria Sponge** and **Chocolate Chip Cookies**.

I've included lots of simple recipes for children to make (with supervision), and some more challenging recipes that require careful timing, and more skill, including patisserie-style desserts, such as **Gâteau Saint Honoré**. Cooks of all levels of experience should find something to make and to challenge them here. Since I first started writing recipes, the equipment available has evolved and improved enormously. Now we have reliable ovens with fan assistance, food processors and electric whisks, non-stick tins and trays, and bread makers. With the help of these aids, baking has become quick, easy and stress-free. All you need is to weigh and measure your ingredients very carefully and follow the tested step-by-step instructions.

I have tried to include recipes for all occasions and I hope you will find plenty of bakes to suit your tastes. But, most of all, I hope that this new collection of my favourite and trusted recipes will help you enjoy homebaking. Cakes are made to be shared so, once you have mastered a recipe, invite your friends and family to enjoy the fruits of your labour with a good pot of tea – happy baking!

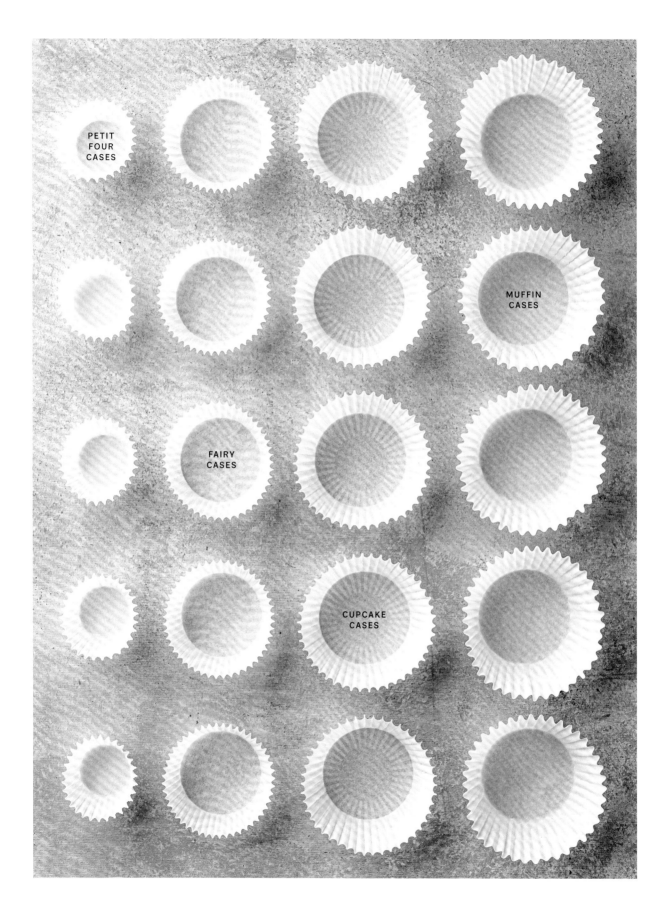

PETIT
FOUR
CASES

MUFFIN
CASES

FAIRY
CASES

CUPCAKE
CASES

BAKING EQUIPMENT

Some people may be put off from baking because they think it requires lots of expensive utensils, but this really isn't the case. Although electric-powered equipment saves time and effort, it's not essential and many of the recipes in this book, such as the traybakes, Victoria sponges, cookies and biscuits, require little more than a set of scales, a wooden spoon to beat the ingredients, a mixing bowl and a cake tin or baking tray, as they use the 'all-in-one' technique. A lot of the equipment you will probably have already, and some you can improvise. If you are buying new equipment, do buy the best you can afford; good-quality baking equipment will last a long time so it will be a worthwhile investment.

MEASURES
You will need a set of measuring spoons including a teaspoon, ½ teaspoon, ¼ teaspoon, tablespoon and dessert spoon. All the amounts given in these recipes are for level spoonfuls unless otherwise stated. To measure liquids, use a transparent heatproof jug that shows both metric and Imperial measures.

SCALES
One piece of equipment that is critical to achieving the perfect bake are measuring scales. Some people prefer old-fashioned balance scales with weights, but they take up a lot of space. Spring balance scales are fine for large amounts but are not accurate for small quantities. There are now a number of very reliable electric and battery-operated digital scales that can measure weights and volumes in metric, Imperial and liquids. Test the scales for accuracy by putting something on them that has the weight printed on it, such as an unopened bag of flour or sugar.

SPOONS
A wooden spoon is vital, but it should have a rounded edge to get into all the bends of the bowl. A large metal spoon for mixing egg whites into a mixture is useful, as its sharper edges flatten the egg foam much less than a wooden spoon does. Use a bendy, rubber or silicone spatula to get all the cake mixture off the sides of the bowl.

WHISKS
Use a balloon whisk or a hand-held electric whisk. It's useful to have two sizes of balloon whisk: a large one for whisking eggs and a small spiral one for small amounts of mixture.

MIXING BOWLS
I have a range of different sized bowls that fit inside each other for easy storage. If you are baking for the first time, invest in one large and one small, preferably Pyrex, mixing bowl with a rounded base so you can get to every bit of mixture with your whisk, spoon or spatula. For all-in-one cakes you will need only one bowl, but it's useful to have at least two as some recipes require you, for example, to whisk egg white separately, then add it to the rest of the mixed cake ingredients.

FOOD MIXERS

A free-standing mixer is not essential but saves time and effort! Choose one that comes with a range of attachments so you can use it to beat and cream cake mixture, knead bread dough, whisk egg white and whip cream. Free-standing table mixers are good for large cakes and are easy to clean but do take up a lot of room. Alternatively, you can use a hand-held electric mixer. I find that I only use the beating and whisking attachments. The great advantage is that hand mixers are inexpensive and they save time, too.

FOOD PROCESSORS

These useful time-saving machines can easily overmix a mixture so take care – if you don't keep a careful eye on them, they can chop nuts and fruit to nothing. It is best to fold in such ingredients by hand. Processors don't get air into the mixture in the same way as food mixers do as they combine ingredients rather than beat them, thus are not suitable for making meringues and fatless sponges.

TINS

Good-quality, solid cake tins will last you a lifetime. Cheap cake tins can be very thin, may warp with use and do not conduct heat evenly. Choosing the right-sized tin for the recipe is crucial to successful baking and particularly critical in sponge making; if the tin is too shallow the cake will spill over the top of the tin as it rises, whereas a tin that is too large will produce a pale, flat-looking cake. I've included a list of all the tins used in this book (right). If you are a first-time baker, don't be put off by the long list! Start off by buying two 18cm (7in) or 20cm (8in) loose-bottomed sandwich tins to make a variety of round cakes; a 30 x 23cm (12 x 9in) traybake tin (if your roasting tin is not the right size); a 450g (1lb) loaf tin; a 900g

(2lb) loaf tin; and a 12-hole muffin tin. As you bake more frequently, add the other tins listed to your collection. Non-stick tins are easier to clean, but it is safer to follow the greasing and lining instructions in the recipes and not to rely solely on their non-stick properties. Choose black-lined tins as they conduct heat more effectively. Avoid tins with thick, insulated bases. They're designed to prevent cakes from burning on the bottom, but they prevent the cake from cooking evenly in most modern ovens.

BAKING TRAYS

Ideally have at least three baking trays. They should be flat, rigid and heavy. Check that they fit inside your oven!

CAKE TINS FOR KEEN BAKERS

deep (4cm/1½in) round cake tins: 15cm (6in), 18cm (7in), 20cm (8in), 23cm (9in), 30cm (12in)
deep (4cm/1½in) loose-bottomed or springform sandwich tins: 18cm (7in), 20cm (8in), 23cm (9in), 25cm (10in)
deep (4cm/1½in) square cake tin: 18cm (7in)
deep (4cm/1½in) traybake or roasting tin: 30 x 23cm (12 x 9in)
square cake tin: 18cm (7in)
square ovenproof baking dish: 28cm (11in)
Swiss roll tin: 33 x 23cm (13 x 9in)
loaf tins: 450g (1lb), 900g (2lb)
deep (5cm/2in) loose-bottomed fluted flan tins: 18cm (7in), 20cm (8in), 23cm (9in), 25cm (10in)
deep (5cm/2in) ovenproof dish: 18 x 23cm (7 x 9in), 18 x 27cm (7 x 10½in)
12-hole muffin tin
12-hole bun tin
12-hole mini muffin tin
ring mould: 1.75 litres (3 pints)
1 French madeleine tray
10 dariol moulds
shallow pie dish: 900ml (1½ pints)
shallow ovenproof dish: 900ml (1½ pints), 1.5 litre (2½ pints)
4 pudding basins: 175ml (6fl oz)
4 individual soufflé dishes or 1 large soufflé dish: 225 ml (8fl oz) or 1.2 litres (2 pints)

BAKING PAPER

A useful cake-making aid that has evolved over time. The baking paper used in this book is non-stick silicone paper, which doesn't require greasing. It comes in a variety of sizes and shapes to make lining tins and trays easy.

If you're using greaseproof paper, you must grease the tin and then the paper (after you've lined the tin).

Also available are tin-liner sheets. They are reusable, tough and come in a variety of tin sizes. They lift off easily and just need to be washed, dried and kept flat when stored.

Most recipes only require the base of the tin to be lined, some the sides and base, so I include here instructions for lining the most frequently used tin shapes in this cookbook.

To line the base of a round cake tin

Using baking paper from a roll, place the base of the tin on the baking paper, draw around it in pencil, then cut out just inside the pencil line. Or you can buy circles of paper in sizes to fit cake tins.

To line the sides of a round cake tin

Cut a strip (or two strips if necessary) of baking paper to reach around the tin and a little extra to overlap the ends. The strip(s) should be about 5cm (2in) wider than the depth of the tin. Fold the bottom edge of the strip up by about 2.5cm (1in), creasing it firmly. Open out the fold and cut slanting lines into the folded paper at about 2.5cm (1in) intervals. Fit the strip(s) around the greased tin (greasing the tin helps to make the lining stick to it). The snipped edge will help the paper fit snugly around the base of any shaped tin. Fit the base paper over the cut part of the side strips, then grease well with a pastry brush.

To line a Swiss roll tin

Place the tin on the baking paper and cut a rectangle about 5cm (2in) bigger than the tin. Snip each corner then press the paper on to the greased tin, folding up the edges to create a paper basket.

To line a loaf tin

Cut a piece of baking paper to fit the widest sides and over the base of the tin with about 5cm (2in) overhang. Press the paper into the greased tin. You do not need to line the ends of the tin, just loosen the cake with a palette knife before turning out.

To line a traybake or roasting tin

Follow the method for lining a Swiss roll tin, or mould aluminium foil into the tin and grease well.

GRIDDLE

Used in this book to make Drop Scones and Singin' Hinny. If you don't have a griddle pan, use a heavy-based, non-stick frying pan instead.

WIRE COOLING RACKS

To cool cakes once they have been baked; they allow air to pass under the cakes or cookies as they cool. If you don't have a wire rack, you can use the rack from a grill pan.

KNIVES

A palette knife has a flexible blade with a rounded end, making it the best tool for spreading and smoothing cake mixture into tins or icing on to cakes. Use one to lift biscuits off baking trays or loosen a cake from the sides of the tin before turning it out on to the wire rack. A fish slice is also good for lifting out traybakes and lifting biscuits off baking trays. For recipes in which the cake is cut into layers, use a long, sharp serrated knife for the cleanest finish.

SIEVE
For sifting flour and icing sugar, and pressing through jam glazes to remove the seeds and solid fruit. Strong stainless steel sieves are good as they come in a variety of sizes and can be put in the dishwasher (wire sieves can become misshapen).

CAKE SKEWER
A long, thin metal skewer is indispensable for testing cooked cakes. Insert it into the centre of the cake, where the mixture is at its most dense. If it comes out clean, the cake is ready. Use a skewer that has flat sides.

ICING SUGAR SHAKER
A canister that has either a fine mesh sieve lid or a lid with tiny holes in. A shaker is ideal for finishing the top of a sponge or tart with a dusting of icing sugar.

ROLLING PIN
For making pastry I find a long wooden rolling pin with no handles is best.

SILICONE FLEXIBLE SPATULAS
For getting the last of the cake mixture out of the bowl.

PASTRY BRUSH
Use a pastry brush for greasing tins and glazing tarts with jam or uncooked scones with milk.

BAKING BEANS
Use ceramic or metal baking beans when a recipe calls for pastry to be baked blind (see opposite for definition). You can also use uncooked dried pasta or pulses.

CAKE SMOOTHER
To make the icing on top and the sides of cakes smooth.

CUTTERS
For biscuits, cookies and scones. Keep a set of plain and fluted round cutters in a range of sizes, and some fun-shaped cutters to make novelty biscuits such as gingerbread men. The most useful sizes of round cutters are 5cm (2in) and 7.5cm (3in). Metal cutters are best but make sure they are thoroughly dry before storing them. If you don't have cutters, use the rim of an appropriately sized glass.

CAKE TURNTABLE
Will help to give a smoother and more even finish when icing cakes.

ICING NOZZLES
I have a box of metal icing nozzles of all sizes, but for the recipes in this book you only need 5mm (¼in) and 1cm (½in) plain nozzles and a large and medium star nozzle. Nozzles can be plastic or metal, and are fitted to a piping bag.

PIPING BAG
Used for decorating cakes with icing and whipped cream. A nylon piping bag is good as it is easily washable. You can make your own piping bag by slotting one small plastic food bag inside another, then snipping off the corners at one point. You can also buy disposable piping bags from cook shops.

DIGITAL THERMOMETER
For sugar syrups and tempering chocolate.

BAKING TERMINOLOGY

Cooking techniques can be confusing as the invention of new technology means that old baking techniques like creaming and beating can be done in more than one way. You will find the following terminology in the book, so I include some short explanations of what they mean.

ALL-IN-ONE METHOD
The easiest cake-making method, suitable for most cakes and traybakes. Measure all the ingredients into a mixing bowl and beat with a free-standing or hand-held mixer or food processor. I find baking spread in a tub, straight from the fridge, gives very good results. (Do not use low-fat spreads as they contain added liquid, which gives a poor result.) If using butter, make sure it is softened.

BAKING BLIND
A method of cooking pastry before the filling is added, it results in the pastry being really crisp. To bake blind, preheat the oven to 200°C/Fan 180°C/Gas 6. Line the flan tin with the pastry, cover with baking paper and fill with ceramic or metal baking beans (or old dried pasta or pulses). Bake for 10–15 minutes. Remove the paper and beans and bake for a further 5 minutes to dry the pastry completely. Remove from the oven and add the chosen filling.

BEAT
In cake making, this can be done either with a wooden spoon or with a free-standing or hand-held food mixer. Beat cake ingredients until they are well blended, but be careful not to over-beat in a machine. It should take a couple of minutes to beat cake mixture until smooth. Beat an egg with a metal fork, breaking up the yolk and blending it into the egg white.

COMBINE (OR MIX)
Mixing ingredients that don't require as much air to be added, such as biscuits. Use a wooden spoon or food processor to do this.

CREAMING METHOD
The beating of butter and sugar together until the mixture turns light and creamy. Cream with either a wooden spoon or food mixer until the colour of the butter and sugar lightens and the texture is fluffy. This is not needed for cakes that can be made with the all-in-one method.

CRIMP
Used in pastry and pie making, it means to press the moistened pastry edges together to seal. You can do this with a finger, the handle of a knife or a fork.

DUST
To sprinkle a fine coating of icing sugar, cocoa powder or flour over a cake or bread using a sieve or sugar shaker.

FOLD
A technique used to keep plenty of air in a cake mixture when adding ingredients such as sifted flour or whisked egg whites. Use a metal spoon or spatula to carefully mix the

ingredients, folding the mixture at the edges over into the centre of the bowl and cutting through the middle until the mixture is evenly combined.

GREASE
Using kitchen paper, cover the insides of the cake tin with a layer of butter or baking spread to prevent the cake mixture from sticking as it cooks. You don't need to grease and line a tin if you are baking pastry as there is enough fat in the dough to prevent it from sticking.

KNEAD
Essential in most bread making, this can be done by hand or with a food mixer fitted with a dough hook. It is the act of mixing together the ingredients to form a smooth, elastic dough. It warms and stretches the dough so that, as the bread bakes, it retains air pockets. If the dough is not kneaded enough, the bread will be dense and heavy.

KNOCK BACK (OR PUNCH DOWN)
Similar to kneading, this is done after proving to get rid of any large air pockets in the dough before it is baked.

LINE
Lining a tin with baking paper to prevent the cake from sticking and ease its removal from the tin after baking. Some cakes require both the base and sides of the tin to be lined, others just the base. Due to the high-fat and low-sugar content in pastry, it does not require the tin to be lined (see note on baking paper on page 13 for instructions on lining tins).

MELTING
Usually golden syrup or black treacle is melted with sugar and fat in a pan, then the other ingredients are added and combined. The mixture is then poured into the tin.

PROVE
After bread dough has been kneaded, it is covered in oiled clingfilm and left in a warm place to allow the yeast to convert the glucose and other carbohydrates into carbon dioxide, causing the dough to rise. It also creates alcohol, giving the dough its flavour. The dough should double in size.

RUBBING IN
I use this method for scones and pastry. Dice the fat and then rub into the flour with your fingertips, or with an electric mixer or food processor, until the mixture resembles fine breadcrumbs.

WHISK (OR WHIP)
This can be done by hand with a balloon whisk, with a hand-held electric whisk or with a food processor. Most often used to describe the whipping of double cream or egg whites to a stiff consistency.

KEY INGREDIENTS

The ingredients listed here are those used most frequently in the book. I think it's useful to know what role each has in the baking process, to help you choose the right type of ingredients for the recipe you are following.

BUTTER AND BAKING SPREAD

For many of the recipes in this book, such as biscuits, shortbread and Genovese sponges, I have used butter. I tend to use salted or lightly salted butter, but you can use whichever you prefer – unsalted works just as well. It's important for the butter to be at the right temperature and consistency before adding it to the mixture.

In cake making, I have used the all-in-one method using chilled baking spread. If you use butter instead, it needs to be softened but not melted before creaming. If you have time, leave the butter at room temperature for at least 30 minutes before using. Even then, it is better to cream the butter on its own to soften it before adding the sugar. Use softened butter for all-in-one cake methods, too.

My own trick to bring refrigerated butter to the right temperature is to cut it into cubes and put them into a bowl of cool/lukewarm tap water (approx. 28°C). Leave for 10 minutes or until a butter cube can be easily compressed. Drain off the water, then the soft butter is ready to use.

If rubbing into pastry, cut cold butter into pieces or grate it into the flour.

It is not always necessary to use butter in baking, unless you specifically require a buttery flavour. Baking spreads have replaced margarines on the domestic market and are more economical than butter. You can use them in any of the recipes here if you prefer; however, I would advise that recipes without heavy flavourings, such as **Fork Biscuits** (page 218) and **The Very Best Shortbread** (page 210) should be made with butter as the buttery flavour is important.

Be careful that you do buy baking spreads that specify they are suitable for baking. Low-fat spreads are not suitable because of their high water content. Baking spreads should be used straight from the fridge.

Some recipes call for lard, white vegetable fat or oil. Cakes made with oil are very easy to bake, and tend to be very moist, but they do need a little extra raising agent in the form of either baking powder or whisked egg whites to prevent heaviness. Choose an oil with as little flavour as possible, such as sunflower or vegetable oil.

FLOURS AND RAISING AGENTS

There are a variety of different flours with different properties for baking. The main distinction is the amount of gluten each contains, and some also have an added raising agent. It's important to use the type of flour stated in the recipe, as the wrong flour will affect drastically the texture and appearance of the cake, pastry or bread. Keep an eye on the use-by date on flours, they do deteriorate over time. Flours, porridge oats and semolina should all be used within four months once the bags or packets have been opened.

In theory, you should always sift flour when baking, particularly cakes, to lighten the flour by incorporating air. Although I have to admit that I rarely sift flour! The only time I do is when I am folding it into a whisked, fatless sponge, when the sifting helps to combine the flour evenly into the mix.

PLAIN AND SELF-RAISING FLOUR

For making cakes, you need to use flour with a low gluten content. It is more starchy and so absorbs the fat well, giving a lighter texture. As the name suggests, self-raising flour contains an added raising agent and so is the most frequently used flour in cake making.

For recipes that do not require the bake to rise (usually biscuits and pastries), plain flour is used. You can also buy wholemeal plain and self-raising flour, which I have used in fruit recipes like **Jane's Fruit Cake** (page 72) and my **Classic Sticky Gingerbread** (page 70).

Wholemeal flour has not had the bran and germ extracted, which gives it a coarser texture that complements dense fruit like currants and raisins, and cooked stone fruits, like apples, plums and apricots, very well.

BREAD FLOURS

When making bread, it is important to use the correct flour. The two main bread flours used in this book are strong white flour and strong wholemeal flour. These are plain flours that have a higher proportion of the protein that forms gluten when mixed with water. This creates air pockets that cause the bread to rise.

I have also used a granary flour to make **Quick Granary Rolls** (page 286). The name

of these flours does vary between brands and they are not always clearly labelled as bread-making flours, so double check that you are buying the right flour!

OTHER FLOURS

I have used other types of flour, including semolina, cornflour and rice flour. These give a crunchier texture that works well in shortbread. I have also used potato flour and buckwheat flour, which has a stronger flavour that is delicious in my **Courgette Loaves** (page 318).

BAKING POWDER

This raising agent is the most commonly added to cake mixture. It consists of an acid (usually cream of tartar) and an alkali (bicarbonate of soda) mixed with a dried starch or flour. When liquid is added the chemicals react, producing carbon dioxide that expands during baking, making the cake rise. Beware, if you add too much baking powder the cake will rise at first and then collapse! Baking powders these days are slow acting, which means it is not a disaster if you make a cake but can't put it in the oven straight away. When making scones or rock cakes, I add extra baking powder to self-raising flour for a good rise.

YEAST

The raising agent used in bread making. I use fast-action yeast, which is a dried yeast that comes in helpful 7g sachets. It's easy to use – simply mix it with the flour and then add the liquid. If you use ordinary dried yeast, follow the manufacturer's instructions when adding liquid. It will require a more lengthy process.

CREAM OF TARTAR

Cream of tartar is not used as a raising agent on its own, but it can be mixed with bicarbonate of soda as the acid ingredient in baking powder.

BICARBONATE OF SODA

Also known as baking soda, this raising agent has a bitter flavour so is best used in recipes with strong flavours, such as gingerbread. It is most effective in recipes where there are natural acids present in the ingredients such as black treacle, lemon juice or buttermilk.

READY-MADE PASTRY

Don't feel guilty about using bought pastry, if you're short of time. There are a number of very good, butter-based pastries to buy now. They can be found in either the refrigerated or frozen sections in the supermarket.

SUGARS

In my cakes, I prefer to use unrefined sugars, such as golden caster and granulated sugar as they have more flavour, but do experiment with the wide range of sugars and sweeteners now available. The only time I would use white caster sugar is for meringues as it makes them really white.

CASTER SUGAR

Most commonly used in cake making, especially for whisked sponges, creamed mixtures and meringues, as its small, regular grains ensure that it blends smoothly, giving an even texture. You can make vanilla sugar by adding two or three vanilla pods to a jar of caster sugar. Leave for two weeks to allow the vanilla to infuse. You can refill the jar as you use the sugar.

GRANULATED SUGAR

This has a coarser texture than caster sugar and is best used in melting and rubbed-in methods. If used in a creamed mixture, it will give a slightly gritty texture and speckled appearance, and will reduce the volume of the cake.

ICING SUGAR

Not generally used in cake mixtures as it will create a hard crust and reduce the volume of the cake. It's most frequently used to make glacé icing and to dust cooked bakes before serving.

MUSCOVADO SUGAR

Made from raw cane sugar, the colour and flavour vary with the molasses content. Light muscovado sugar can be used to make many cakes as it creams well. It is natural, so I prefer it to soft brown sugar. Use it for brown sugar meringues, using half light muscovado and half caster sugar. Dark muscovado sugar can be overpowering but works well in gingerbreads and rich fruit cakes. To prevent muscovado sugar going damp, put a sheet of kitchen paper in the bag or jar and seal.

DEMERARA SUGAR

This is traditionally unrefined, but it has a lower molasses content than muscovado sugar. It is best suited to cakes made with the melting method to dissolve its large crystals, and to being sprinkled on top of cakes or added to cheesecake bases for extra crunch.

NIBBED SUGAR

'Nibbed' is an old-fashioned term meaning coarsely chopped. Nibs are the rough-shaped 'shavings' formed when sugar cubes are cut. I use it to top cakes before baking, but you can use crushed sugar cubes instead as nibbed sugar is difficult to get hold of.

GOLDEN SYRUP, BLACK TREACLE AND HONEY

Light, sweet golden syrup and darker, strong black treacle, which has added molasses, are both made from crystallised refined sugar. Nature's equivalent, honey, is the oldest sweetener in the world. Use clear or runny honey in recipes as it dissolves more quickly.

MALT EXTRACT

Made from powdered malt that has been reduced into a syrup, this is added to breads to add a sweet flavour and to aid the action of carbon dioxide.

CONDENSED MILK

Milk that has had half the water content removed and sugar added, sold in cans. I have used it as a sweetener in some recipes to give a fudgey flavour.

When heated with butter and muscovado sugar it turns to a thick caramel, used in **Millionaires' Shortbread** (page 253).

MILK, CREAM AND CHEESE

MILK

Recipes use semi-skimmed milk, unless otherwise stated. Full-fat milk will obviously add a richness to baking, but skimmed milk works just as well, if you prefer it.

CREAM

Cream is best whipped from cold.

You have the option of using whipping cream for filling cakes, as it is healthier and cheaper than double cream, but you can use either. Double cream is best for piping because it holds its shape longer than whipping cream. Use whipped double cream if you are adding other flavourings, like brandy. Whipping cream gives a lighter texture to mousses.

As a more economical and healthier filling for a cake, I often use a mix of half whipped cream and half low-fat yoghurt. Remember that yoghurt is wetter than cream, so use a full-fat yoghurt if you want a firmer filling.

CHEESE

For cheesecakes, use full-fat cream cheese.

Curd cheese is useful too, and has a slightly tart flavour, or you can use ricotta instead. This book does use hard cheese too, mainly Cheddar and Parmesan, in savoury scones and biscuits, including **Puff Pastry Cheese Straws** (page 232) and **Dorchester Biscuits** (page 228).

EGGS

I use large eggs throughout, unless otherwise stated, and always free-range or organic. Allow eggs to come to room temperature before using. Store leftover egg whites in the fridge in a container covered in clingfilm. Spoon a little cold water over leftover yolks to prevent a skin from forming, then cover with clingfilm. Keep for up to one week.

CHOCOLATE

DARK CHOCOLATE

There are a number of brands of dark chocolate that contain a high proportion of cocoa solids. Although they are delicious to eat, their high percentage of cocoa solids does not make them ideal for baking as the flavour can be too bitter. The finest-quality block chocolate always contains a high proportion of cocoa butter. The more cocoa butter the chocolate contains, the softer and creamier it will be. Some cheaper brands replace cocoa butter with palm or vegetable oils.

The cocoa-solids and cocoa-butter content will affect the consistency of your cake or icing. The cake might not rise properly, the icing might separate or not set, or heavier ingredients such as chocolate chips might sink to the bottom if there is not enough fat to hold them in place as the cake cooks. The cocoa flavour might also be too overpowering.

I recommend using a dark chocolate that contains about 39 per cent cocoa solids, such as Bournville. This will ensure a ratio of cocoa solids to cocoa butter that will produce a cake or icing with the correct consistency and flavour. There is no need to buy an expensive brand for baking unless the recipe specifies.

MILK CHOCOLATE

This has the addition of full-cream milk and sugar, so is much sweeter and has a milder cocoa flavour. Milk chocolate is only ideal for decorating as the chocolate flavour is lost in baking.

WHITE CHOCOLATE

Contains cocoa butter but not the dark cocoa solids. The amounts of cocoa butter used varies between brands, and some cheaper ones replace the cocoa butter with vegetable oil. When buying milk and white chocolate for cooking, choose Belgian chocolate and check that it does not contain vegetable oil.

COCOA POWDER

This is a very good and inexpensive ingredient in baking, but always sift it with the dry ingredients or mix with a little boiling water before using. Don't use drinking chocolate instead as the added sugar gives it a mild, sweet flavour not suitable for baking.

MELTING, CHOPPING AND GRATING

When melting chocolate, it is essential that you do not let it overheat. Break the chocolate into small pieces in a heatproof bowl that fits snugly over a pan of hot, but not boiling, water. If the water boils, the chocolate can be become solid and lose its shine. Also, make sure the base of the bowl does not touch the water. Heat liquids with the melting chocolate, do not add them to the chocolate once it has melted as this may cause the chocolate to 'seize'. White chocolate is more likely to separate on heating so keep the heat low. You can melt chocolate in the microwave, but again heat gently on a defrost or low setting to avoid burning.

If a recipe calls for chopped or grated chocolate, put the bar in the fridge to chill first and make sure the grater or knife are cold and completely dry. You can chop chocolate in a food processor but be careful not to overwork it, as the chocolate might melt or stick together.

BAKING TIPS

All the recipes in the book include individual cake-making instructions and for certain recipes I have given specific tips that are useful to know. However, there is some general advice that can be applied.

Always read the recipe carefully, checking that you have enough time and all the ingredients before you begin.

—

Weigh ingredients using accurate measures and scales and follow the order of the recipe making sure nothing is missed out – ticking off ingredients and instructions as you complete them helps prevent you from missing anything.

—

Mix ingredients by hand or in the food processor until the mixture is the specified colour and texture. Make sure you follow a recipe using the right utensils when it instructs you to beat, whisk or fold ingredients; these are different techniques and have specific effects on the cake mixture consistency – the success of the cake depends on this!

—

Always preheat the oven before starting to make a cake. Check your oven – if it is electric, see whether it is a fan oven or not. It must be at the correct temperature by the time the cake is ready to go in. Make sure the oven shelves are in the right position beforehand – unless specified otherwise, cook cakes in the centre of the oven.

—

Be patient and don't open the oven door or move the cake in the first stages of baking, as this can cause the cake to sink in the middle.

—

Don't overload your oven with trays of biscuits as they will cook unevenly – biscuits on a high shelf or at the edges of a tray can brown too quickly, while the others are still uncooked. There needs to be a good circulation of air as they bake. If you put more than one cake in the oven at a time, they will take a little longer to cook.

—

Most cakes are cooked when they begin to shrink away from the sides of the cake tin, and when the centre of the cake springs back after being pressed lightly with a finger.

—

Check the recipe to see what colour the cooked cake or biscuits should be. Test fruit cakes by inserting a skewer into the centre of the cake; it should come out clean. If there is any cake mixture stuck to the skewer, it needs a little longer in the oven. Biscuits and scones are cooked when they are lightly and evenly coloured on top; underneath, biscuits should be lightly coloured and scones golden.

—

Cover cakes with foil if they are browning too quickly, and perhaps reduce the oven temperature a little. Oven temperature settings do vary.

—

Follow each recipe for individual cooling instructions. Generally, sponge cakes should be left to cool for a few minutes before turning out on to a wire rack. The sides of the cake will shrink away from the tin, making them easier to remove. For sponge cakes, turn the cake the right side up on the wire rack and then cover with the cake tin. This prevents the moisture evaporating while the cake cools, but doesn't make it soggy. Leave fruit cakes to cool completely in their tins.

——

Don't leave biscuits and cookies on their trays to cool completely, as they can stick. Remove them with a palette knife while still warm.

——

To turn cakes out of a loose-bottomed or springform cake tin, stand the base on something like a large can so that the sides can slip down, leaving the cake still standing on the tin base.

——

Make sure a cake, bake or biscuit is completely cold before decorating, unless the recipe specifies otherwise. Fill when you are ready to serve. I like to keep the decoration simple, but there are so many options available now that you can get creative and experiment with lots of different toppings.

——

For many cakes, if you have time, it is good to brush it with an apricot glaze before icing. Make the glaze by pushing warmed apricot jam through a sieve. The glaze will prevent crumbs getting into the icing, and the icing will remain glossy as the cake won't absorb its moisture. Apricot glaze is also useful when covering a cake with almond paste: when spread over the cake before the paste is applied it acts as 'glue'.

——

Most cakes should be eaten soon after making but they can be kept fresh for a short time in an airtight container, or wrapped in foil or clingfilm. Sponges that have a low fat content or no fat (such as Swiss roll) do not keep well and should be eaten on the day or wrapped well and then filled and eaten the following day. Bakes with a fresh cream filling or icing should be kept in the fridge. Biscuits, flapjacks and bars made with the melting method do keep well but should be stored in an airtight container to prevent them going soggy.

——

Freeze undecorated cakes and biscuits wrapped tightly in foil, clingfilm or freezer-proof bags, as soon as they are cold, to preserve their freshness. Keep them frozen for no longer than 3 months.

——

Open-freeze (freeze unwrapped) iced or decorated cakes until hard, then wrap well. Refresh small cakes such as scones by warming them in a moderate oven after thawing.

——

Don't store cakes and biscuits in the same tin as the moisture from the cake will make the biscuits soggy. If biscuits do go soggy, refresh them in a moderate oven for 5–10 minutes, then cool and eat.

——

If fruit sinks to the bottom of the cake, it means that either the mixture was too runny to support the fruit, the fruit was too wet or the wrong fat was used (see page 19 for information on baking fats). If not enough fat is added, the cake may be dry.

——

If cakes crack on top during baking, it means that the oven was too hot or the cake was placed on too high a shelf.

—

A cake may sink if too much baking powder was used, the cake was taken out of the oven before it was cooked or the oven door was opened before the cake mixture had time to set. It may also not rise properly if the mixture was over-beaten (so that the air was beaten out), or if not enough raising agent was added.

—

Make pastry either by hand in a mixing bowl or in a food processor, but be careful not to over-whiz otherwise the dough will be tough.

—

Once a pastry case is lined the dough freezes very well, making it perfect to have in the freezer ready for a special occasion.

—

When proving and rising bread, do not prove in too hot a place otherwise the yeast will be killed and the rising process will stop.

—

CONVERSION TABLES

WEIGHTS

METRIC	IMPERIAL
5g	$\frac{1}{8}$oz
10g	$\frac{1}{4}$oz
15g	$\frac{1}{2}$oz
20g	$\frac{3}{4}$oz
30g	1oz
35g	$1\frac{1}{4}$oz
40g	$1\frac{1}{2}$oz
55g	2oz
65g	$2\frac{1}{2}$oz
75g	3oz
80g	$3\frac{1}{4}$oz
90g	$3\frac{1}{2}$oz
115g	4oz
125g	$4\frac{1}{2}$oz
150g	5oz
175g	6oz
180g	$6\frac{1}{4}$oz
200g	7oz
225g	8oz
250g	9oz
275g	10oz
300g	$10\frac{1}{2}$oz
325g	$11\frac{1}{2}$oz
350g	12oz
375g	13oz
400g	14oz
425g	15oz
450g	1lb
500g	1lb 2oz
550g	$1\frac{1}{4}$lb
600g	1lb 5oz
650g	1lb 7oz
675g	$1\frac{1}{2}$lb
700g	1lb 9oz
750g	1lb 10oz
800g	$1\frac{3}{4}$oz
850g	1lb 14oz
900g	2lb
1.3kg	3lb
1.8kg	4lb
2.25kg	5lb

MEASUREMENTS

METRIC	IMPERIAL
5mm	$\frac{1}{4}$in
1cm	$\frac{1}{2}$in
2cm	$\frac{3}{4}$in
2.5cm	1in
3cm	$1\frac{1}{4}$in
4cm	$1\frac{1}{2}$ in
5cm	2in
6.5cm	$2\frac{1}{2}$in
7cm	$2\frac{3}{4}$in
7.5cm	3in
9cm	$3\frac{1}{2}$in
10cm	4in
11cm	$4\frac{1}{2}$in
12.5cm	5in
15cm	6in
18cm	7in
20cm	8in
23cm	9in
25cm	10in
28cm	11in
30cm	12in
33cm	13in
35cm	14in

VOLUME

METRIC	IMPERIAL
30ml	1fl oz
50ml	2fl oz
75ml	2½fl oz
85ml	3fl oz
100ml	3½fl oz
125ml	4fl oz
150ml	5fl oz (¼ pint)
175ml	6fl oz
200ml	7fl oz (⅓ pint)
225ml	8fl oz
240ml	8½fl oz
250ml	9fl oz
300ml	10fl oz (½ pint)
350ml	12fl oz
400ml	14fl oz
450ml	15fl oz (¾ pint)
500ml	18fl oz
600ml	1 pint / 20fl oz
700ml	1¼ pints
900ml	1½ pints
1 litre	1¾ pints
1.2 litres	2 pints
1.25 litres	2¼ pints
1.5 litres	2½ pints
1.75 litres	3 pints
2 litres	3½ pints
2.25 litres	4 pints
2.5 litres	4½ pints
2.75 litres	5 pints
3.4 litres	6 pints
3.9 litres	7 pints
4.5 litres	8 pints (1 gallon)

OVEN TEMPERATURES

°C	Fan °C	°F	Gas Mark
120	100	250	½
140	120	275	1
150	130	300	2
160	140	325	3
180	160	350	4
190	170	375	5
200	180	400	6
220	200	425	7
230	210	450	8
240	220	475	9

CHAPTER ONE

CLASSIC CAKES

This must be the best known and loved of all family cakes. The all-in-one method takes away the hassle of creaming, and ensures success every time. Baking spreads give an excellent result, but the cake won't keep as long.

LARGE ALL-IN-ONE VICTORIA SANDWICH

CUTS INTO 6 GENEROUS SLICES

225g (8oz) baking spread, straight from the fridge
225g (8oz) caster sugar
4 large eggs
225g (8oz) self-raising flour
1 level teaspoon baking powder

For the filling and topping
about 4 tablespoons strawberry jam
150ml (5fl oz) pouring double cream, whipped
a little caster sugar, for sprinkling

Preheat the oven to 180°C/Fan 160°C/Gas 4. Lightly grease two deep 20cm (8in) loose-bottomed sandwich tins and line the base of each with non-stick baking paper.

———

Measure all the cake ingredients into a large bowl and beat for about 2 minutes with an electric mixer until beautifully smooth and lighter in colour. The time will vary depending on the efficiency of the mixer. Divide the mixture evenly between the tins and level the surfaces.

———

Bake in the preheated oven for about 25 minutes, or until well risen, golden and the cakes are shrinking away from the sides of the tin. Leave to cool in the tins for a few minutes then turn out, peel off the baking paper and finish cooling on a wire rack.

———

When completely cold, sandwich the cakes together with the jam and whipped cream. Sprinkle with caster sugar to serve.

TIP

Here are the ingredients and baking times for smaller cakes so that you don't have to calculate the quantities. Follow the instructions for the Large All-in-one Victoria Sandwich.

For an 18cm (7in) Victoria Sandwich, use 175g (6oz) baking spread, 175g (6oz) caster sugar, 3 large eggs, 175g (6oz) self-raising flour and ¾ teaspoon baking powder. Bake in two 18cm (7in) greased and lined sandwich tins for about 25 minutes.

For a 15cm (6in) Victoria Sandwich, use 115g (4oz) baking spread, 115g (4oz) caster sugar, 2 large eggs, 115g (4oz) self-raising flour and ½ teaspoon baking powder. Bake in two 15cm (6in) greased and lined sandwich tins for about 20 minutes.

This is a simple but delicious alternative to the classic Victoria Sandwich that's perfect for coffee time.

COFFEE VICTORIA SANDWICH

CUTS INTO 6 GENEROUS SLICES

4 large eggs
2 heaped teaspoons instant
    coffee granules
225g (8oz) baking spread,
    straight from the fridge
225g (8oz) caster sugar
225g (8oz) self-raising flour
1 level teaspoon baking
    powder

For the filling and topping
55g (2oz) butter, softened
175g (6oz) icing sugar, sifted
1 tablespoon strong coffee
1 tablespoon milk (optional)

Preheat the oven to 180°C/Fan 160°C/Gas 4. Lightly grease two deep 20cm (8in) loose-bottomed sandwich tins and line the base of each with non-stick baking paper.

—

Break the eggs into a large bowl and beat with a fork. Stir in the instant coffee until dissolved. Add all the remaining cake ingredients and beat for about 2 minutes with an electric mixer until beautifully smooth and lighter in colour. The time will vary depending on the efficiency of the mixer. Divide the mixture evenly between the tins and level the surfaces.

—

Bake in the preheated oven for about 25 minutes or until well risen and the cakes are shrinking away from the sides of the tin. Leave to cool in the tins for a few minutes, then turn out, peel off the baking paper and finish cooling on a wire rack.

—

To make the butter cream filling and topping, blend together the butter, icing sugar and coffee until smooth, adding the milk, if necessary. When the cakes are completely cold, use half the butter cream to sandwich the cakes together. Spread the remaining butter cream on top.

TIP
To make strong coffee, you can dissolve 1 heaped teaspoon instant coffee granules in 1 tablespoon hot water.

This light chocolate cake is sandwiched together with a white butter cream and looks as good as it tastes.

CHOCOLATE VICTORIA SANDWICH

CUTS INTO 6 GENEROUS SLICES

2 tablespoons cocoa
　　powder
3 tablespoons boiling water
225g (8oz) baking spread,
　　straight from the fridge
225g (8oz) caster sugar
4 large eggs
225g (8oz) self-raising flour
1 level teaspoon baking
　　powder

For the filling and topping
55g (2oz) butter, softened
175g (6oz) icing sugar, sifted
1 tablespoon milk
coarsely grated dark
　　chocolate, to decorate

Preheat the oven to 180°C/Fan 160°C/Gas 4. Lightly grease two deep 20cm (8in) loose-bottomed sandwich tins and line the base of each with non-stick baking paper.

—

Blend the cocoa and water in a large bowl then leave to cool slightly. Measure all the remaining cake ingredients into the bowl and beat for about 2 minutes with an electric mixer until beautifully smooth and lighter in colour. The time will vary depending on the efficiency of the mixer. Divide the mixture evenly between the tins and level the surfaces.

—

Bake in the preheated oven for about 25 minutes or until well risen and the cakes are shrinking away from the sides of the tin. Leave to cool in the tins for a few minutes then turn out, peel off the baking paper and finish cooling on a wire rack.

—

To make the butter cream filling and topping, blend together the butter, icing sugar and milk until smooth. When the cake is completely cold, use half the butter cream to sandwich the cakes together, then spread the remaining butter cream on top and decorate with the grated chocolate.

To make an Orange or Lemon Victoria Sandwich, follow the recipe for a Large All-in-one Victoria Sandwich (page 34), adding the grated zest of an orange or lemon to the cake mixture. Sandwich the cooked cakes together with whipped cream and either orange marmalade or lemon curd, instead of the strawberry jam, and sprinkle the top with a little caster sugar.

A family classic. You could decorate this roll with butter cream and use it for a Christmas log.

CHOCOLATE ROULADE

SERVES 8

4 large eggs
115g (4oz) caster sugar,
    plus extra for sprinkling
65g (2½oz) self-raising flour
40g (1½oz) cocoa powder,
    plus extra for dusting

For the filling
115g (4oz) dark chocolate,
    broken into pieces
3 tablespoons raspberry jam
300ml (½ pint) pouring
    double cream, whipped

Preheat the oven to 220°C/Fan 200°C/Gas 7. Grease a 33 x 23cm (13 x 9in) Swiss roll tin and line with non-stick baking paper.

—

Whisk the eggs and sugar in a large bowl until the mixture is light and frothy and the whisk leaves a trail when lifted out. Sift the flour and cocoa into the mixture, carefully folding them in at the same time. Turn the mixture into the prepared tin and give it a gentle shake so that the mixture finds its own level, making sure that it spreads evenly into the corners.

—

Bake in the preheated oven for about 10 minutes, or until the sponge begins to shrink from the sides of the tin.

—

While the cake is cooking, place a piece of baking paper a little bigger than the size of the tin on a work surface and sprinkle it with caster sugar. Invert the cake straight from the oven on to the sugared paper. Quickly loosen the paper on the bottom of the cake and peel it off. Trim the edges of the sponge with a sharp knife and make a score mark 2.5cm (1in) in from one shorter edge, being careful not to cut right through. Roll the cake firmly from the scored end, with the paper inside, and leave to cool.

—

Place the chocolate in a small heatproof bowl. Place the bowl over a pan of simmering water, making sure the base of the bowl is not touching the water, until melted. Warm the jam gently in a small pan until easily spreadable. If it is too warm it will soak straight into the sponge.

—

Carefully unroll the cooled cake. Remove the paper and spread the sponge with jam, then the whipped cream. Drizzle half the melted chocolate over the cream and swirl into it. Re-roll the sponge, then drizzle the remaining chocolate over the top and dust with cocoa powder to serve.

This is a rich, densely textured sponge cake. It is essential that the butter is a creamy spreading consistency before mixing the ingredients together.

MADEIRA CAKE

SERVES 6

175g (6oz) butter, softened
175g (6oz) caster sugar
225g (8oz) self-raising flour
55g (2oz) ground almonds
4 large eggs
finely grated zest of 1 lemon
a thin slice of candied
    lemon peel

Preheat the oven to 180°C/Fan 160°C/Gas 4. Line the base of an 18cm (7in) deep round cake tin with non-stick baking paper.

—

Measure all the ingredients except the candied peel into a large mixing bowl. Whisk with an electric whisk until thoroughly mixed.

—

Spoon into the prepared tin and level the surface. Place the slice of candid peel in the centre. Bake in the preheated oven for 1–1¼ hours, until well risen, lightly golden and a skewer inserted into the centre comes out clean. Leave to cool in the tin for 10 minutes then turn out, peel off the baking paper and finish cooling on a wire rack.

TIP
If a fruit or Madeira cake has a slight dip in the centre when it comes out of the oven, turn upside down on to baking paper on a wire rack. The action of gravity and the weight of the cake will level the top while it cools.

This fatless sponge is a nice alternative to a round cake at teatime.
The filling can be easily jazzed-up to serve the Swiss Roll as a dessert.

SWISS ROLL

SERVES 8

4 large eggs
115g (4oz) caster sugar,
    plus extra for sprinkling
115g (4oz) self-raising flour

For the filling
4 tablespoons strawberry
    or raspberry jam

Preheat the oven to 220°C/Fan 200°C/Gas 7. Grease a 33 x 23cm (13 x 9in) Swiss roll tin and line with non-stick baking paper.

Whisk the eggs and sugar together in a large bowl until the mixture is light and frothy and the whisk leaves a trail when lifted out. Sift the flour into the mixture, carefully folding it in at the same time. Turn the mixture into the prepared tin and give it a gentle shake so that the mixture finds its own level, making sure that it spreads evenly into the corners.

Bake in the preheated oven for about 10 minutes, or until the sponge is golden brown and begins to shrink from the sides of the tin. While the cake is cooking, place a piece of baking paper a little bigger than the size of the tin on a work surface and sprinkle it with caster sugar.

Invert the cake on to the sugared paper. Quickly loosen the paper on the bottom of the cake and peel it off. Trim the edges of the sponge with a sharp knife and make a score mark 2.5cm (1in) in from one shorter edge, being careful not to cut right through.

Leave to cool slightly, then spread with the jam. If the cake is too hot the jam will soak straight into the sponge. Roll up the cake firmly from the scored end.

To make a smaller Swiss Roll, use 3 large eggs and 75g (3oz) each of sugar and flour. Bake in a greased and lined 28 x 18cm (11 x 7in) Swiss roll tin.

To make a Coffee Swiss Roll, fill the basic Swiss Roll with coffee butter cream made with 75g (3oz) softened butter, 225g (8oz) sifted icing sugar, 2 teaspoons milk and 2 teaspoons strong coffee.

To make a Raspberry or Strawberry Swiss Roll, fill the basic Swiss Roll with 300ml (½ pint) whipped cream and sliced strawberries or whole raspberries, or both!

This recipe is delicious flavoured with orange too. Substitute an orange for the lemon and orange marmalade for the lemon curd.

LEMON SWISS ROLL

SERVES 8

4 large eggs
115g (4oz) caster sugar,
    plus extra for sprinkling
finely grated zest of 1 lemon
115g (4oz) self-raising flour

For the filling
4 tablespoons lemon curd

Preheat the oven to 220°C/Fan 200°C/Gas 7. Grease a 33 x 23cm (13 x 9in) Swiss roll tin and line with non-stick baking paper.

—

Whisk the eggs, sugar and lemon zest in a large bowl until the mixture is light and frothy and the whisk leaves a trail when lifted out. Sift the flour into the mixture, carefully folding it in at the same time. Turn the mixture into the prepared tin and give it a gentle shake so that the mixture finds its own level, making sure that it spreads evenly into the corners.

—

Bake in the preheated oven for about 10 minutes, or until the sponge is golden brown and begins to shrink from the sides of the tin. While the cake is cooking, place a piece of baking paper a little bigger than the size of the tin on a work surface and sprinkle it with caster sugar.

—

Invert the cake on to the sugared paper. Quickly loosen the paper on the bottom of the cake and peel it off. Trim the edges of the sponge with a sharp knife and make a score mark 2.5cm (1in) in from one shorter edge, being careful not to cut right through.

—

Leave to cool slightly, then spread with the lemon curd. If the cake is too hot the lemon curd will soak straight into the sponge. Roll up the cake firmly from the scored end.

This is a version of a cake that has been a favourite with my family for many years. Expect it to dip slightly in the centre. It can be served with coffee or as a dessert with cream and is best eaten warm.

AMERICAN APPLE AND APRICOT CAKE

SERVES 8

250g (9oz) self-raising flour
1 teaspoon baking powder
225g (8oz) caster sugar
2 large eggs
½ teaspoon almond extract
150g (5oz) butter, melted
225g (8oz) cooking apples, peeled, cored and thickly sliced (prepared weight)
115g (4oz) ready-to-eat dried apricots, snipped into pieces
30g (1oz) flaked almonds

Preheat the oven to 160°C/Fan 140°C/Gas 3. Grease a 20cm (8in) loose-bottomed deep, round cake tin and line the base with non-stick baking paper.

—

Measure the flour, baking powder, sugar, eggs, almond extract and melted butter into a large bowl. Mix well to combine, then beat well for 1 minute. Add the apples and apricots and gently mix them in with a spoon.

—

Spoon the mixture into the prepared tin, gently level the surface and sprinkle with the flaked almonds. Bake in the preheated oven for 1–1½ hours, until the cake is golden, firm to the touch and beginning to shrink away from the side of the tin. Leave to cool in the tin for a few minutes then turn out, peel off the baking paper and put on to a plate to serve warm.

This Canadian-inspired cake is a real treat for a special gathering. Fill and cover ahead of time, so that the cake keeps moist.

MAPLE SYRUP CAKE

CUTS INTO 6-8 GENEROUS SLICES

225g (8oz) butter, softened
225g (8oz) light
    muscovado sugar
finely grated zest of 1 orange
4 large eggs
100ml (3½fl oz) maple syrup
350g (12oz) self-raising flour
1 level teaspoon baking
    powder
½ level teaspoon ground
    ginger
55g (2oz) pecan nuts,
    chopped

For the filling and topping
450ml (¾ pint) pouring
    double cream
2 tablespoons maple syrup
zest of 1 orange, to decorate

Preheat the oven to 160°C/Fan 140°C/Gas 3. Grease a 20cm (8in) deep round cake tin and line the base with non-stick baking paper.

——

Measure all the cake ingredients except the pecan nuts into a large bowl and beat until evenly blended. Stir in the chopped pecan nuts.

——

Spoon the mixture into the prepared tin and level the surface. Bake in the preheated oven for about 1½ hours, until well risen, golden and springy to the touch. Leave to cool in the tin for a few minutes then turn out, peel off the baking paper and finish cooling on a wire rack.

——

To make the filling and topping, whip the cream until it just holds its shape, then fold in the maple syrup.

——

Cut the cake into three horizontally using a serrated or bread knife. Sit one cake on a plate and spread with some of the cream, right to the edge. Continue stacking the cakes and spreading with the cream. Finally, smooth the cream evenly over the top and sides of the whole cake and decorate the top with the orange zest. Keep chilled in the fridge.

The walnuts in this cake really complement the coffee flavour and provide extra bite to contrast the moist cake and the smooth butter cream.

COFFEE AND WALNUT SPONGE CAKE

SERVES 6

115g (4oz) butter, softened
115g (4oz) caster sugar
2 large eggs
115g (4oz) self-raising flour
½ level teaspoon baking
    powder
55g (2oz) chopped walnuts
1 tablespoon strong coffee

For the filling and topping
75g (3oz) butter, softened
225g (8oz) icing sugar, sifted
2 teaspoons milk
2 teaspoons strong coffee
6 walnut halves, to decorate

Preheat the oven to 180°C/Fan 160°C/Gas 4. Grease two 18cm (7in) sandwich tins and line the base of each tin with non-stick baking paper.

—

Measure all the cake ingredients into a bowl and beat until thoroughly blended and smooth.

—

Divide the mixture between the sandwich tins and level the surfaces. Bake in the preheated oven for 20–25 minutes, or until well risen and the top of the cakes spring back when lightly pressed with a finger. Leave to cool in the tins for a few minutes then turn out, peel off the baking paper and finish cooling on a wire rack.

—

To make the filling and topping, beat together the butter, icing sugar, milk and coffee in a bowl until smooth. When the cakes are completely cold sandwich together with half of the filling and use the rest for the top of the cake. Decorate with the walnut halves.

TIP
To make strong coffee, use 2 teaspoons instant coffee granules mixed with 1 tablespoon hot water.

Make sure you use deep sandwich tins, as the shallower tins tend to overflow.

CAPPUCCINO CAKE

SERVES 8

55g (2oz) cocoa powder
6 tablespoons boiling water
3 large eggs
50ml (2fl oz) milk
175g (6oz) self-raising flour
¾ level teaspoon baking
    powder
115g (4oz) butter, softened
275g (10oz) caster sugar

For the filling and topping
300ml (½ pint) pouring
    double cream
1 teaspoon instant coffee
    granules, dissolved in 2
    teaspoons hot water
a little cocoa powder
    or drinking chocolate,
    for dusting

Preheat the oven to 180°C/Fan 160°C/Gas 4. Grease two 20cm (8in) loose-bottomed deep sandwich tins and line the base of each tin with non-stick baking paper.

——

Measure the cocoa powder into a large mixing bowl, add the boiling water and mix well until it has a paste-like consistency. Add all the remaining ingredients to the bowl and beat until just combined. The mixture will be a fairly thick batter (be careful not to over-beat).

——

Divide the cake mixture between the prepared tins and gently level the surfaces. Bake in the preheated oven for 25–30 minutes, until the cakes are well risen and beginning to shrink away from the sides of the tins. Leave to cool in the tins for a few minutes, then turn out, peel off the baking paper and finish cooling on a wire rack.

——

To finish the cake, whip the cream until it just holds its shape, then stir in the dissolved coffee. Use half the cream to fill the cake and spread the remainder over the top. Gently smooth the surface with a palette knife and dust with sifted cocoa powder or drinking chocolate.

TIP
This cake is best eaten fresh. Store it in the fridge if necessary.

This is a lovely moist cake. Keep it in the fridge and eat within a week.

LEMON YOGHURT CAKE

SERVES 8

300g (10½oz) caster sugar
55g (2oz) butter, softened
3 large eggs, separated
225g (8oz) Greek yoghurt
finely grated zest of 1 lemon
175g (6oz) self-raising flour

For the icing
115g (4oz) icing sugar, sifted
about 1½ tablespoons fresh
   lemon juice

Preheat the oven to 180°C/Fan 160°C/Gas 4. Grease a 20cm (8in) deep round cake tin and line the base with non-stick baking paper.

—

Beat together the sugar, butter and egg yolks in a bowl. Add the yoghurt and lemon zest and beat until smooth. Gently fold in the flour.

—

Whisk the egg whites to a soft peak, then carefully fold into the cake mixture.

—

Turn into the prepared tin and bakc in the preheated oven for 1–1¼ hours, or until the cake is well risen and firm to the touch. Leave to cool in the tin for a few minutes then turn out, peel off the baking paper and finish cooling on a wire rack.

—

For the icing, mix together the sifted icing sugar and the lemon juice and pour over the cold cake. Smooth over with a palette knife and leave to set.

You can use either marzipan or homemade or bought almond paste for this famous chequerboard cake.

BATTENBERG CAKE

SERVES 8

115g (4oz) butter, softened
115g (4oz) caster sugar
2 large eggs
55g (2oz) ground almonds
115g (4oz) self-raising flour
½ level teaspoon baking
    powder
a few drops of almond
    extract
red food colouring

To finish
about 3–4 tablespoons
    apricot jam
225g (8oz) almond paste
    or marzipan (see page 398
    for almond paste recipe)

TIP
If you haven't got a Battenberg tin, grease an 18cm (7in) square cake tin. Cut out a piece of non-stick baking paper that is 7.5cm (3in) longer than one side of the tin. Fold the paper in half widthways. Open out the paper and push up the centre fold to a 4cm (1½in) pleat. Line the base of the tin with this, making any adjustments to ensure the pleat runs down the centre of the tin.

Preheat the oven to 160°C/Fan 140°C/Gas 3. Grease an 18cm (7in) Battenberg tin and line the base with non-stick baking paper.

Measure the butter, sugar, eggs, ground almonds, flour, baking powder and almond extract into a large bowl and beat for about 2 minutes until smooth.

Spoon half the mixture into the right half of the prepared tin as neatly as possible. Add a few drops of red food colouring to the remaining mixture to turn it a deep pink colour, then spoon this into the left half of the tin. Try to get the join between the 2 mixtures as neat as possible. Smooth the surface of each half.

Bake in the preheated oven for 35–40 minutes, or until the cake is well risen, springy to the touch and has shrunk slightly from the sides of the tin. Leave to cool in the tin for a few minutes, then turn out, peel off the baking paper and finish cooling on a wire rack.

Trim the edges of the cake and then cut into 4 equal strips – 2 pink and 2 plain.

Gently heat the apricot jam in a small pan. Use the warmed jam to stick the 4 strips of cake together to make a chequerboard effect. Brush the top of the assembled cake with apricot jam.

Roll out the almond paste or marzipan into an oblong the length of the cake and sufficiently wide to wrap around the cake. Invert the cake on to the almond paste or marzipan, then brush the remaining 3 sides with apricot jam. Press the almond paste or marzipan neatly around the cake, arranging the join in one corner. Score the top of the cake with a criss-cross pattern and crimp the edges with your fingers to decorate.

This cake is always popular and a great idea for charity events or family get togethers. I'm afraid, though, that it sounds much healthier than it really is!

CARROT CAKE

SERVES 8

225g (8oz) self-raising flour
1 level teaspoon baking
    powder
150g (5oz) light muscovado
    sugar
55g (2oz) chopped walnuts
115g (4oz) carrots, coarsely
    grated
2 ripe bananas, mashed
2 large eggs
150ml (¼ pint) sunflower
    or vegetable oil

For the topping
175g (6oz) full-fat cream
    cheese
55g (2oz) butter, softened
115g (4oz) icing sugar, sifted
a few drops of vanilla extract
walnut halves, to decorate

Preheat the oven to 180°C/Fan 160°C /Gas 4. Grease a 20cm (8in) deep round cake tin and line the base with non-stick baking paper.

—

Measure all the cake ingredients into a large bowl and beat well until thoroughly blended and smooth.

—

Turn into the prepared tin and level the surface. Bake in the preheated oven for about 50–60 minutes, until the cake is well risen and shrinking away from the sides of the tin. Leave to cool in the tin for a few minutes then turn out, peel off the baking paper and finish cooling on a wire rack.

—

For the topping, measure all the ingredients, except the walnuts, into a bowl or food processor, and blitz until smooth. Spread over the top of the cake, swirling with a spatula for a decorative effect. Decorate with the walnut halves and chill a little before serving. Store in the fridge as the topping is soft.

The same crunchy topping can be used on traybakes and teabreads. The secret is to pour the crunchy topping over the cake while it is still warm so that the lemon soaks in and the sugar stays on top.

CRUNCHY TOP LEMON CAKE

SERVES 8

115g (4oz) butter, softened
175g (6oz) caster sugar
175g (6oz) self-raising flour
¾ level teaspoon baking
    powder
2 large eggs, beaten
4 tablespoons milk
finely grated zest of 1 lemon

For the topping
juice of 1 lemon
115g (4oz) caster or
    granulated sugar

Preheat the oven to 180°C/Fan 160°C/Gas 4. Grease an 18cm (7in) deep round cake tin and line the base with non-stick baking paper.

—

Measure all the cake ingredients into a large bowl and beat for about 2 minutes until smooth and well blended.

—

Turn the mixture into the prepared tin and level the surface. Bake in the preheated oven for about 35–40 minutes, or until the cake has shrunk slightly from the sides of the tin and springs back when lightly pressed with a finger.

—

While the cake is baking, make the crunchy topping. Measure the lemon juice and sugar into a bowl and stir until blended. When the cake comes out of the oven, spread the lemon paste over the top while the cake is still hot. Leave to cool completely in the tin, then turn out and peel off the baking paper.

TIP
If a softened cake has sunk disastrously in the middle, cut this out, fill with softened fruits and whipped cream, and serve as a dessert.

A lovely light sponge cake, this is always popular and is especially good on the day it's made.

DOUBLE ORANGE CAKE

SERVES 8

175g (6oz) butter, softened
175g (6oz) caster sugar
3 large eggs, beaten
175g (6oz) self-raising flour
¾ level teaspoon
    baking powder
finely grated zest and juice
    of 1 large orange

To finish
about 2 tablespoons
    apricot jam
115g (4oz) icing sugar
finely grated zest and juice
    of ½ orange

Preheat the oven to 180°C/Fan 160°C/Gas 4. Grease a 20cm (8in) deep round cake tin then line the base with non-stick baking paper.

—

Measure all the cake ingredients into a large bowl and beat until thoroughly blended.

—

Turn into the prepared tin and level the surface. Bake in the preheated oven for about 35 minutes, until well risen and springy to the touch. Leave to cool in the tin for a few minutes then turn out, peel off the baking paper and finish cooling on a wire rack.

—

Measure the apricot jam into a small pan and gently warm through. Brush the jam over the top of the cake.

—

Sift the icing sugar into a bowl and mix in the orange juice to a coating consistency. Pour over the top of the cake and gently spread out with a small palette knife. Leave to set then decorate with the pared orange zest.

CHAPTER TWO

SPICED CAKES

Gingerbread is said to be one of the oldest forms of cake in the world. Most European countries have their own version. One of the major advantages of homemade gingerbread is that it improves with keeping.

ICED GINGERBREAD
CUTS INTO 16 SQUARES # WITH STEM GINGER

115g (4oz) butter, softened
115g (4oz) light
    muscovado sugar
2 large eggs
150g (5oz) black treacle
150g (5oz) golden syrup
225g (8oz) plain flour
1 level teaspoon
    ground ginger
1 level teaspoon ground
    mixed spice
½ level teaspoon
    bicarbonate of soda
2 tablespoons milk

For the icing
175g (6oz) icing sugar
3 tablespoons stem
    ginger syrup
1 bulb stem ginger,
    finely chopped

Preheat the oven to 160°C/Fan 140°C/Gas 3. Grease an 18cm (7in) deep square cake tin, then line the base with non-stick baking paper.

Measure the butter, sugar, eggs, treacle and golden syrup into a bowl and beat until thoroughly mixed. Sift the flour with the spices and fold into the mixture. Add the bicarbonate of soda to the milk, then stir this into the mixture.

Pour into the prepared tin and level the surface. Bake in the preheated oven for 1 hour.

Reduce the oven temperature to 150°C/Fan 130°C/Gas 2 and bake for a further 15–30 minutes, or until well risen and firm to the touch. Leave to cool in the tin for 10 minutes then turn out, peel off the baking paper and finish cooling on a wire rack.

For the icing, sift the icing sugar into a bowl and add the stem ginger syrup and enough water to make a spreading consistency (about 3 teaspoons). Mix to give a smooth icing. Add the chopped stem ginger and pour the icing over the cake. Leave to set before cutting into squares.

A favourite from the north of England, parkin definitely improves with keeping, so try to store it for at least a week before cutting.

TRADITIONAL PARKIN

CUTS INTO 16 SQUARES

175g (6oz) black treacle
150g (5oz) butter
115g (4oz) dark
    muscovado sugar
175g (6oz) plain flour
2 level teaspoons
    ground ginger
1 level teaspoon
    ground cinnamon
1 level teaspoon freshly
    grated nutmeg
275g (10oz) porridge oats
1 large egg
150ml (5fl oz) milk
1 level teaspoon
    bicarbonate of soda

Preheat the oven to 180°C/Fan 160°C/Gas 4. Grease an 18cm (7in) deep square cake tin then line the base with non-stick baking paper.

Measure the treacle, butter and sugar into a medium pan and heat gently until the butter has melted and the sugar has dissolved. Allow to cool slightly.

Sift the flour and spices into a large bowl and add the porridge oats. Mix together the egg and milk and stir in the bicarbonate of soda. Add to the dry ingredients, along with the treacle mixture and stir well to mix.

Pour into the prepared tin and bake in the preheated oven for about 1 hour, or until firm to the touch. Leave to cool in the tin for 10 minutes then turn out, peel off the baking paper and finish cooling on a wire rack.

Wrap the cold parkin in baking paper and store in a cake tin for a week before cutting into 16 squares.

A thin layer of sweet almond paste is baked through the centre of this cake and works very well with the warming flavours of cinnamon and clove.

ALMOND SPICE CAKE

SERVES 8

115g (4oz) almond paste or
   marzipan (see page 398
   for almond paste recipe)
175g (6oz) butter, softened
175g (6oz) caster sugar
3 large eggs
225g (8oz) self-raising flour
1 level teaspoon baking
   powder
½ level teaspoon ground
   cinnamon
¼ level teaspoon ground
   cloves
115g (4oz) flaked almonds,
   toasted

For the topping
55g (2oz) butter
115g (4oz) light
   muscovado sugar
2 tablespoons double cream

Preheat the oven to 180°C/Fan 160°C/Gas 4. Grease an 18cm (7in) deep round cake tin, then line the base with non-stick baking paper.

Roll out the almond paste or marzipan to an 18cm (7in) circle, then set aside.

Measure the butter, sugar, eggs, flour, baking powder and spices into a bowl and beat until thoroughly blended. Fold in 75g (3oz) of the toasted flaked almonds.

Spoon half of the cake mixture into the prepared tin and level the surface. Lightly place the circle of almond paste on top, then add the remaining cake mixture and level the surface.

Bake in the preheated oven for 1–1¼ hours, or until well risen and golden brown and the surface springs back when lightly pressed with a finger. Leave to cool in the tin for 5 minutes, then turn out, peel off the baking paper and finish cooling on a wire rack.

For the topping, heat the butter, sugar and cream in a saucepan until blended, then bring to the boil. Stand the wire rack on a baking tray to catch any drips and drizzle the icing over the cake. Sprinkle with the remaining toasted flaked almonds, then leave to set for 10–15 minutes.

If possible store the cake for two days, wrapped in baking paper and foil, before icing. This allows the cake to mature and become moist and sticky.

STICKY GINGER AND ORANGE CAKE

SERVES 8

115g (4oz) golden syrup
115g (4oz) black treacle
250ml (9fl oz) water
115g (4oz) butter, softened
115g (4oz) caster sugar
finely grated zest of 1 orange
1 large egg, beaten
275g (10oz) plain flour
1½ level teaspoons
    bicarbonate of soda
1 level teaspoon
    ground cinnamon
1 level teaspoon
    ground ginger

For the icing
115g (4oz) icing sugar
juice of 1 orange

Preheat the oven to 180°C/Fan 160°C/Gas 4. Grease a 23cm (9in) deep round cake tin, then line the base and sides with non-stick baking paper.

Measure the golden syrup and treacle into a pan along with the water and bring to the boil.

Meanwhile, put the remaining cake ingredients into a mixing bowl and beat well until thoroughly blended. Add the syrup and treacle mixture and beat again until smooth.

Pour the mixture into the prepared tin and level the surface. Bake in the preheated oven for about 50 minutes, or until a skewer inserted into the centre comes out clean. Leave to cool in the tin for 10 minutes, then turn out, peel off the baking paper and finish cooling on a wire rack.

To make the icing, sift the icing sugar into a bowl and add enough orange juice to make a smooth, fairly thick mixture. Stand the wire rack on a baking tray to catch any drips, then spoon the icing over the top of the cake and leave to set for about 1 hour.

This keeps and freezes extremely well. Sometimes you get a dip in the middle of the gingerbread, which indicates that you have been a bit heavy-handed with the syrup and treacle. It just means it tastes even more moreish!

CLASSIC STICKY GINGERBREAD

CUTS INTO 16 PIECES

225g (8oz) butter
225g (8oz) light
   muscovado sugar
225g (8oz) golden syrup
225g (8oz) black treacle
225g (8oz) self-raising flour
225g (8oz) wholemeal
   self-raising flour
4 level teaspoons
   ground ginger
2 large eggs
300ml (½ pint) milk

Preheat the oven to 160°C/Fan 140°C/Gas 3. Grease a 30 x 23cm (12 x 9in) traybake or roasting tin, then line the base and sides with non-stick baking paper.

Measure the butter, sugar, golden syrup and black treacle into a medium pan and heat gently until the mixture has melted evenly. Allow to cool slightly.

Put the flours and ground ginger into a large bowl and stir together lightly. Beat the eggs into the milk. Pour the cooled butter and syrup mixture into the flour, along with the egg and milk mixture, and beat until smooth.

Pour the mixture into the prepared tin and tilt gently to level the surface. Bake in the preheated oven for 50 minutes, until well risen, golden and springy to the touch. Leave to cool in the tin for a few minutes then turn out, peel off the baking paper and finish cooling on a wire rack.

When cold, cut into 16 squares.

This is a traditional name for a cake that is so delicious that everyone will come back for another slice. Good for a hungry family, this is not a rich cake, so it is best eaten as fresh as possible.

CUT AND COME AGAIN CAKE

SERVES 8

350g (12oz) self-raising flour
1 level teaspoon ground
    mixed spice
175g (6oz) butter, softened
175g (6oz) caster sugar
3 large eggs, beaten
175g (6oz) currants
115g (4oz) sultanas
115g (4oz) raisins
3 tablespoons milk

Preheat the oven to 180°C/Fan 160°C/Gas 4. Grease a 20cm (8in) deep round cake tin, then line the base with non-stick baking paper.

—

Measure all the ingredients into a large bowl and beat until thoroughly mixed.

—

Turn into the prepared tin and level the surface. Bake in the preheated oven for 1¼–1½ hours, or until a skewer inserted into the centre of the cake comes out clean. Leave to cool in the tin for 10 minutes then turn out, peel off the baking paper and finish cooling on a wire rack.

In Victorian times, cakes were made larger than they are now, and so one-pound quantities – hence the name – would have been used. In this version, the ingredients are in half-pound quantities.

POUND CAKE

SERVES 8

115g (4oz) red or natural
  glacé cherries, quartered
225g (8oz) butter, softened
225g (8oz) light
  muscovado sugar
4 large eggs
225g (8oz) self-raising flour
225g (8oz) raisins
225g (8oz) sultanas
1 level teaspoon ground
  mixed spice
1 tablespoon brandy

Preheat the oven to 150°C/Fan 130°C/Gas 2. Grease a 20cm (8in) deep round cake tin, then line the base with non-stick baking paper.

Place the cherries in a sieve and rinse under running water. Drain well then dry thoroughly on kitchen paper. Measure all the ingredients into a large bowl and beat together until thoroughly combined.

Turn the mixture into the prepared tin and level the surface. Bake in the preheated oven for 2–2¼ hours, covering the top with baking paper after an hour to prevent the cake becoming too brown. When cooked, the cake should be firm to the touch and a skewer inserted into the centre will come out clean. Leave to cool in the tin for 30 minutes, then turn out, peel off the baking paper and finish cooling on a wire rack.

CHAPTER THREE

CHOCOLATE BAKES

These small loaves are great to take on a picnic. You can vary the thickness of the slices, depending on how much of a sweet tooth your guests have!

BROWNIE LOAVES WITH WHITE CHOCOLATE CHIPS

MAKES 2 LOAVES

55g (2oz) ground almonds
225g (8oz) baking spread,
    straight from the fridge
175g (6oz) self-raising flour
225g (8oz) light
    muscovado sugar
55g (2oz) cocoa powder
5 large eggs
1 level teaspoon baking
    powder
150g (5oz) white
    chocolate chips

For the icing
175g (6oz) dark chocolate,
    broken into pieces
50g butter

Preheat the oven to 180°C/Fan 160°C/Gas 4. Grease and line two 450g (1lb) loaf tins with non-stick baking paper.

Measure all the brownie loaf ingredients, except the white chocolate chips, into a large bowl. Whisk together using an electric hand whisk until light and fluffy. Stir in 125g (4½oz) of the chocolate chips.

Spoon into the prepared tins and level the surfaces. Bake in the preheated oven for about 1 hour, or until well risen and the top of the loaves spring back when lightly pressed. Leave to cool in the tin for a few minutes, then turn out on to a wire rack and peel off the baking paper.

To make the icing, melt the dark chocolate and butter in a heatproof bowl over a pan of simmering water. Leave to cool slightly. Fold in the remaining white chocolate chips before spreading over the tops of the loaves to make a ripple effect.

Cut each loaf into slices to serve.

TIP
The loaves freeze well.

A really simple brownie recipe – just measure all the ingredients into a bowl and give it a good mix! Be careful not to overcook your brownies: they should have a slightly gooey texture. The outside crust should be on the crisp side, though, thanks to the high proportion of sugar.

CHOCOLATE CHIP BROWNIES

CUTS INTO 24 PIECES

275g (10oz) butter, softened
375g (13oz) caster sugar
4 large eggs
75g (3oz) cocoa powder
115g (4oz) self-raising flour
115g (4oz) dark
   chocolate chips

Preheat the oven to 180°C/Fan 160°C/Gas 4. Grease a 30 x 23cm (12 x 9in) traybake or roasting tin, then line the base and sides with non-stick baking paper.

Measure all the ingredients into a large bowl and beat until evenly blended.

Spoon the mixture into the prepared tin, scraping the sides of the bowl with a plastic spatula. Gently spread the mixture to the corners of the tin and level the surface. Bake in the preheated oven for 40–45 minutes, or until the brownies have a crusty top and a skewer inserted into the centre comes out clean. (Cover loosely with foil for the last 10 minutes if the mixture is browning too much.) Leave to cool in the tin.

Cut into 24 pieces and store in an airtight tin.

With a little coffee, some chopped walnuts and the addition of dark chocolate chips, these brownies have a rich, 'grown-up' flavour. Cooked brownie mixture, like gingerbread, is likely to dip in the middle, but this all adds to the charm.

DARK INDULGENT CHOCOLATE AND WALNUT BROWNIES

CUTS INTO 24 PIECES

350g (12oz) dark chocolate, broken into pieces
225g (8oz) butter
2 level teaspoons instant coffee granules
2 tablespoons hot water
3 large eggs
225g (8oz) caster sugar
1 teaspoon vanilla extract
75g (3oz) self-raising flour
175g (6oz) walnuts, chopped
225g (8oz) dark chocolate chips

Preheat the oven to 190°C/Fan 170°C/Gas 5. Grease a 30 x 23cm (12 x 9in) traybake or roasting tin then line the base with non-stick baking paper.

Place the chocolate and butter in a large heatproof bowl set over a pan of simmering water until melted, stirring occasionally. Leave to cool.

Dissolve the coffee in the hot water in a large bowl and leave to cool for 5 minutes. Add the eggs, sugar and vanilla extract and mix together.

Gradually beat the chocolate mixture into the coffee mixture, then fold in the flour, walnuts and chocolate chips.

Pour the mixture into the prepared tin and level the surface. Bake in the preheated oven for 40–45 minutes, or until the brownies have a crusty top and a skewer inserted into the centre comes out clean. Leave the brownies to cool in the tin.

Cut into 24 pieces. Store in an airtight tin.

I have given a generous amount of icing to fill and ice this cake, as death by chocolate should be sheer luxury and a complete indulgence! The icing is very easy to make, but take care not to overheat it or it will lose its shine.

DEATH BY CHOCOLATE CAKE

SERVES 8

275g (10oz) plain flour
3 level tablespoons
   cocoa powder
1½ level teaspoons
   bicarbonate of soda
1½ level teaspoons
   baking powder
200g (7oz) caster sugar
3 tablespoons golden syrup
3 large eggs, beaten
225ml (8fl oz) sunflower oil
225ml (8fl oz) milk

For the icing
450g (1lb) dark chocolate,
   broken into pieces
200g (7oz) unsalted butter

To finish
55g (2oz) Belgian white
   chocolate, coarsely grated
55g (2oz) dark chocolate,
   coarsely grated

TIP
Don't store the cake in the fridge, or the icing will lose its shine – a cool place is fine.

Preheat the oven to 160°C/Fan 140°C/Gas 3. Grease two 20cm (8in) deep loose-bottomed cake tins, then line the base of each with non-stick baking paper.

Sift the flour, cocoa powder, bicarbonate of soda and baking powder into a large bowl. Add the sugar and mix well. Make a well in the centre of the dry ingredients and add the golden syrup, eggs, oil and milk. Beat well, using a wooden spoon, until smooth.

Pour into the prepared tins and level the surfaces. Bake in the preheated oven for about 35 minutes, or until well risen and the tops of the cakes spring back when lightly pressed with a finger. Leave to cool in the tins for a few minutes then turn out, peel off the baking paper and finish cooling on a wire rack. When cold, cut each cake in half horizontally using a serrated or bread knife.

To make the icing, place the chocolate in a large heatproof bowl. Place the bowl over a pan of simmering water until the chocolate has melted, making sure that the base of the bowl is not touching the water and you do not overheat the chocolate. Remove from the heat, add the butter and leave to melt into the chocolate.

Stand the wire rack on a baking tray to catch any drips, then sandwich the cake layers together with the icing. Pour the remaining icing over the top of the cake and use a small palette knife to smooth it evenly over the top and around the sides. Leave to set.

Decorate with the grated white and dark chocolates.

There are quite a few stages to this cake, so it's not one to tackle if you're in a hurry, but you can make the cake in advance and freeze it. Be very light-handed when folding in the flour and melted butter, or the butter will sink and result in a heavy cake. Eat as a dessert, with a fork. There are two sizes of leaf gelatine available; we use 11g sheets.

CHOCOLATE MOUSSE CAKE

SERVES 8

30g (1oz) butter
6 large eggs
175g (6oz) caster sugar
115g (4oz) self-raising flour
30g (1oz) cocoa powder
2 tablespoons cornflour

For the mousse filling
2 sheets of platinum-grade
   leaf gelatine
175g (6oz) dark chocolate,
   broken into pieces
2 tablespoons brandy
2 large eggs, separated
300ml (½ pint) pouring
   double cream, whipped
   to soft peaks

For the decoration
200g (7oz) dark chocolate
150g (5oz) Belgian
   white chocolate

To finish
150ml (¼ pint) pouring
   double cream, whipped
icing sugar, for dusting

Preheat the oven to 180°C/Fan 160°C/Gas 4. Grease a 23cm (9in) deep loose-bottomed cake tin, then line the base with non-stick baking paper.

Put the butter in a small pan and heat gently until melted, then leave to cool slightly.

Beat the eggs and sugar together at full speed until the mixture is pale and creamy and thick enough to leave a trail when the whisk is lifted from the mixture.

Sift the flour, cocoa and cornflour together.

Carefully fold half the flours into the egg mixture. Pour half the cooled butter around the edge of the mixture and carefully fold in. Gradually fold in the remaining flours, then the remaining butter.

Pour the mixture into the prepared tin and level the surface. Bake in the preheated oven for 35–40 minutes, or until well risen and the top of the cake springs back when lightly pressed with a finger. Leave to cool in the tin for a few minutes then turn out, peel off the baking paper and finish cooling on a wire rack. Wash the cake tin and, when the cake is cold, cut it in half horizontally using a serrated or bread knife and put the bottom half back in the tin.

Recipe continued overleaf

To make the mousse filling, half fill a small bowl with water. Add the sheets of gelatine and leave to become soft for about 5 minutes.

Meanwhile, melt the chocolate with the brandy in a heatproof bowl set over a pan of simmering water, making sure the base of the bowl is not touching the water, stirring occasionally. Once the melted chocolate has cooled slightly, squeeze any water from the gelatine sheets and stir into the chocolate mixture, along with the egg yolks. Fold in the whipped cream.

Whisk the egg whites until stiff but not dry, then gently fold into the chocolate mixture. Pour the mousse on top of the cake in the tin. Gently level the surface and top with the remaining cake. Cover and leave to set in the fridge for a minimum of 4 hours.

While the mousse is setting, shave the dark chocolate and white chocolate with a vegetable peeler for the decoration and keep them separate.

When the mousse is set, ease around the sides of the mousse with a small palette knife, then stand the base of the cake tin on a large can. Ease the sides of the tin down, then slip the cake off the cake tin base and on to a serving plate.

Cover the top and sides of the cake with whipped cream and arrange the dark and white chocolate shavings to cover the cake completely, in any pattern you like! Finish with a little dusting of sifted icing sugar.

The origin of this pie is rather uncertain, but it has become a very popular dessert in cafés and bistros. Like many American recipes, it is rich, so serve in small slices.

MISSISSIPPI MUD PIE

SERVES 6-8

For the base
115g (4oz) digestive
   biscuits, crushed
55g (2oz) butter, melted
30g (1oz) demerara sugar

For the filling
200g (7oz) dark chocolate,
   broken into pieces
115g (4oz) butter
1 heaped teaspoon instant
   coffee granules
1 tablespoon boiling water
300ml (½ pint) single cream
175g (6oz) dark
   muscovado sugar
6 large eggs, beaten

To finish
150ml (¼ pint) pouring
   double cream, whipped

Preheat the oven to 180°C/Fan 160°C/Gas 4. Grease a 20cm (8in) deep loose-bottomed cake tin or springform tin.

To make the base, mix together the crushed digestive biscuits, melted butter and sugar. Spoon into the prepared tin and press the biscuit mixture out in an even layer, using the back of a metal spoon.

To make the filling, place the chocolate, butter, instant coffee granules and water in a large pan over a gentle heat until the butter and chocolate have melted, stirring occasionally. Remove from the heat and beat in the cream, sugar and eggs.

Pour the mixture on to the biscuit crust and bake in the preheated oven for about 1¼ hours, or until set. Leave to cool completely in the tin, then turn out and decorate the top with whipped cream.

*This will become your favourite chocolate cake recipe – it is the best!
It is speedy to make and the easy filling doubles as an icing. The cake
is moist and has a 'grown-up' chocolate flavour.*

VERY BEST CHOCOLATE FUDGE CAKE

SERVES 8

55g (2oz) sifted cocoa
    powder
6 tablespoons boiling water
3 large eggs
50ml (2fl oz) milk
175g (6oz) self-raising flour
1 rounded teaspoon
    baking powder
115g (4oz) butter, softened
275g (10oz) caster sugar

For the filling and icing
3 tablespoons apricot jam
150g (5oz) dark chocolate,
    broken into pieces
150ml (¼ pint) double cream

Preheat the oven to 180°C/Fan 160°C/Gas 4. Grease two 20cm (8in) deep sandwich tins then line the base of each tin with non-stick baking paper.

Blend the cocoa and boiling water in a large bowl then add the remaining cake ingredients and beat until the mixture is a smooth, thickish batter.

Divide the cake mix equally between the prepared tins and level the surfaces. Bake in the preheated oven for about 25–30 minutes, or until well risen and the tops of the cakes spring back when lightly pressed with a finger. Leave to cool in the tins for a few minutes then turn out, peel off the baking paper and finish cooling on a wire rack.

Warm the apricot jam in a very small pan, then spread a little over the base of one cake and the top of the other.

To make the icing, melt the chocolate with the cream in a heatproof bowl set over a pan of simmering water, stirring occasionally. Remove the bowl from the heat and leave to cool until it is on the point of setting, then spread on top of both cakes. Sandwich the cakes together and use a palette knife to spread the icing on the top. Keep in a cool place until ready to serve.

TIP

The cake can be frozen (iced or un-iced) for up to 1 month. Store in a round freezer-proof container about 2.5cm (1in) bigger than the diameter of the cake. Sit the cake on the inside of the lid and place the container over the top. Seal, label and freeze. If the cake is frozen iced, the icing will not be quite as shiny once thawed. To defrost, release the lid but leave in position and thaw for 4 hours at room temperature.

Chocolate and orange are a favourite combination and this is a light sponge that everyone will enjoy.

ORANGE CHOCOLATE CAKE

SERVES 6-8

175g (6oz) self-raising flour
175g (6oz) baking spread,
    straight from the fridge
20g (¾oz) cocoa powder
175g (6oz) caster sugar
1 teaspoon baking powder
3 large eggs
finely grated zest of 1 orange

For the icing
250g (9oz) orange
    chocolate, broken
    into pieces
125g (4½oz) butter, softened
225g (8oz) icing sugar

Preheat the oven to 180°C/Fan 160°C/Gas 4. Grease and line two 20cm (8in) sandwich cake tins with non-stick baking paper.

Measure all the cake ingredients into a large bowl. Whisk with an electric hand whisk until light and fluffy.

Spoon into the tins and level the surfaces. Bake in the preheated oven for 25 minutes, or until well risen and the top of the cakes spring back when lightly pressed with a finger. Leave to cool in the tin for 10 minutes, then turn out on to a wire rack and peel off the baking paper.

To make the icing, melt 200g (7oz) of the orange chocolate in a heatproof bowl set over a pan of simmering water, making sure the base of the bowl is not touching the water, stirring occasionally. Remove the bowl from the heat.

Whisk the butter and icing sugar together in a large bowl with an electric hand whisk until light and fluffy. Whisk in the melted chocolate.

Spread half the icing over one cake and sandwich the two cakes together. Spread the remaining icing on top. Roughly chop the remaining orange chocolate and scatter over the top of the cake.

This family weekend cake has a nice texture and looks spectacular, marbled with white and brown. It must be eaten fresh.

MARBLED CHOCOLATE RING CAKE

SERVES 8

225g (8oz) butter, softened
225g (8oz) caster sugar
4 large eggs
225g (8oz) self-raising flour
1 level teaspoon
    baking powder
1½ level tablespoons
    cocoa powder
1½ tablespoons
    boiling water

For the icing
150g (5oz) dark chocolate,
    broken into pieces
115g (4oz) butter
55g (2oz) Belgian milk
    chocolate, broken
    into pieces

Preheat the oven to 180°C/Fan 160°C/Gas 4. Grease a 1.75 litre (3 pint) or 24cm (9½in) ring mould then line with strips of non-stick baking paper.

Measure all the cake ingredients, except the cocoa and boiling water, into a large bowl. Beat until thoroughly blended. Dot about half of this mixture, in teaspoons, into the base of the prepared tin.

Mix the cocoa powder and boiling water together in a small bowl, then mix into the remaining cake mixture. Dot this mixture over and between the plain mixture in the tin until all is used up.

Swirl a little with a knife, then carefully level the surface. Bake in the preheated oven for about 40 minutes, or until well risen and the top of the cake springs back when lightly pressed with a finger. Leave to cool in the tin for a few minutes then turn out, peel off the baking paper and finish cooling on a wire rack.

To make the icing, melt the dark chocolate with 2 tablespoons water and the butter in a heatproof bowl set over a pan of simmering water, stirring occasionally. Pour the icing over the cake, then leave to set for about 1 hour.

Melt the milk chocolate in a small heatproof bowl set over a pan of simmering water, making sure the base of the bowl is not touching the water, stirring occasionally. Spoon into a paper piping bag, cut off the tip of the bag and drizzle the chocolate over the top of the dark chocolate icing. Leave to set.

Achieving a lovely shine to your mirror cake will make this an impressive cake to behold. It is worth trying! The cake will keep well in the fridge without losing its shine.

CHOCOLATE MIRROR CAKE

SERVES 8

4 large eggs
125g (4½oz) caster sugar
125g (4½oz) self-raising
  flour, sifted
55g (2oz) butter, melted
  and cooled

For the icing
7 sheets of platinum-grade
  leaf gelatine
225g (8oz) caster sugar
75g (3oz) cocoa powder
75ml (2½fl oz) double cream
125ml (4fl oz) water
55g (2oz) dark chocolate,
  broken into pieces

TIP
There are two sizes of
leaf gelatine available;
we use 11g sheets.

Preheat the oven to 180°C/Fan 160°C/Gas 4. Grease a 23cm (9in) round springform tin and line the base with non-stick baking paper.

Place the eggs and sugar in a large mixing bowl. Whisk together using an electric hand whisk until thick ribbon stage. Gently fold the flour into the egg mixture until well combined. Pour the butter around the edge of the bowl, then carefully fold into the mixture.

Pour into the prepared tin and level the surface. Bake in the preheated oven for about 30 minutes, or until pale golden and coming away from the sides of the tin. Leave to cool in the tin for a few minutes, then turn out, peel off the baking paper and finish cooling on a wire rack.

To make the icing, place the gelatine leaves in a bowl of cold water for 5 minutes until soft. Measure the remaining ingredients, except the dark chocolate, into a saucepan. Place over a gentle heat until melted, then bring up to the boil, stirring until smooth. Remove from the heat and add the chocolate, stirring to melt and incorporate. Leave to cool for 5 minutes.

Remove the gelatine leaves from the water and squeeze out any excess liquid. Place the gelatine in the warm chocolate mixture and stir until dissolved. Pour the icing through a sieve into a bowl and leave to thicken at room temperature for about 15 minutes, or until a thick pouring consistency. Depending on the heat of your kitchen, you may need to pop it in the fridge.

Place a baking tray under the cooled sponge on the wire rack and pour the icing all over the surface and sides until completely covered. Leave for 30 minutes for the icing to set before transferring to a serving plate.

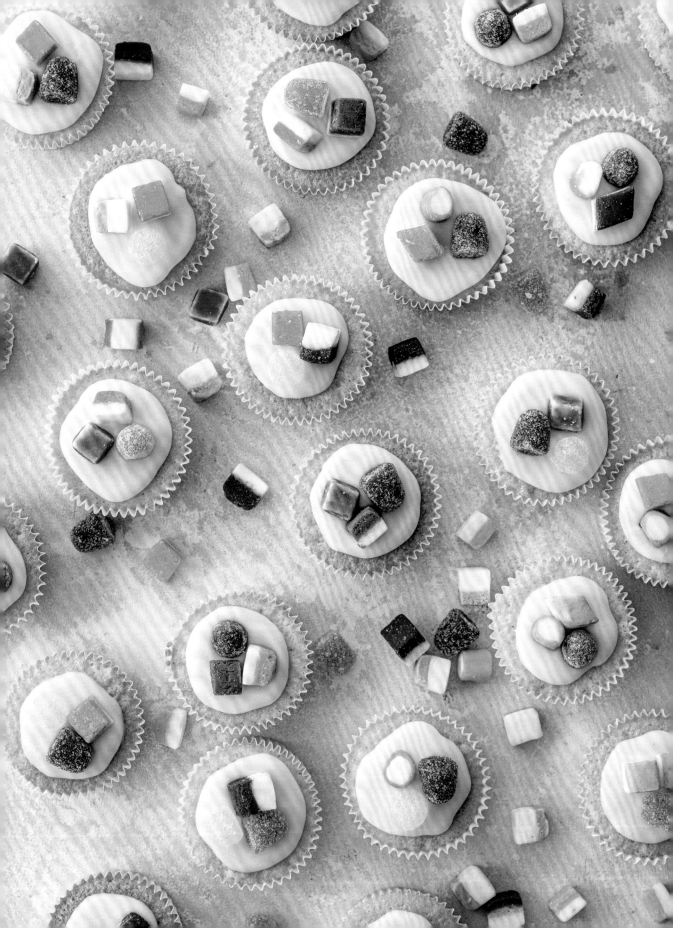

CHAPTER FOUR

CUPCAKES
AND OTHER
SMALL BAKES

Cupcakes are great for teatime, or arranged stacked on a cake stand instead of a large traditional birthday cake or even a wedding cake. Cupcakes are a different shape to fairy cakes – the cases are deeper and have less angular sides.

CUPCAKES

MAKES 12 CAKES

100g (4oz) butter, softened
150g (5oz) self-raising flour
150g (5oz) caster sugar
3 tablespoons milk
2 large eggs
½ teaspoon vanilla extract

For the icing
(choose one type of icing or
	halve the ingredients and
	make a mixture of both)

Butter icing
100g (4oz) butter, softened
225g (8oz) icing sugar, sifted
½ teaspoon vanilla extract

Glacé icing
juice of 1 lemon, warmed
225g (8oz) icing sugar, sifted

To decorate
combination of plain or
	white chocolate curls
	or shavings, silver hearts,
	hundreds and thousands,
	marshmallows and
	silver balls

Preheat the oven to 180°C/Fan 160°C/Gas 4. Put muffin cases into a 12-hole muffin tin.

—

Measure all the cupcake ingredients into a large bowl and beat until the mixture is well blended and smooth.

—

Fill each muffin case with the mixture and bake in the preheated oven for 20–25 minutes, until risen and golden brown. Lift the paper cases out of the tin and cool them on a wire rack until completely cold before icing.

—

To make the butter icing, beat together all the ingredients to give a creamy, thick icing, then smooth it over the cold cupcakes. To make the glacé icing, gradually add the warmed lemon juice to the icing sugar to give a glossy icing.

—

Decorate the cupcakes with chocolate curls or shavings, silver hearts, hundreds and thousands, marshmallows or silver balls.

To make Fruity Celebration Cupcakes, follow the ingredients and method for Rich Fruit Cake (page 133) and cook at 160°C/Fan 140°C/Gas 3 for about 1 hour. Ice with fondant icing (page 400).

TIPS

If you are making a double quantity of cupcakes or using a smaller tin, you can prepare the cupcake mixture in one go and spoon it into the paper cases ready to go into the oven. They will come to no harm, as raising agents react more slowly nowadays. Bake one tray of cupcakes at a time.

Try adding 2 tablespoons cocoa powder or 1 teaspoon strong coffee to the butter icing to make chocolate or coffee icing. When making the glacé icing, warming the lemon juice before mixing with the icing sugar helps it set better.

Butterfly cakes are quick and easy to make, they look pretty and are very effective for a children's party.

BUTTERFLY CAKES

MAKES 12 CAKES

115g (4oz) butter, softened
115g (4oz) caster sugar
2 large eggs
115g (4oz) self-raising flour
½ level teaspoon baking
     powder

For the icing
175g (6oz) butter, softened
350g (12oz) icing sugar,
     sifted, plus extra
     for dusting

Preheat the oven to 200°C/Fan 180°C/Gas 6. Place fairy cake cases in a 12-hole bun tin.

—

Measure all the cake ingredients into a large bowl and beat well for 2–3 minutes until the mixture is well blended and smooth.

—

Fill each paper case with the mixture and bake in the preheated oven for 15–20 minutes, until the cakes are well risen and golden brown. Lift the paper cases out of the bun tin and cool them on a wire rack.

—

To make the icing, beat the butter and icing sugar together until well blended. Cut a slice from the top of each cake and cut this slice in half. Pipe a swirl of butter cream into the centre of each cake and place the half slices of cake on top to resemble butterfly wings. Dust the cakes with icing sugar to finish.

To make Chocolate Butterfly Cakes, follow the recipe above but make chocolate icing by mixing 2 tablespoons cocoa powder with 3 tablespoons boiling water. Allow to cool slightly, then beat in 175g (6oz) softened butter and 350g (12oz) sifted icing sugar until well blended. To make them really chocolatey, you can replace 30g (1oz) of self-raising flour from the cake ingredients with 30g (1oz) cocoa powder.

To make Orange or Lemon Butterfly Cakes, add the grated zest of 1 orange or lemon to the cake mixture in step 2. Ice them with a butter cream made from butter, icing sugar and a little orange or lemon juice, then dust with icing sugar.

For this recipe, you will need dariole moulds, which are available from specialist cook shops and department stores.

ENGLISH MADELEINES

MAKES 10 MADELEINES

115g (4oz) butter, softened
115g (4oz) caster sugar
2 large eggs
115g (4oz) self-raising flour
½ level teaspoon baking
 powder
2–3 drops of vanilla extract

To finish
4 tablespoons raspberry
 or strawberry jam
55g (2oz) desiccated
 coconut
5 red or natural glacé
 cherries, halved

Preheat the oven to 180°C/Fan 160°C/Gas 4. Grease ten dariole moulds and line the base of each with non-stick baking paper. Stand the tins on a baking tray.

Measure the cake ingredients into a large bowl and beat until the mixture is well blended and smooth.

Spoon the mixture into the dariole moulds, filling them about half full. Bake in the preheated oven for about 20 minutes, until well risen and firm to the touch. Leave to cool in the moulds for 5 minutes, then turn out, peel off the baking paper and finish cooling on a wire rack.

When the cakes are cool, trim the bases so that they stand firmly. Push the raspberry or strawberry jam through a sieve, then warm in a small pan. Spread the coconut out on a large plate. Use a fork to spear the bases of the cakes to hold them. Brush them with the warm jam, then roll in the coconut to coat. Decorate each madeleine with half a glacé cherry.

These shell-shaped cakes are made using a madeleine tin, available from specialist kitchen shops and department stores. It is worth greasing and flouring the tins well so that the cakes come out cleanly. They are best on the day of making and, in France, are traditionally dipped into tea to eat.

FRENCH MADELEINES

MAKES ABOUT 30 MADELEINES

150g (5oz) self-raising flour, plus extra for dusting
150g (5oz) butter
3 large eggs
150g (5oz) caster sugar
½ level teaspoon baking powder
finely grated zest of 1 lemon
icing sugar, to dust (optional)

Preheat the oven to 220°C/Fan 200°C/Gas 7. Grease a madeleine tray, dust with flour and shake off any excess.

Melt the butter in a small pan and allow to cool slightly.

Measure the eggs and sugar into a large bowl and whisk until pale and thick.

Sift in half the flour with the baking powder and lemon zest and fold in gently. Pour in half the melted butter around the edge of the bowl and fold in. Repeat the process with the remaining flour and butter.

Spoon the mixture into the prepared moulds so that it is just below the rim. Bake in the preheated oven for 8–10 minutes, until well risen, golden and springy to the touch. Ease out of the tins with a small palette knife and cool on a wire rack.

Grease and flour the tins again and repeat until all the mixture has been used up.

Dust with icing sugar to serve, if you like.

These large muffins look quite impressive. They're best eaten on the day of baking.

CHOCOLATE CHIP AMERICAN MUFFINS

MAKES 12 MUFFINS

250g (9oz) self-raising flour
1 level teaspoon baking
   powder
55g (2oz) butter, softened
75g (3oz) caster sugar
175g (6oz) dark chocolate
   chips
2 large eggs
1 teaspoon vanilla extract
250ml (9fl oz) milk

Preheat the oven to 200°C/Fan 180°C/Gas 6. Place muffin cases in a 12-hole muffin tin.

Measure the flour and baking powder into a large bowl. Add the butter and rub into the flour, using your fingertips, until the mixture resembles fine breadcrumbs. Stir in the sugar and chocolate chips.

Mix together the eggs, vanilla extract and milk, then pour all in one go into the dry ingredients. Mix quickly with a wooden spoon to blend. The mixture should have a lumpy consistency.

Spoon the mixture into the paper cases, filling almost to the top. Bake in the preheated oven for 20–25 minutes, or until well risen and firm to the touch. Leave to cool for a few minutes in the tray, then lift out and cool for a little longer on a wire rack.

This makes special little cakes, ideal for children's parties.

ICED FAIRY CAKES

MAKES 24 CAKES

115g (4oz) butter, softened
115g (4oz) caster sugar
2 large eggs
115g (4oz) self-raising flour
½ level teaspoon baking
    powder

For the icing
225g (8oz) icing sugar, sifted
2–3 tablespoons warm
    water
sweets, to decorate

Preheat the oven to 200°C/Fan 180°C/Gas 6. Place fairy cake cases in two 12-hole bun tins.

Measure all the cake ingredients into a large bowl and beat for 2–3 minutes until the mixture is well blended and smooth.

Fill each paper case with the mixture and bake in the preheated oven for 15–20 minutes, until the cakes are well risen and golden brown. Lift the paper cases out of the bun tin and cool them on a wire rack.

Place the icing sugar in a bowl and gradually blend in the warm water until you have a fairly stiff icing. Spoon over the top of the cakes and decorate with sweets.

To make Orange Fairy Cakes, follow the recipe above and add the grated zest of 1 orange with the other ingredients. To make the icing, gradually blend the icing sugar with the juice of 1 orange until you have a fairly stiff icing.

These spicy little currant cakes, enclosed in a flaky pastry, come from the north of England. You can use ready-made puff pastry, if you wish.

ECCLES CAKES

MAKES ABOUT 8 CAKES

For the flaky pastry
225g (8oz) plain flour
175g (6oz) butter
a squeeze of lemon juice
8 tablespoons cold water

For the filling
55g (2oz) butter, softened
55g (2oz) light
    muscovado sugar
½ level teaspoon
    ground mixed spice
55g (2oz) candied peel,
    chopped
115g (4oz) currants

To finish
1 large egg white, beaten
a little caster sugar

First make the flaky pastry. Measure the flour into a bowl. Divide the butter into 4 equal portions and rub one portion of it into the flour, using your fingertips, until the mixture resembles fine breadcrumbs. Add the lemon juice and water and mix with a round-bladed knife to form a soft dough.

___

On a lightly floured work surface, gently knead the dough until smooth. Roll out into an oblong three times as long as it is wide. Dot a second portion of the butter in small pieces over the top two-thirds of the pastry. Fold the bottom third of the pastry up over the middle third and the top third down, then seal the edges well with the edge of your hand. Wrap the pastry in clingfilm and put in the fridge to relax for about 15 minutes.

___

Re-roll the pastry as before, always starting with the folds of the dough to the left, until the remaining portions of butter have been used up. Wrap the pastry again in clingfilm and leave in the fridge for at least 30 minutes before using.

___

Preheat the oven to 220°C/Fan 200°C/Gas 7.

___

To make the filling, mix the butter, sugar, spice, chopped peel and currants in a bowl. Roll out the pastry thinly and cut into eight rounds about 15cm (6in) in diameter (use a saucer as a guide). If using ready-made puff pastry, remember to roll it out very thinly otherwise it will be too thick when cooked.

___

Place a good tablespoon of the filling into the centre of each round, dampen the pastry edges with water, then draw together to enclose the filling. Turn the pastry over and flatten gently with the rolling pin so that the currants just show through. Re-shape to a round with your hands, if necessary. Make 3 small cuts in the top of each cake, brush with the beaten egg white and sprinkle with caster sugar.

—

Transfer the cakes to a baking tray and bake in the preheated oven for 10–15 minutes until golden. Leave to cool on the baking tray for a few minutes before lifting on to a wire rack to cool completely.

TIP

For light pastry, incorporate as much air as possible by sifting flour from a height, cutting butter in small pieces with a knife, and lifting your hands well above the bowl when rubbing in.

Traditionally a red jam is used for the centre of these cakes, which are buttery and very delicious.

APRICOT SWISS CAKES

MAKES 18 CAKES

225g (8oz) butter, softened
75g (3oz) icing sugar, sifted,
    plus extra for dusting
200g (7oz) self-raising flour
55g (2oz) cornflour

To finish
a little apricot jam

Preheat the oven to 180°C/Fan 160°C/Gas 4. Place 18 fairy cake cases in two 12-hole bun tins.

Place the butter in a large bowl. Add the icing sugar and beat well until really soft and fluffy. Stir in the flours and mix until smooth. Spoon the mixture into a large piping bag fitted with a large star nozzle.

Pipe circles of the mixture into the base of each paper case and bake in the preheated oven for 15–20 minutes, or until pale golden brown. Remove the paper cases from the tin and cool them on a wire rack.

Put a small amount of apricot jam on the centre of each cake. Dust lightly with sifted icing sugar.

American muffins (very different to English muffins) are hugely popular. These are best served warm, traditionally at breakfast time.

BLUEBERRY MUFFINS

MAKES 12 MUFFINS

250g (9oz) self-raising flour
1 level teaspoon baking
   powder
55g (2oz) butter, softened
75g (3oz) caster sugar
175g (6oz) blueberries
finely grated zest of 1 lemon
2 large eggs
250ml (9fl oz) milk

Preheat the oven to 200°C/Fan 180°C/Gas 6. Place muffin cases in a 12-hole muffin tin.

—

Measure the flour and baking powder into a large bowl. Add the butter and rub into the flour, using your fingertips, until the mixture resembles fine breadcrumbs. Stir in the sugar, blueberries and lemon zest.

—

Mix together the eggs and milk, then pour all in one go into the dry ingredients. Mix quickly to blend. The mixture should have a lumpy consistency.

—

Spoon the mixture into the paper cases, filling almost to the top. Bake in the preheated oven for 20–25 minutes, until well risen, golden and firm to the touch. Leave to cool for a few minutes in the tray, then lift out the paper cases and cool for a few minutes on a wire rack. Serve warm.

CHAPTER FIVE

CELEBRATION CAKES

This is a wonderful, rich traditional fruit cake. It can be made up to three months in advance. Make sure you allow plenty of time to 'feed' the cake with brandy and let it mature. I've included a table overleaf to show the different ingredient quantities needed to make variously sized cakes.

CLASSIC RICH CHRISTMAS CAKE

SERVES 12

115g (4oz) red or natural glacé
   cherries, quartered
115g (4oz) ready-to-eat dried
   apricots, snipped into pieces
275g (10oz) currants
175g (6oz) sultanas
175g (6oz) raisins
55g (2oz) candied peel,
   finely chopped
3 tablespoons brandy
225g (8oz) plain flour
¼ level teaspoon freshly
   grated nutmeg
½ level teaspoon ground
   mixed spice
225g (8oz) butter, softened
225g (8oz) dark muscovado
   sugar
4 large eggs
55g (2oz) chopped almonds
scant 1 tablespoon black treacle
finely grated zest of 1 lemon
finely grated zest of 1 orange

To finish
brandy, to feed the cake
675g (1½lb) almond paste
   or marzipan (see page 398
   for almond paste recipe)
675g (1½lb) fondant or
   ready-to-roll icing
   (page 400)

Begin this cake the night before you want to bake it. Place the cherries in a sieve and rinse under running water. Drain well then dry thoroughly on kitchen paper. Measure all the fruits and chopped peel into a large bowl. Mix in the brandy, cover and leave in a cool place overnight.

Preheat the oven to 140°C/Fan 120°C/Gas 1. Grease a 20cm (8in) deep round cake tin, then line the base and sides with a double layer of baking paper.

Measure the flour, spices, butter, sugar, eggs, almonds, treacle and lemon and orange zests into a large bowl. Beat well, then fold in the soaked fruits.

Spoon the mixture into the prepared tin and spread out evenly with the back of a spoon. Cover the top of the cake loosely with a double layer of baking paper. Bake in the preheated oven for about 4½–4¾ hours, or until the cake feels firm to the touch and a skewer inserted into the centre comes out clean. Leave the cake to cool in the tin.

When cool, pierce the cake at intervals with a fine skewer and feed with a little brandy. Wrap the completely cold cake in a double layer of baking paper, and again in foil, and store in a cool place, feeding at intervals with more brandy. Don't remove the lining paper when storing as this helps to keep the cake moist. Cover the cake with almond paste or marzipan about a week before icing.

Recipe continued overleaf

To decorate
almond paste (leftover from putting over the cake)
green food colouring
icing sugar, sifted
ribbon, holly or your favourite decorations

Cover the cake with fondant or ready-to-roll icing. Colour the almond paste (left over from putting the almond paste on the cake) dark green. Roll out on a board that has been lightly sprinkled with icing sugar and cut into 2.5cm (1in) wide strips. Cut these into diamonds and then, with the base of an icing nozzle, remove half circles from the sides of the diamonds to give holly-shaped leaves. Make vein marks on the leaves with a sharp knife, bend the leaves over the handles of wooden spoons and leave to dry. Decorate the top of the cake with the almond-paste holly leaves, dust lightly with icing sugar and finish by tying a ribbon around the sides of the cake.

	15cm (6in) round / 12.5cm (5in) square	18cm (7in) round / 15cm (6in) square	20cm (8in) round / 18cm (7in) square	23cm (9in) round / 20cm (8in) square	25cm (10in) round / 23cm (9in) square	28cm (11in) round / 25cm (10in) square	30cm (12in) round / 28cm (11in) square	33cm (13in) round / 30cm (12in) square
Glacé cherries	55g (2oz)	75g (3oz)	115g (4oz)	150g (5oz)	175g (6oz)	225g (8oz)	275g (10oz)	350g (12oz)
Ready-to-eat dried apricots	55g (2oz)	75g (3oz)	115g (4oz)	150g (5oz)	175g (6oz)	225g (8oz)	275g (10oz)	350g (12oz)
Currants	150g (5oz)	200g (7oz)	275g (10oz)	400g (14oz)	450g (1lb)	550g (1¼lb)	750g (1½lb)	800g (1¾lb)
Sultanas	75g (3oz)	115g (4oz)	175g (6oz)	225g (8oz)	275g (10oz)	350g (12oz)	450g (1lb)	550g (1¼lb)
Raisins	75g (3oz)	115g (4oz)	175g (6oz)	225g (8oz)	275g (10oz)	350g (12oz)	450g (1lb)	550g (1¼lb)
Candied peel	30g (1oz)	40g (1½oz)	55g (2oz)	65g (2½oz)	75g (3oz)	115g (4oz)	150g (5oz)	175g (6oz)
Brandy	1½ tbsp	2 tbsp	3 tbsp	4 tbsp	5 tbsp	6 tbsp	7 tbsp	8 tbsp
Plain flour	115g (4oz)	175g (6oz)	225g (8oz)	275g (10oz)	400g (14oz)	450g (1lb)	500g (1lb 2oz)	550g (1¼lb)
Grated nutmeg	⅛ tsp	scant ¼ tsp	¼ tsp	scant ½ tsp	½ tsp	½ tsp	¾ tsp	1 tsp
Ground mixed spice	¼ tsp	scant ½ tsp	½ tsp	¾ tsp	¾ tsp	1 tsp	1¼ tsp	1½ tsp
Softened butter	115g (4oz)	175g (6oz)	225g (8oz)	275g (10oz)	400g (14oz)	450g (1lb)	500g (1lb 2oz)	550g (1¼lb)
Dark musc. sugar	115g (4oz)	175g (6oz)	225g (8oz)	275g (10oz)	400g (14oz)	450g (1lb)	500g (1lb 2oz)	550g (1¼lb)
Large eggs	2	3	4	5	7	8	9	10
Chopped almonds	30g (1oz)	40g (1½oz)	55g (2oz)	65g (2½oz)	75g (3oz)	115g (4oz)	150g (5oz)	175g (6oz)
Black treacle	½ tbsp	rounded ½ tbsp	scant 1 tbsp	1 tbsp	1½ tbsp	2 tbsp	3 tbsp	4 tbsp
Zest lemon	½	½	1	1½	2	2	3	3
Zest orange	½	½	1	1½	2	2	3	3
Baking times (approx.)	3½ hrs	4 hrs	4½ hrs	4¾ hrs	5 hrs	5½ hrs	6 hrs	6½ hrs

Unlike traditional Christmas cakes, this mixture produces a light, yet succulent cake. The pineapple makes it lovely and moist.

VICTORIAN CHRISTMAS CAKE

SERVES 14

350g (12oz) red or natural
  glacé cherries, quartered
1 × 227g can pineapple in
  natural juice, drained
  and chopped
350g (12oz) ready-to-eat
  dried apricots, snipped
  into pieces
115g (4oz) almonds,
  roughly chopped
finely grated zest of
  2 lemons
350g (12oz) sultanas
250g (9oz) self-raising flour
250g (9oz) caster sugar
250g (9oz) butter, softened
75g (3oz) ground almonds
5 large eggs

To decorate
whole almonds
red or natural glacé cherries
glacé pineapple (available
  from health-food shops)
115g (4oz) icing sugar, sifted

Preheat the oven to 160°C/Fan 140°C/Gas 3. Grease a 23cm (9in) deep round cake tin, then line the base and sides with a double layer of non-stick baking paper.

Place the cherries in a sieve and rinse under running water, then drain well. Dry the drained cherries and the pineapple very thoroughly on kitchen paper. Place in a bowl with the apricots, chopped almonds, lemon zest and sultanas and gently mix together.

Measure the remaining cake ingredients into a large bowl and beat well for 1 minute until smooth. Lightly fold in the fruit and nuts.

Turn the mixture into the prepared cake tin and level the surface. Decorate the top with the whole almonds, halved glacé cherries and pieces of glacé pineapple. Bake in the preheated oven for about 2¼ hours, or until golden brown. A skewer inserted into the centre of the cake should come out clean. Cover the cake loosely with foil after 1 hour to prevent the top becoming too dark. Leave to cool in the tin for about 30 minutes then turn out, peel off the baking paper and finish cooling on a wire rack.

Mix the icing sugar with a little water and drizzle over the cake to glaze.

Individual fruit cakes are particularly welcome gifts for those who live on their own or have small appetites.

TINY FRUIT CAKES

MAKES 3 CAKES

40g (1½oz) red or natural glacé cherries, quartered
55g (2oz) raisins
55g (2oz) sultanas
55g (2oz) currants
30g (1oz) ready-to-eat dried apricots, snipped into pieces
15g (½oz) candied peel, chopped
2 teaspoons brandy, rum or sherry, plus extra for feeding the cake
15g (½oz) almonds, chopped
15g (½oz) ground almonds
finely grated zest of ¼ lemon
75g (3oz) plain flour
½ level teaspoon mixed ground spice
55g (2oz) dark muscovado sugar
55g (2oz) butter, softened
2 teaspoons black treacle
1 large egg
1 tablespoon flaked almonds

For the icing
3 tablespoons apricot jam
225g (8oz) almond paste or marzipan (see page 398 for almond paste recipe)
225g (8oz) fondant or ready-to-roll icing (page 400)

Place the cherries in a sieve and rinse under running water. Drain well then dry thoroughly on kitchen paper. Measure all the dried fruits and chopped peel into a large bowl, add the brandy, rum or sherry, cover the bowl tightly and leave overnight.

Preheat the oven to 160°C/Fan 140°C/Gas 3. Grease and line three 7 × 6cm (2¾ × 2¼in) baking rings with non-stick baking paper. Place them on a baking tray lined with non-stick paper.

Measure the chopped and ground almonds, lemon zest, flour, mixed spice, sugar, butter, treacle and egg into a large bowl and mix together. Beat thoroughly for about 2 minutes until the mixture is smooth. Add the soaked fruit and any liquid and stir to mix in thoroughly. Spoon the mixture into the prepared rings. Level the surfaces, then sprinkle with the flaked almonds.

Bake in the preheated oven for about 1–1¼ hours, or until a fine skewer inserted into the centre comes out clean. Allow the cakes to cool in the rings. Pierce the top of the cakes in several places with a skewer and spoon in a little brandy, rum or sherry.

Remove the cakes from the rings but do not remove the baking paper as this helps to keep the cakes moist. Wrap in more baking paper and then some foil, and store in a cool place for a week.

Sieve the apricot jam and warm it slightly, then brush it over the surface of the cakes. Cover with almond paste or marzipan and icing in the usual way. Decorate as liked.

I've often been asked for this recipe, which doesn't have to be made in advance or fed with brandy. The cake is light and moist.

FAST MINCEMEAT CHRISTMAS CAKE

150g (5oz) butter, softened
150g (5oz) light
    muscovado sugar
2 large eggs
225g (8oz) self-raising flour
400g (14oz) luxury
    mincemeat
175g (6oz) currants
55g (2oz) almonds, chopped

To decorate
675g (1½lb) almond paste
    or marzipan (see page 398
    for almond paste recipe)
1 quantity of royal icing
    (page 399)

Preheat the oven to 160°C/Fan 140°C/Gas 3. Grease a 20cm (8in) deep round cake tin, then line the base and sides with non-stick baking paper.

—

Measure all the cake ingredients into a large bowl and beat well for 1 minute until thoroughly mixed.

—

Turn into the prepared tin and level the surface. Bake in the preheated oven for about 1¾ hours, or until a skewer inserted into the centre comes out clean and the cake is shrinking from the sides of the tin. Cover the cake with foil after 1 hour if beginning to brown too much. Leave to cool in the tin for 10 minutes then turn out, peel off the baking paper and finish cooling on a wire rack.

—

Cover the cake with almond paste about a week before icing. Make up the royal icing and spread some of the icing thickly over the sides of the cake, smoothing with a palette knife. Spoon more royal icing on top of the cake. Smooth a strip in the centre (this is where the ribbon will go) then pull the remainder into peaks with the back of a spoon. Leave the icing to harden for a few hours, then decorate the cake with ribbon.

I'm often asked for the boiled fruit cake with condensed milk that Granny used to make – here it is. Although I add fat to make it even tastier!

QUICK BOILED FRUIT CAKE

SERVES 10-12

1 × 397g can full-fat
  condensed milk
150g (5oz) butter
225g (8oz) raisins
225g (8oz) sultanas
175g (6oz) currants
175g (6oz) red or
  natural glacé cherries,
  roughly chopped
225g (8oz) self-raising flour
2 level teaspoons ground
  mixed spice
1 level teaspoon
  ground cinnamon
2 large eggs

Preheat the oven to 150°C/Fan 130°C/Gas 2. Grease an 18cm (7in) deep round cake tin, then line the base and sides with non-stick baking paper.

Pour the condensed milk into a heavy-based pan and add the butter, dried fruit and glacé cherries. Place over a low heat until the butter has melted into the condensed milk. Stir well, then simmer gently for 5 minutes. Remove from the heat and set aside to cool for about 10 minutes, stirring occasionally.

Measure the flour and spices into a large bowl and make a well in the centre. Add the eggs and the cooled fruit mixture and quickly mix together until well blended.

Turn into the prepared tin and level the surface. Bake in the preheated oven for about 1¾–2 hours, or until the cake is well risen, golden brown and the top feels firm. A skewer inserted into the centre should come out clean. Leave to cool in the tin for 10 minutes then turn out, peel off the baking paper and finish cooling on a wire rack.

This has become the traditional Easter cake, but originally it was given by servant girls to their mothers when they went home on Mothering Sunday. The almond-paste balls represent the eleven apostles (excluding Judas).

EASTER SIMNEL CAKE

SERVES 12

115g (4oz) red or natural glacé cherries, quartered
225g (8oz) baking spread, straight from the fridge
225g (8oz) light muscovado sugar
4 large eggs
225g (8oz) self-raising flour
225g (8oz) sultanas
115g (4oz) currants
115g (4oz) ready-to-eat dried apricots, snipped into pieces
55g (2oz) candied peel, chopped
finely grated zest of 2 lemons
2 level teaspoons ground mixed spice

For the filling and topping
500g (1lb 2oz) almond paste or marzipan (see page 398 for almond paste recipe)
2 tablespoons apricot jam
1 large egg, beaten, to glaze

Preheat the oven to 150°C/Fan 130°C/Gas 2. Grease a 20cm (8in) deep round cake tin then line the base and sides with non-stick baking paper.

Place the cherries in a sieve and rinse under running water. Drain well then dry thoroughly on kitchen paper.

Measure all the cake ingredients into a large mixing bowl and beat well until thoroughly blended. Place half the mixture in the prepared tin and level the surface.

Take one-third of the almond paste or marzipan and roll it out to a circle the size of the tin and place on top of the cake mixture.

Spoon the remaining cake mixture on top and level the surface. Bake in the preheated oven for about 2½ hours until well risen, evenly brown and firm to the touch. Cover with foil after 1 hour if the top is browning too quickly. Leave to cool in the tin for 10 minutes then turn out, peel off the baking paper and finish cooling on a wire rack.

When the cake is cool, brush the top with a little warmed apricot jam. Roll half the remaining almond paste into a ball, then roll out to a 20cm (8in) circle. Press firmly on the top and crimp the edges to decorate. Mark a criss-cross pattern on the almond paste with a sharp knife. Form the remaining almond paste into 11 balls.

Brush the almond paste with beaten egg and arrange the almond paste balls around the edge of the cake. Brush the tops of the balls with beaten egg, too, then place the cake under a hot grill to turn the almond paste golden.

This cake is robust enough to pack for a picnic and also makes a good alternative Christmas cake. Instead of dried cranberries, you can use the same weight of red or natural quartered glacé cherries, but wash and dry them thoroughly.

CRANBERRY AND APRICOT FRUIT CAKE

SERVES 12-14

1 × 227g can pineapple
  in natural juice, drained
  and roughly chopped
350g (12oz) ready-to-eat
  dried apricots, snipped
  into pieces
350g (12oz) dried
  cranberries
350g (12oz) sultanas
115g (4oz) almonds,
  roughly chopped
75g (3oz) ground almonds
finely grated zest of
  2 lemons
250g (9oz) self-raising flour
250g (9oz) caster sugar
250g (9oz) butter, softened
5 large eggs

To decorate
55g (2oz) whole almonds

Preheat the oven to 150°C/Fan 130°C/Gas 2. Grease a 23cm (9in) deep round cake tin, then line the base and sides with non-stick baking paper.

—

Dry the pineapple thoroughly on kitchen paper. Combine all the fruits, nuts (chopped and ground) and lemon zest in a large bowl and mix together well.

—

Measure the remaining ingredients into a large mixing bowl and beat until smooth. Fold in the fruit and nuts, then spoon the mixture into the prepared tin. Level the top with the back of a spoon and decorate with concentric circles of regularly spaced almonds.

—

Bake in the preheated oven for about 2½ hours, or until the cake is nicely browned. If it shows signs of becoming too browned before it is cooked, cover the top loosely with foil. When cooked, the cake should show signs of shrinking away from the sides of the tin and a skewer inserted into the centre of the cake should come out clean. Leave to cool in the tin for about 30 minutes then turn out, leaving the baking paper in place, and finish cooling on a wire rack.

TIPS

Like most fruit cakes, this improves on storing and can be made up to 1 week ahead. Leave the baking paper in place, wrap the cake closely in clingfilm and store in an airtight container.

To freeze the cake, wrap closely in clingfilm as above, seal inside a plastic bag (this takes up less space than a plastic freezer box), then label and freeze for up to 3 months. To defrost, put the cake, fully wrapped, in the fridge overnight or remove from the plastic bag and thaw for 8 hours at room temperature.

I use this for Christmas, birthdays and all special occasions – it's a winner. Start preparing the cake the night before you want to bake it, as the dried fruits need to be soaked in brandy so that they become plump.

RICH FRUIT CAKE

SERVES 12-14

175g (6oz) red or natural
    glacé cherries, quartered
350g (12oz) currants
225g (8oz) sultanas
225g (8oz) raisins
175g (6oz) ready-to-eat
    dried apricots, snipped
    into pieces
75g (3oz) candied peel,
    finely chopped
4 tablespoons brandy,
    plus extra to feed the cake
400g (14oz) plain flour
½ level teaspoon grated
    nutmeg
½ level teaspoon ground
    mixed spice
400g (14oz) butter,
    softened
400g (14oz) dark
    muscovado sugar
5 large eggs
65g (2½oz) almonds,
    chopped
1 tablespoon black treacle
finely grated zest of 1 lemon
finely grated zest of 1 orange

To decorate
55g (2oz) whole almonds
55g (2oz) red or natural
    glacé cherries, rinsed,
    dried and halved

Place the cherries in a sieve and rinse under running water. Drain well then dry thoroughly on kitchen paper. Place the cherries, currants, sultanas, raisins, apricots and chopped peel in a large bowl, stir in the brandy, cover and leave in a cool place overnight.

The next day, preheat the oven to 140°C/Fan 120°C/Gas 1. Grease a 23cm (9in) deep round cake tin, then line the base and sides with a double layer of non-stick baking paper.

Measure the flour, grated nutmeg, mixed spice, butter, sugar, eggs, chopped almonds, black treacle and grated lemon and orange zests into a large bowl and beat to mix thoroughly. Fold in the soaked fruits, then spoon the mixture into the prepared cake tin and level the surface. Decorate the top with the whole almonds and halved glacé cherries, pushing them lightly into the top of the cake mixture.

Cover the top of the cake loosely with a double layer of non-stick baking paper and bake in the preheated oven for 4–4½ hours, until the cake feels firm to the touch and a skewer inserted into the centre comes out clean. Leave to cool in the tin then, when the cake is almost cold, turn out, peel off the baking paper and finish cooling on a wire rack.

Pierce the base at intervals with a fine skewer and feed with a little brandy. Once the cake is completely cold, wrap it in a double layer of baking paper and then in foil. Store in a cool place for up to 3 months, feeding at intervals with more brandy.

This is a version of a French Christmas log, which is suitable for serving as a dessert or with coffee.

BÛCHE DE NOËL

SERVES 10

1 unfilled Chocolate Roulade
(see page 38)

For the filling
1 tablespoon instant
coffee granules
2 tablespoons hot milk
225g (8oz) unsweetened
chestnut purée
2 tablespoons brandy
55g (2oz) caster sugar
150ml (¼ pint) pouring
double cream, whipped

For the topping
300 ml (½ pint) pouring
double cream, whipped
cocoa powder, for dusting

First make the Chocolate Roulade. Roll with baking paper inside and leave to cool.

———

While it is cooling, make the filling. Dissolve the coffee in the hot milk. Sieve the chestnut purée into a bowl and beat in the coffee mixture, brandy and sugar until the mixture is smooth. Fold the whipped cream into the chestnut purée mixture.

———

Carefully unroll the chocolate Swiss roll. Remove the paper and spread the chestnut filling all over the cake, then re-roll. Cut a small slice off at an angle from one of the ends of the roll, then place the roll on a serving plate or board and attach the slice to look like a branch.

———

Spread the whipped cream over the cake to cover completely, using a small palette knife in long strokes to give the bark effect. Dust lightly with cocoa and decorate with Christmassy decorations of your choice.

A lemon cake is perfect for a christening. Colour the icing pale pink or pale blue, if you like, or maybe a pale primrose yellow.

SPONGE CHRISTENING CAKE

75g (3oz) butter
6 large eggs
175g (6oz) caster sugar
150g (5oz) self-raising flour
2 level tablespoons
    cornflour

For the filling
300ml (½ pint) pouring
    double cream, whipped
4 tablespoons lemon curd

To finish
icing sugar, for dusting
700g (1lb 9oz) fondant
    or ready-to-roll icing
    (see page 400 for
    fondant recipe)
crystallised flowers
    (page 401)
ribbon, to decorate

Preheat the oven to 180°C/Fan 160°C/Gas 4. Grease a 23cm (9in) deep round cake tin, then line the base with non-stick baking paper.

Melt the butter in a small pan, then leave to cool slightly.

Measure the eggs and sugar into a large heatproof bowl and whisk over hot water with an electric whisk on high speed until the mixture becomes pale and creamy and leaves a trail on the surface when the whisk is lifted. Remove from the heat and continue to whisk until the mixture is cold.

Sift the flours together into a bowl. Fold half of the flours into the egg mixture, then carefully pour half the cooled butter around the edge of the mixture and lightly fold in. Repeat with the remaining flour and butter.

Pour into the prepared tin and level the surface. Bake in the preheated oven for about 40 minutes, or until well risen, firm to the touch and beginning to shrink away from the sides of the tin. Leave to cool in the tin for a few minutes then turn out, peel off the baking paper and finish cooling on a wire rack.

Cut the cake into three horizontally using a serrated or bread knife. Reserve 3–4 tablespoons of the whipped cream then mix the remainder with the lemon curd and use to sandwich the slices together. Spread the reserved cream around the sides and over the top of the cake.

Dust the work surface with icing sugar and roll out the fondant icing large enough to cover the cake completely. Fold the icing over the rolling pin and carefully lift on to the cake, gently smoothing the sides. Trim the extra icing from the base of the cake. Decorate with crystallised flowers and ribbon.

This cake serves about 100 people and makes a super dessert for a wedding breakfast served with raspberry coulis. You can make this recipe all in one go, but you will need huge bowls. The separate quantities needed to make each layer individually have also been included, which some might find an easier method – also useful if you want to make one of the layers for a practice run. The cakes can be frozen for up to 2 months, but the icing should be made the day before the wedding.

AMERICAN CHOCOLATE
SERVES 100 WEDDING CAKE

Total ingredients needed
1.6kg (3lb 9oz) dark chocolate, broken into pieces
30 large eggs, separated
8 large eggs, whole
1.25kg (2½lb) caster sugar
840g (1lb 14oz) ground almonds
7½ teaspoons freshly made black coffee

For the filling and icing
225g (8oz) apricot jam
1.25kg (2½lb) dark chocolate
450g (1lb) unsalted butter

To decorate
edible foliage and flowers

To make each layer separately see ingredient quantities overleaf

Preheat the oven to 190°C/Fan 170°C/Gas 5. Lightly grease a 15cm (6in), 23cm (9in) and 30cm (12in) deep round cake tin then line the base and sides of each tin with non-stick baking paper.

To make the cakes, melt the chocolate in a bowl set over a pan of simmering water, making sure the base of the bowl is not touching the water, stirring occasionally. Remove from the heat and leave to cool slightly.

Measure the yolks, whole eggs and sugar into a large bowl and beat until thick and light. Add the melted chocolate along with the almonds and coffee.

In a separate bowl, whisk the egg whites until stiff but not dry. Fold carefully into the chocolate mixture.

Divide the mixture between the prepared tins and bake in the preheated oven (they can all go into the oven at once; put the large cake on the middle shelf and the two smaller cakes on the top shelf). The small cake will take about 45 minutes, the medium cake 1–1¼ hours and the large cake 1½ –1¾ hours (cover loosely with foil after 1 hour). Test the centre of each with a skewer, which should come out just about clean. Leave to cool in the tins for a few minutes then turn out, peel off the baking paper and finish cooling on a wire rack. At this point, the cakes can be frozen.

Recipe continued overleaf

15cm (6in) cake
175g (6oz) dark chocolate,
    broken into pieces
3 large eggs, separated
1 large egg, whole
150g (5oz) caster sugar
75g (3oz) ground almonds
½ teaspoon freshly made
    black coffee

For the filling and icing
2 tablespoons apricot jam
225g (8oz) dark chocolate,
    broken into pieces
75g (3oz) unsalted butter

23cm (9in) cake
525g (1lb 3oz) dark chocolate,
    broken into pieces
10 large eggs, separated
2 large eggs, whole
425g (15oz) caster sugar
275g (10oz) ground almonds
2½ teaspoons freshly made
    black coffee

For the filling and icing
75g (3oz) apricot jam
350g (12oz) dark chocolate,
    broken into pieces
150g (5oz) unsalted butter

30cm (12in) cake
900g (2lb) dark chocolate,
    broken into pieces
17 large eggs, separated
5 large eggs, whole
700g (1lb 9oz) caster sugar
475g (1lb 1oz) ground almonds
4½ teaspoons freshly made
    black coffee

For the filling and icing
115g (4oz) apricot jam
550g (1¼lb) dark chocolate,
    broken into pieces
225g (8oz) unsalted butter

Turn the cold cakes upside down so that the flat side is uppermost. Push the apricot jam through a sieve, then brush over the tops and sides of the cakes.

To make the icing, melt the chocolate gently in a heatproof bowl over a pan of simmering water, making sure the base of the bowl is not touching the water, stirring occasionally. Add the butter and stir until the butter has melted.

Stand each cake on the wire rack on a baking tray to catch any drips, then pour over the chocolate icing. Smooth the top and sides with a palette knife and then leave to set in a cool place.

Transport the cake as separate layers and assemble and decorate in situ. Place the largest cake on a cake board or serving plate then carefully stack the other two cakes on top. Decorate with fresh edible flowers and foliage to match the wedding bouquet. Serve with raspberry coulis.

TIPS
The cakes will freeze un-iced for up to a month or can be made up to 7 days ahead. It is normal for the cakes to have crusty tops when baked – trim if necessary. Use a good-quality chocolate for the icing. I find better quality chocolates give a smoother finish. The high chocolate and sugar content make the cakes susceptible to burning, so do keep an eye on them. You may need to cover them with foil or baking paper. The cakes are firm enough to stack as they are but use thin cake boards slightly smaller than each layer if you feel happier. Don't ice the cake more than a day before the wedding to prevent it losing its sheen. Once iced, keep the cake in a cool place, but not in the fridge.

This is a very close-textured 'fudgy' cake that needs no filling. There is no flour in this recipe; ground almonds give the flavour and texture.

DIVINE CHOCOLATE BIRTHDAY CAKE

SERVES ABOUT 10

6 large eggs, 5 of them
    separated
215g (7½oz) caster sugar
265g (9½oz) dark chocolate,
    broken into pieces
1 level teaspoon instant
    coffee granules
1 teaspoon hot water
150g (5oz) ground almonds

For the icing
4 tablespoons apricot jam
225g (8oz) dark chocolate,
    broken into pieces
115g (4oz) unsalted butter

Preheat the oven to 190°C/Fan 170°C/Gas 5. Grease a 23cm (9in) deep round cake tin, then line the base with non-stick baking paper.

Place the egg yolks and whole egg in a large bowl with the sugar and beat together until thick and light in colour.

Melt the chocolate in a heatproof bowl set over a pan of simmering water, making sure the base of the bowl is not touching the water, stirring occasionally. Dissolve the coffee granules in the hot water and add to the melted chocolate. Cool slightly, then stir into the egg mixture along with the ground almonds.

In a separate bowl, whisk the egg whites until stiff but not dry. Carefully fold into the egg and chocolate mixture.

Turn into the prepared tin and gently level the surface. Bake in the preheated oven for about 50 minutes, or until well risen and a skewer inserted into the centre comes out clean. Leave to cool in the tin for 10 minutes then turn out, peel off the baking paper and finish cooling on a wire rack. Measure the apricot jam into a small saucepan and allow to melt over a low heat. Brush over the cake.

To make the icing, melt the chocolate gently in a heatproof bowl set over a pan of simmering water, making sure the base of the bowl is not touching the water, stirring occasionally. Remove from the heat, add the butter and stir until the icing has the consistency of thick pouring cream.

Stand the wire rack on a baking tray to catch any drips, then pour the icing over the cake, smoothing it over the top and sides with a palette knife. Allow to set, then decorate as you like.

A super and impressive large celebration cake.

RED VELVET CAKE

SERVES 16

For the sponges
300ml (½ pint) sunflower oil
500g (1lb 2oz) plain flour
2 tablespoons cocoa
    powder
4 teaspoons baking powder
2 teaspoons bicarbonate
    of soda
500g (1lb 2oz) light
    muscovado sugar
1 teaspoon fine salt
400ml (14fl oz) buttermilk
4 teaspoons vanilla extract
30ml (1fl oz) red food
    colouring gel or about
    ¼ teaspoon food colouring
    paste (use a professional
    food colouring paste if
    you can; a natural liquid
    colouring won't work and
    may turn the sponge green)
4 large eggs

For the icing
250g (9oz) butter, softened
750g (1lb 10oz) icing sugar
350g (12oz) full-fat
    cream cheese
1 teaspoon vanilla extract

TIP
The sponge cakes can
be made up to 3 days
ahead and will stay moist
if wrapped in clingfilm,
or you can wrap well and
freeze for up to 2 months.

Preheat the oven to 180°C/160°C fan/Gas 4. Grease and line the base of two 20cm (8in) cake tins with non-stick baking paper.

—

Measure half each of the flour, cocoa powder, baking powder, bicarbonate of soda, sugar and salt into a bowl and mix well.

—

Mix half each of the buttermilk, oil, vanilla, food colouring and 100ml water in a jug. Add 2 eggs and whisk until smooth. Pour the wet ingredients into the dry ingredients and whisk until well combined. The cake mixture should be bright red; it will get a little darker as it cooks. If it's not as vivid as you'd like, add a touch more colouring.

—

Divide the cake mixture evenly between the two tins and level the surfaces. Bake in the preheated oven for 25–30 minutes, or until well risen and the cakes are shrinking away from the sides of the tins. Cool in the tins for 10 minutes, then turn out on to a wire rack, peel off the baking paper and leave to cool.

—

Repeat these steps with the remaining ingredients, until you have four cakes in total.

—

To make the icing, place the butter in a large bowl and sift in half the icing sugar. Roughly mash together with a spatula, then whiz with a hand-held mixer until smooth. Add the cream cheese and vanilla, sift in the remaining icing sugar, mash together again, then blend once more with the hand-held mixer.

—

To assemble the cake, stick one of the sponges to a cake stand or board with a little of the soft icing. Use roughly half the icing to stack the remaining cakes on top, spreading a generous amount between each layer. Pile the remaining icing on top of the assembled cake and use a palette knife to ease it over the edges, covering the entire surface of the cake.

CHAPTER SIX

SPECIAL CAKES

This Hungarian cake is not quick to make, but it does look spectacular. The caramel topping will soften due to the moisture from the cake, so serve it within 12 hours.

DOBOS TORTE

SERVES 8

For the sponge
4 large eggs
175g (6oz) caster sugar
150g (5oz) self-raising
  flour, sifted

*For the chocolate
  butter cream*
2 large egg whites
115g (4oz) icing sugar
225g (8oz) unsalted
  butter, softened
115g (4oz) dark chocolate,
  broken into pieces

For the caramel
75g (3oz) granulated
  or caster sugar
3 tablespoons water

Preheat the oven to 220°C/Fan 200°C/Gas 7. Mark six 20cm (8in) circles on non-stick baking paper and lay on baking trays.

To make the sponge, whisk the eggs and sugar in a large bowl until the mixture is light and foamy and leaves a trail. Lightly fold in the flour, a little at a time.

Divide the mixture between the 6 marked circles, spreading the mixture out evenly. Bake in the preheated oven for 6–8 minutes, until pale golden and springy to the touch. With a sharp knife, trim the circles. Peel off the paper and leave to cool on a wire rack.

To make the chocolate butter cream, whisk the egg whites and icing sugar in a heatproof bowl set over a pan of simmering water until the mixture holds its shape. Cream the butter until really soft, then add the egg white mixture to it a little at a time. Melt the chocolate gently in a heatproof bowl set over a pan of hot water, making sure the base of the bowl is not touching the water, stirring occasionally. Cool slightly then add to the butter cream and mix well until evenly blended.

Take one of the sponge circles and place on a sheet of baking paper, ready to be topped with caramel. To make the caramel, dissolve the sugar in the water over a low heat, then increase the heat and boil the syrup until it reaches a deep straw colour. Allow it to cool slightly then pour over the sponge circle. When the caramel on top of the sponge is just beginning to set, mark it and cut into 16 portions with an oiled knife.

Sandwich the remaining five circles of sponge together with the butter cream. Spread butter cream around the sides, and pipe butter cream rosettes on the top. Place a caramel-topped wedge of cake at an angle on each rosette to form the top layer.

Nusskuchen comes in many forms, but always contains hazelnuts. This one is filled with a delicious apple mixture and topped with melted chocolate.

NUSSKUCHEN
SERVES 6

40g (1½oz) shelled hazelnuts
115g (4oz) butter, softened
115g (4oz) caster sugar
2 large eggs, separated
1 level teaspoon instant
   coffee granules
1 tablespoon warm milk
115g (4oz) self-raising flour

For the filling
450g (1lb) dessert apples,
   peeled, cored and sliced
2 tablespoons apricot jam
grated zest and juice of
   ½ lemon

To finish
55g (2oz) dark chocolate,
   broken into pieces

Preheat the oven to 190°C/Fan 170°C/Gas 5. Grease and base line a 20cm (8in) sandwich tin with non-stick baking paper.

Place the hazelnuts on a baking tray and put in the oven for about 10 minutes. Tip on to a tea towel and rub them together to remove the skins. (Some stubborn ones may need to go back into the oven but don't worry about getting every last bit of skin off, it's not necessary.) Place the nuts in a food processor and grind.

Measure the butter and sugar into a bowl and beat together until light and fluffy. Gradually beat in the egg yolks and stir in the prepared nuts. Dissolve the coffee in the warm milk then stir into the nut mixture. Carefully fold in the flour.

In a separate bowl, whisk the egg whites until they form soft peaks, then gently fold into the cake mixture.

Turn into the prepared tin and level the surface. Bake in the preheated oven for 25 minutes, or until well risen and the top of the cake springs back when lightly pressed with a finger. Leave to cool in the tin for a few minutes, then turn out, peel off the baking paper and finish cooling on a wire rack.

Meanwhile, prepare the filling. Place the apples in a pan with the apricot jam and lemon zest and juice. Cover and cook very gently until the apples are soft but still retain their shape. Leave to cool.

Cut the cake in half horizontally using a serrated or bread knife, then sandwich the slices together with the cooled apple mixture.

Melt the chocolate gently in a heatproof bowl set over a pan of simmering water, making sure the base of the bowl is not touching the water. Spread over the top of the cake and leave to set.

This chocolate cake is said to have been invented in Vienna by the chef Franz Sacher in 1832. It is quite dense and rich, so serve in small wedges.

SACHERTORTE

SERVES 12

150g (5oz) dark chocolate, broken into pieces
150g (5oz) unsalted butter, softened
115g (4oz) caster sugar
½ teaspoon vanilla extract
5 large eggs, separated
75g (3oz) ground almonds
40g (1½oz) plain flour

For the topping and icing
6 tablespoons apricot jam
150g (5oz) dark chocolate, broken into pieces
200ml (⅓ pint) double cream
30g (1oz) milk chocolate, broken into pieces

Preheat the oven to 180°C/Fan 160°C/Gas 4. Grease and base line a 23cm (9in) deep round cake tin with non-stick baking paper.

Melt the chocolate for the cake gently in a heatproof bowl set over a pan of simmering water, making sure the base of the bowl is not touching the water, stirring occasionally, then cool slightly.

Beat the butter until really soft in a large bowl, then gradually beat in the sugar until the mixture is light and fluffy. Add the cooled chocolate and the vanilla extract and beat again. Add the egg yolks, one at a time, beating between each addition, then fold in the ground almonds and flour.

In a separate bowl, whisk the egg whites until stiff but not dry. Add about one-third to the chocolate mixture and stir in vigorously. Gently fold in the remaining egg whites. Pour into the prepared tin and level the surface. Bake in the preheated oven for 45–50 minutes, until well risen and the top springs back when lightly pressed with a finger. Leave to cool in the tin for a few minutes then turn out, peel off the baking paper and finish cooling on a wire rack.

Heat the apricot jam in a small pan, then brush evenly over the top and sides of the cold cake. Allow to set.

To make the topping, melt the dark chocolate gently with the cream in a small pan. Stir occasionally. Allow to cool for 1–2 minutes to thicken slightly, then pour on to the cake. Spread it gently over the top and down the sides, and leave to set.

For the icing, melt the milk chocolate gently in a heatproof bowl set over a pan of hot water. Spoon into a small icing bag and snip off the corner. Pipe 'Sacher' across the cake and leave to set.

A Parisian speciality, this gâteau was named in honour of Saint Honoré, the patron saint of bakers. It's an absolute classic but does take time and skill to make.

GÂTEAU SAINT HONORÉ

SERVES 8

For the pâte sucrée
115g (4oz) plain flour
55g (2oz) butter, softened
55g (2oz) caster sugar
2 large egg yolks

For the choux pastry
55g (2oz) butter
150ml (¼ pint) water
65g (2½oz) plain flour
2 large eggs, beaten

For the crème pâtissière
6 egg yolks
115g (4oz) caster sugar
55g (2oz) plain flour
1 level tablespoon cornflour
500ml (18fl oz) full-fat milk
1 teaspoon vanilla extract
150ml (¼ pint) pouring
   double cream,
   lightly whipped

**For the caramel and
   spun sugar**
225g (8oz) granulated sugar
75ml (2½fl oz) water

Grease 3 baking trays.

To make the pâte sucrée, measure the flour, butter and sugar into a food processor and whiz briefly until the mixture resembles fine breadcrumbs. Add the egg yolks and pulse until just blended to form a dough. Knead the mixture gently until smooth. Wrap in clingfilm and leave to rest in the fridge for about 30 minutes.

Preheat the oven to 190°C/Fan 170°C/Gas 5.

Roll out the pâte sucrée on a lightly floured work surface to an 18cm (7in) round. Place on one of the prepared baking trays, crimp the edges and prick all over with a fork

Bake in the preheated oven for 15–20 minutes, or until the pastry is a pale golden brown. Leave to cool on the baking tray for a few minutes, then turn out and finish cooling on a wire rack. Increase the oven temperature to 220°C/Fan 200°C/Gas 7.

Next make the choux pastry. Measure the butter and water into a medium pan, heat gently until the butter has melted, then bring slowly to the boil. Remove the pan from the heat, add the flour all at once and beat until the mixture forms a soft ball. Allow the flour mixture to cool slightly, then gradually beat in the eggs, beating well between each addition to give a smooth, shiny paste. Spoon the dough into a piping bag fitted with a 1cm (½in) plain nozzle. Pipe an 18cm (7in) ring of choux pastry on to the second baking tray and pipe 16 pieces about the size of a walnut on the third baking tray. Bake in the preheated oven for about 10 minutes, then reduce the temperature to 190°C/Fan 170°C/Gas 5 and cook for a further 20 minutes until well risen, golden brown and crisp.

Recipe continued overleaf

The sugar syrup used to make the caramel and spun sugar can easily burn skin. Please take extra care when handling, particularly if there are children in the house at the time.

To make the spun sugar, cover your working area with sheets of oiled foil, and cover a rolling pin with foil and oil it lightly. Have ready 2 forks taped together back to back. Dip the prongs of the forks in the caramel and, holding the covered rolling pin in the other hand, flick the forks back and forth over the rolling pin, to form long strands of sugar. Repeat with the remaining caramel, then place on an oiled baking tray until needed.

Remove the tray from the oven and pierce the choux ring and the buns at intervals underneath, to allow the steam to escape. Return to the oven for about 5 minutes to dry out completely. Cool on a wire rack.

To make the crème pâtissière, place the yolks, sugar and flours in a large bowl. Whisk, using an electric whisk until the mixture is thick and has become paler. Heat the milk in a medium-sized saucepan until scalding then add the vanilla extract. Slowly pour this milk into the egg mixture and continue whisking until smooth. Pour back into the saucepan and stir constantly over a medium heat. Cook until the mixture is very thick and smooth. Spoon into a bowl, cover the surface with non-stick baking paper to stop a skin forming and leave to cool.

Whisk the cooled crème pâtissière until smooth, then fold in the cream. Cover tightly with clingfilm and chill thoroughly.

Pipe a little of the crème pâtissière into the choux ring and buns, using the holes made in the bases to allow the steam to escape. Leave in a cool place while making the caramel.

To make the caramel, measure the sugar and water into a heavy-based pan. Heat gently until the sugar has dissolved, brushing down the sides of the pan with hot water from time to time. Bring to the boil and boil the syrup until it turns a golden colour. Immediately plunge the base of the pan into cold water to stop the caramel darkening further. Place the pan in a large bowl and fill the bowl with boiling water, to keep the caramel fluid.

Put the pâte sucrée on a plate and position the choux ring on top. One by one, dip the base of each choux bun in the caramel and place on the choux ring, holding it in place for a few seconds to secure. Continue with the remaining buns. Spoon a little caramel over the top of each bun.

Spoon the remaining crème pâtissière into the choux case and, if you like, decorate with spun sugar (see Tip). If you have decorated the gâteau with spun sugar, serve it within the hour, as the sugar will gradually start to disintegrate due to the moisture.

This cake is perfect not just for Wimbledon, but for all summer occasions. It uses no flour, and the semolina used instead gives it a slightly crunchy, close texture. The cake must be eaten on the day of filling.

WIMBLEDON CAKE

SERVES 6-8

6 large eggs, separated
200g (7oz) caster sugar
finely grated zest and juice
   of 2 oranges
150g (5oz) semolina

For the filling and topping
115g (4oz) strawberries
1 passion fruit
150ml (¼ pint) pouring
   double cream, whipped
icing sugar, to finish

Preheat the oven to 180°C/Fan 160°C/Gas 4. Grease a 20cm (8in) deep round cake tin then line the base with non-stick baking paper.

Measure the egg yolks, sugar, orange zest and juice and the semolina into a bowl and beat until pale and thick using an electric hand whisk. In a separate clean bowl, whisk the egg whites until they are stiff but not dry, then gently fold into the orange and semolina mixture. Turn into the prepared tin and level the surface.

Bake in the preheated oven for about 40 minutes, or until well risen and the top of the cake springs back when lightly pressed with a finger. Leave to cool in the tin for a few minutes then turn out, peel off the baking paper and finish cooling on a wire rack.

Reserve a few strawberries to decorate the top of the cake, then slice the remainder. Halve the passion fruit and scoop out the pulp.

Cut the cake in half horizontally using a serrated or bread knife, then sandwich the halves together with the sliced strawberries, passion fruit pulp and whipped cream.

Just before serving, decorate with the reserved strawberries, sliced or left whole, and sift some icing sugar over the top.

Made with semolina and ground almonds instead of flour, this cake has a lovely light but 'short' texture. It keeps better than an ordinary sponge cake and is delicious with different fruits. For an even more luscious cake, double the quantities of cream and lemon curd to smooth over the top of the cake as well as fill it.

LEMON GRIESTORTE

SERVES 6–8

3 large eggs, separated
115g (4oz) caster sugar
finely grated zest and juice
    of ½ lemon
55g (2oz) fine semolina
15g (½oz) ground almonds

For the filling
150ml (¼ pint) pouring
    double cream
4 tablespoons lemon curd
115g (4oz) raspberries
    (optional)

To finish
icing sugar

Preheat the oven to 180°C/Fan 160°C/Gas 4. Grease a 20cm (8in) deep round cake tin and line the base and sides with non-stick baking paper.

Measure the egg yolks and sugar into a bowl and whisk until pale and light in texture. Add the lemon juice and continue to whisk until the mixture is thick. Fold in the grated lemon zest, semolina and ground almonds. In a separate bowl, whisk the egg whites until they form soft peaks, then fold into the mixture until evenly blended.

Turn into the prepared tin and bake in the preheated oven for 30–35 minutes, or until well risen and a pale golden brown. Leave to cool in the tin for a few minutes then turn out, peel off the baking paper and finish cooling on a wire rack.

Whisk the cream until it holds its shape, then fold in the lemon curd.

Cut the cake in half horizontally using a serrated or bread knife, then sandwich the halves together with the lemon cream and raspberries, if using. Dust the top with icing sugar to serve.

These small cakes can be fiddly to make, but are delicious and have a sponge that is moist and light. They are the sort of cake that would be on sale in the very best of French patisseries.

CHOCOLATINES

MAKES 9 CHOCOLATINES

For the genoese sponge
40g (1½oz) butter
3 large eggs
75g (3oz) caster sugar
65g (2½oz) self-raising flour
1 level tablespoon cornflour

For the crème au
* beurre chocolat*
115g (4oz) dark chocolate,
   broken into pieces
55g (2oz) granulated sugar
4 tablespoons water
2 large egg yolks
175g (6oz) unsalted
   butter, softened

To finish
75g (3oz) mixed nuts,
   toasted and finely
   chopped

Preheat the oven to 180°C/Fan 160°C/Gas 4. Grease an 18cm (7in) shallow square cake tin then line the base with non-stick baking paper.

To make the sponge, gently melt the butter in a pan, then set aside to cool slightly.

Measure the eggs and sugar into a large bowl and whisk at full speed until the mixture is pale, mousse-like and thick enough so that a trail is left when the whisk is lifted from the mixture.

Sift the flours together into a bowl. Carefully fold half the flour into the egg mixture then gently pour half the cooled butter around the edge of the mixture and fold in. Repeat with the remaining flour and butter.

Pour the mixture into the prepared tin and level the surface. Bake in the preheated oven for 35–40 minutes, or until well risen and the top of the cake springs back when lightly pressed with a finger. Leave to cool in the tin for a few minutes then turn out, peel off the baking paper and finish cooling on a wire rack.

To make the crème au beurre chocolat (chocolate butter cream), place the chocolate in a large heatproof bowl. Place the bowl over a pan of simmering water until melted, making sure that the base of the bowl is not touching the water.

Measure the granulated sugar and water into a small heavy-based pan. Heat very gently until the sugar has dissolved. Bring to the boil then boil steadily for about 5 minutes until the syrup is clear and forms a slim thread when pulled apart between 2 teaspoons.

Put the egg yolks into a bowl and give them a quick stir to break them up. Pour the syrup in a thin stream on to the egg yolks, whisking all the time. Continue to whisk until the mixture is thick and cold. In another bowl, cream the butter until very soft and gradually beat in the egg yolk mixture. Stir in the cooled, melted chocolate to flavour.

Cut the cold sponge in half horizontally using a serrated or bread knife, then sandwich the halves together with a thin layer of the chocolate butter cream. Trim the cake edges and cut neatly into 6cm (2¼in) squares. Spread the top and sides of each cake with most of the remaining butter cream and press the chopped, toasted nuts around the sides. Finish by piping the tops of the squares with tiny rosettes of the remaining butter cream.

TIP
Leftover egg whites can be stored in a covered container in the fridge for up to three weeks, or frozen for up to six months.

*These are a coffee-flavoured variation of the chocolatines on page 156.
I've often seen them in smart Parisian patisseries. The recipe traditionally
does not use self-raising flour, but I always do, because it gets a better result.*

MOKATINES
MAKES 8 MOKATINES

For the genoese sponge
40g (1½oz) butter
3 large eggs
75g (3oz) caster sugar
65g (2½oz) self-raising flour
1 level tablespoon cornflour

*For the crème au
    beurre moka*
40g (1½oz) caster sugar
2 tablespoons water
1 large egg yolk
75g (3oz) butter, softened
1 tablespoon strong coffee

For the soft coffee icing
3 tablespoons apricot jam
55g (2oz) butter
3 tablespoons milk
1 level tablespoon instant
    coffee granules
225g (8oz) icing sugar, sifted

Preheat the oven to 180°C/Fan 160°C/Gas 4. Grease an 18cm (7in) shallow square cake tin then line the base with non-stick baking paper.

To make the sponge, gently melt the butter in a pan, then set to one side to cool slightly. Measure the eggs and sugar into a large bowl and whisk at full speed until the mixture is pale and mousse-like, and thick enough so that a trail is left when the whisk is lifted from the mixture.

Sift the flours together into a bowl. Carefully fold half the flour into the egg mixture, gently pour half the cooled butter around the edge of the mixture and then fold in. Repeat with the remaining flour and butter.

Pour the mixture into the prepared tin and level the surface. Bake in the preheated oven for 35–40 minutes, or until well risen and the top of the cake springs back when lightly pressed with a finger. Leave to cool in the tin for a few minutes then turn out, peel off the baking paper and finish cooling on a wire rack.

To make the crème au beurre moka (coffee butter cream), measure the sugar and water into a small heavy-based pan. Heat very gently until the sugar has dissolved. Bring to the boil then boil steadily for about 5 minutes until the syrup is still clear and forms a slim thread when pulled apart between 2 teaspoons.

Recipe continued overleaf

Put the egg yolk into a bowl and give it a quick stir to break it up. Pour the syrup in a thin stream over the yolk, whisking all the time. Continue to whisk until the mixture is thick and cold. In another bowl, cream the butter until very soft and gradually beat in the egg yolk mixture. Stir in the coffee to flavour.

Cut the cold cake in half horizontally using a serrated or bread knife, then sandwich the halves together with a thin layer of the coffee butter cream. Trim the cake edges and neatly cut in half, then cut each half into 4 to give 8 oblongs. Sieve the apricot jam into a small pan and warm gently. Brush the top and sides of the cakes with the hot apricot jam.

To make the soft coffee icing, measure the butter, milk and coffee into a small pan and heat gently until the butter has melted. Add the sifted icing sugar and beat until smooth and glossy. Leave to thicken slightly, then use most of the soft icing to pour over each cake, smoothing the sides quickly if necessary. Leave to set, then decorate with the remaining piped soft coffee icing.

TIP

Store eggs in a cool place, larder or fridge, pointed end down, and away from strong-smelling foods such as fish. Bring them to room temperature before using.

This is one of my favourite coffee cakes, and it looks spectacular, too.

GÂTEAU MOKA AUX AMANDES

SERVES 8

3 large eggs
115g (4oz) caster sugar
75g (3oz) self-raising flour

*For the crème au
    beurre moka*
75g (3oz) caster sugar
4 tablespoons water
2 large egg yolks
175g (6oz) butter, softened
1–2 tablespoons strong
    coffee

To finish
175g (6oz) shredded or
    flaked almonds, toasted
icing sugar, for dusting
    (optional)

Preheat the oven to 190°C/Fan 170°C/Gas 5. Grease a 23cm (9in) deep round cake tin, then line the base with non-stick baking paper.

Measure the eggs and sugar into a large bowl and whisk at full speed until the mixture is pale in colour and thick enough to just leave a trail when the whisk is lifted. Sift the flour over the surface of the mixture and gently fold in with a metal spoon or spatula.

Turn into the prepared tin and level the surface. Bake in the preheated oven for about 30 minutes, or until well risen and the top of the cake springs back when lightly pressed with a finger. Leave to cool in the tin for a few minutes then turn out, peel off the baking paper and finish cooling on a wire rack.

To make the crème au beurre moka (coffee butter cream), measure the sugar and water into a small, heavy-based pan. Heat very gently until the sugar has dissolved. Bring to the boil then boil steadily for about 5 minutes until it has reached a temperature of 107°C on a sugar thermometer, or until the syrup forms a slim thread when pulled apart between 2 teaspoons. Place the egg yolks in a bowl and give them a quick stir to break them up. Pour the syrup in a thin stream on to the egg yolks, whisking all the time. Continue to whisk until the mixture is thick and cold. In another bowl, cream the butter until very soft and gradually beat in the egg yolk mixture. Stir in the coffee to flavour.

Cut the cake in half horizontally using a serrated or bread knife, then sandwich the halves together with a thin layer of the coffee butter cream. Spread butter cream over the top and sides of the cake, retaining some for decoration, then press the toasted almonds all over the cake. Dust lightly with icing sugar and finish by piping rosettes of butter cream around the top.

This is a light walnut sponge filled with strawberries and cream, often served on the Continent as a pudding. For a lighter filling, you can use full-fat crème fraîche and you could use wild strawberries when they are in season.

SWISS STRAWBERRY
SERVES 8
AND WALNUT CAKE

3 large eggs
115g (4oz) caster sugar
75g (3oz) self-raising flour
55g (2oz) walnuts, finely
  chopped

For the filling and topping
300ml (½ pint) pouring
  double cream, whipped
450g (1lb) strawberries,
  roughly chopped,
  plus extra kept whole
  for decoration

Preheat the oven to 180°C/Fan 160°C/Gas 4. Grease a 20cm (8in) deep round cake tin, then line the base with non-stick baking paper.

Measure the eggs and sugar into a large bowl and beat until the mixture is thick and mousse-like and leaves a trail when the whisk is lifted out of the mixture. Sift the flour on to the mixture and lightly fold in along with the chopped walnuts.

Turn into the prepared cake tin and level the surface. Bake in the preheated oven for about 40–45 minutes, or until well risen and the top of the cake springs back when lightly pressed with a finger. Leave to cool in the tin for a few minutes then turn out, peel off the baking paper and finish cooling on a wire rack.

When cold, cut the cake into three horizontally using a serrated or bread knife, then sandwich the slices together with a good amount of whipped cream and strawberries. Spread the remaining cream over the top and the sides of the cake and decorate with the reserved strawberries.

CHAPTER SEVEN

TRAYBAKES

This is the simplest of cakes to make. When cooked and cold, sift a little icing sugar over the top to finish, if you like.

BASIC ALL-IN-ONE TRAYBAKE

CUTS INTO 16 PIECES

225g (8oz) baking spread, straight from the fridge
225g (8oz) caster sugar
275g (10oz) self-raising flour
1 level teaspoon baking powder
4 large eggs
4 tablespoons milk

To finish
a little sifted icing sugar (optional)

Preheat the oven to 180°C/Fan 160°C/Gas 4. Grease a 30 x 23cm (12 x 9in) traybake or roasting tin then line the base with non-stick baking paper.

Measure all the ingredients into a large bowl and mix with an electric hand whisk until well blended.

Turn the mixture into the prepared tin and level the surface. Bake in the preheated oven for about 35–40 minutes, or until the cake has shrunk from the sides of the tin and springs back when pressed in the centre with your fingertips. Leave to cool in the tin.

Cut into 16 pieces and peel off the baking paper.

To make a larger traybake, follow the method above. Grease a 36 x 29cm (14½ x 11½in) traybake or roasting tin and line the base with non-stick baking paper. Measure 350g (12oz) baking spread, 350g (12oz) caster sugar, 450g (1lb) self-raising flour, 1 level teaspoon baking powder, 6 large eggs and 6 tablespoons milk into a large bowl and beat until well blended. Bake in the preheated oven for 40–45 minutes, or until the cake has shrunk from the sides of the tin and springs back when pressed in the centre with your fingertips. Leave to cool in the tin before cutting into 24 pieces and removing the baking paper.

You can vary a basic traybake quite simply – in this case by adding a subtle lemon flavour and a lemon glacé icing.

ICED LEMON TRAYBAKE

CUTS INTO 16 PIECES

225g (8oz) baking spread,
   straight from the fridge
225g (8oz) caster sugar
275g (10oz) self-raising flour
1 level teaspoon baking
   powder
4 large eggs
4 tablespoons milk
grated zest of 2 lemons

For the icing
3 tablespoons fresh
   lemon juice
225g (8oz) icing sugar, sifted

Preheat the oven to 180°C/Fan 160°C/Gas 4. Grease a 30 x 23cm (12 x 9in) traybake or roasting tin then line the base with non-stick baking paper.

Measure all the sponge ingredients into a large bowl and mix with an electric hand whisk until well blended.

Turn the mixture into the prepared tin and level the surface. Bake in the preheated oven for about 35–40 minutes, or until the cake has shrunk from the sides of the tin and springs back when pressed in the centre with your fingertips. Leave to cool in the tin, then turn out and peel off the baking paper.

To make the icing, mix together the lemon juice and icing sugar to give a runny consistency. Spread out evenly over the cake and leave to set before cutting into 16 pieces.

Chocolate cakes are always popular, and this is a particularly simple version, which is great for family teas or lunch boxes.

ICED CHOCOLATE TRAYBAKE

CUTS INTO 16 PIECES

4 level tablespoons
    cocoa powder
4 tablespoons boiling water
225g (8oz) baking spread,
    straight from the fridge
225g (8oz) caster sugar
225g (8oz) self-raising flour
1 level teaspoon baking
    powder
4 large eggs
1 tablespoon milk

For the icing and decoration
4 tablespoons apricot jam
150g (5oz) dark chocolate,
    broken into pieces
6 tablespoons water
350g (12oz) icing sugar,
    sifted
1 teaspoon sunflower oil
chocolate curls (page 402)

Preheat the oven to 180°C/Fan 160°C/Gas 4. Grease a 30 x 23cm (12 x 9in) traybake or roasting tin then line the base with non-stick baking paper.

—

Blend the cocoa and boiling water together in a large bowl then allow to cool slightly. Add all the remaining sponge ingredients and mix with an electric hand whisk until well blended.

—

Turn the mixture into the prepared tin and level the surface. Bake in the preheated oven for about 35–40 minutes, or until the cake has shrunk from the sides of the tin and springs back when pressed in the centre with your fingertips. Leave to cool in the tin, then turn out and peel off the baking paper.

—

Warm the apricot jam in a pan and brush all over the cake.

—

To make the icing, melt the chocolate in a pan with the water, heating gently until melted and smooth. Leave to cool slightly, then beat in the icing sugar and oil. Pour over the cake and smooth gently with a palette knife. Leave to set for about 30 minutes, then decorate with chocolate curls before cutting into 16 pieces.

TIP
Brushing the cold cake with apricot jam before icing gives the cake a lovely flavour and prevents crumbs from the cake getting into the icing.

*Bought mixtures of chopped nuts might include a high proportion of peanuts.
I always prefer to make up my own mix from shelled nuts.*

AMERICAN SPICED
CUTS INTO 16 PIECES # CARROT TRAYBAKE

275g (10oz) self-raising flour
350g (12oz) caster sugar
1 level teaspoon baking
    powder
75g (3oz) unsalted
    mixed nuts, chopped
3 level teaspoons
    ground cinnamon
2 level teaspoons
    ground ginger
300ml (½ pint) sunflower oil
275g (10oz) carrots,
    coarsely grated
4 large eggs
1 teaspoon vanilla extract

For the topping
400g (14oz) full-fat
    cream cheese
4 teaspoons clear honey
2 teaspoons fresh
    lemon juice
mixed unsalted nuts,
    chopped, to decorate

Preheat the oven to 180°C/Fan 160°C/Gas 4. Grease a
30 x 23cm (12 x 9in) traybake or roasting tin then line the
base with non-stick baking paper.

Measure all the dry cake ingredients into a large bowl. Add
the oil, grated carrots, eggs (one at a time) and vanilla extract,
beating between each addition.

Pour into the prepared tin and level the surface. Bake in the
preheated oven for about 50–60 minutes, or until the cake is
well risen, golden brown in colour and firm to the touch. Leave
to cool in the tin for 10 minutes, then turn out, peel off the
baking paper and finish cooling on a wire rack.

To make the topping, mix together the cream cheese, honey
and lemon juice. Add a little extra lemon juice, if necessary, to
make a spreading consistency. Spread evenly over the cake with
a palette knife, then sprinkle with the chopped nuts to decorate.

TIP
You can store the iced cake in the fridge for up to 2 weeks.

Coffee and walnuts go particularly well together, but you can use other nuts for this recipe if you prefer.

COFFEE AND WALNUT TRAYBAKE

CUTS INTO 16 PIECES

225g (8oz) baking spread, straight from the fridge
225g (8oz) light muscovado sugar
275g (10oz) self-raising flour
1 level teaspoon baking powder
4 large eggs
2 tablespoons milk
2 tablespoons strong coffee (see Tip)
75g (3oz) walnuts, chopped

For the icing
75g (3oz) butter, softened
225g (8oz) icing sugar, sifted
2 teaspoons milk
2 teaspoons strong coffee
30g (1oz) walnuts, chopped

Preheat the oven to 180°C/Fan 160°C/Gas 4. Grease a 30 x 23cm (12 x 9in) traybake or roasting tin then line the base with non-stick baking paper.

Measure all the sponge ingredients into a large bowl and mix with an electric hand whisk until well blended.

Turn the mixture into the prepared tin and level the surface. Bake in the preheated oven for about 35–40 minutes or until the cake has shrunk from the sides of the tin and springs back when pressed in the centre with your fingertips. Leave to cool in the tin, then turn out and peel off the baking paper.

To make the icing, beat together the butter with the icing sugar, milk and coffee. Spread evenly over the cold cake using a palette knife, then decorate with the chopped walnuts.

TIP
To make strong coffee, you can mix 2 teaspoons coffee granules with 2 tablespoons water.

A simple, delicate apple traybake. Lovely as it is or warmed and served with crème fraîche.

APPLE AND VANILLA TRAYBAKE

CUTS INTO 16 PIECES

225g (8oz) cooking apples, peeled, cored and thinly sliced (prepared weight)
juice of ½ lemon
350g (12oz) self-raising flour
1 level teaspoon baking powder
350g (12oz) caster sugar
4 large eggs
2 teaspoons vanilla extract
225g (8oz) butter, melted

For the icing
175g (6oz) icing sugar, sifted
finely grated zest of 1 lemon
2–3 tablespoons boiling water

Preheat the oven to 180°C/Fan 160°C/Gas 4. Grease a 30 x 23cm (12 x 9in) traybake or roasting tin then line the base with non-stick baking paper.

—

Place the apple slices in a large bowl and squeeze the lemon juice over them.

—

Measure the flour, baking powder and sugar into a large bowl. Beat the eggs together with the vanilla extract and stir into the flour along with the melted butter. Whisk with an electric hand whisk until well blended.

—

Spread half this mixture into the tin. Arrange the apples over the top, then carefully cover with the rest of the mixture – but don't worry if the apples show through a little. Bake in the preheated oven for 50–60 minutes, or until the cake is golden, firm to the touch and shrinks away slightly from the sides of the tin. Leave to cool in the tin for 15 minutes, then turn out and remove the baking paper.

—

To make the icing, measure the icing sugar into a bowl. Add the lemon zest and enough boiling water to mix to a paste. Spoon into a piping bag and pipe over the top of the cake in a thick zig-zag shape.

Treacle can be difficult to weigh accurately, as it tends to stick to the scale pan. Weighing it on top of the sugar overcomes this problem.

GINGER AND TREACLE
CUTS INTO 16 PIECES SPICED TRAYBAKE

225g (8oz) baking spread, straight from the fridge
175g (6oz) light muscovado sugar
200g (7oz) black treacle
300g (10½oz) self-raising flour
1 level teaspoon baking powder
1 level teaspoon ground mixed spice
1 level teaspoon ground allspice
4 large eggs
4 tablespoons milk
3 finely chopped bulbs stem ginger from a jar

For the icing
75g (3oz) icing sugar, sifted
3 tablespoons stem ginger syrup from the jar
3 finely chopped bulbs stem ginger from a jar

Preheat the oven to 180°C/Fan 160°C/Gas 4. Grease a 30 x 23cm (12 x 9in) traybake or roasting tin then line the base with non-stick baking paper.

—

Put all the sponge ingredients into a large bowl and mix with an electric hand whisk until well blended.

—

Turn the mixture into the prepared tin and level the surface. Bake in the preheated oven for 35–40 minutes, or until the cake has shrunk from the sides of the tin and springs back when pressed in the centre with your fingertips. Leave to cool in the tin for a few minutes, then turn out, peel off the baking paper and finish cooling on a wire rack.

—

To make the icing, measure the icing sugar into a bowl, add the ginger syrup and mix until the icing is smooth and has a spreading consistency. Pour the icing over the cake, spread it gently to the edges with a small palette knife and sprinkle with the chopped stem ginger to decorate. Allow the icing to set before slicing the traybake into pieces.

TIP
This traybake freezes very well un-iced, and in fact improves with freezing.

This really is a top favourite. It is always moist and crunchy. The cake needs to be still warm when the topping is added so that it absorbs the lemon syrup easily, leaving the sugar on top. Do allow the cake to cool a little, though – if it is too hot, the syrup will tend to run straight through.

LEMON DRIZZLE TRAYBAKE

CUTS INTO 16 PIECES

225g (8oz) baking spread, straight from the fridge
225g (8oz) caster sugar
275g (10oz) self-raising flour
1 level teaspoon baking powder
4 large eggs
4 tablespoons milk
finely grated zest of 2 lemons

For the crunchy topping
175g (6oz) granulated sugar
juice of 2 lemons

Preheat the oven to 180°C/Fan 160°C/Gas 3. Grease a 30 x 23cm (12 x 9in) traybake or roasting tin then line the base with non-stick baking paper.

Measure all the sponge ingredients into a large bowl and mix with an electric hand whisk until well blended.

Turn the mixture into the prepared tin and level the surface. Bake in the preheated oven for about 35–40 minutes, or until the cake has shrunk from the sides of the tin and springs back when pressed in the centre with your finger tips.

Leave to cool in the tin for a few minutes, then turn out, carefully peel off the baking paper and leave to cool a little on a wire rack.

To make the crunchy topping, mix the granulated sugar and lemon juice in a small bowl to give a runny consistency. Stand the wire rack with the traybake on a tray to catch any drips and spoon the lemon syrup evenly over the traybake while it is still a little warm. Leave to finish cooling on the wire rack.

To make a Lemon Poppy Seed Traybake, add 30g (1oz) poppy seeds with the other traybake ingredients.

Children will adore this traybake. Double chocolate and marshmallows, what could be better?

DOUBLE CHOC CHIP AND MARSHMALLOW TRAYBAKE

CUTS INTO 16 PIECES

4 tablespoons cocoa
   powder
4 tablespoons boiling water
4 large eggs
225g (8oz) baking spread,
   straight from the fridge
225g (8oz) caster sugar
225g (8oz) self-raising flour
1 level teaspoon baking
   powder
115g (4oz) dark
   chocolate chips

For the icing
40g (1½oz) cocoa
   powder, sifted
55g (2oz) butter, softened
3–4 tablespoons milk
125g (4½oz) icing sugar,
   sifted

To decorate
30g (1oz) mini
   marshmallows
75g (3oz) Maltesers,
   crushed or chopped

Preheat the oven to 180°C/160°C Fan/Gas 4. Grease a 30 x 23cm (12 x 9in) traybake or roasting tin then line the base with non-stick baking paper.

—

To make the sponge, measure the cocoa powder and boiling water into a large bowl and mix until smooth. Add all the remaining sponge ingredients, except the chocolate chips, and mix with an electric hand whisk until light and fluffy. Stir in the chocolate chips.

—

Turn the mixture into the prepared tin and level the surface. Bake in the middle of the oven for about 35 minutes, or until the cake has shrunk from the sides of the tin and springs back when pressed in the centre with your fingertips. Leave to cool in the tin, then turn out and peel off the baking paper.

—

To make the icing, measure the cocoa, butter, milk and icing sugar into a bowl. Beat well to a light, smooth consistency then spread over the top of the cool cake.

—

Scatter the marshmallows and Maltesers over the top to decorate.

CHAPTER EIGHT

BAKING FOR CHILDREN

Lovely little tarts for a kids' party. Children love to have small mouthfuls of food and this is a great recipe for starting them off on pastry.

MINI JAM TARTS
MAKES 18 DEEP TARTS

115g (4oz) plain flour
55g (2oz) butter
1 tablespoon icing sugar
1 large egg yolk
1 tablespoon water
½ jar raspberry jam
 or lemon curd

Preheat the oven to 200°C/180°C Fan/Gas 6. You will need 2 x 12 mini muffin tins or 1 x 24 mini muffin tin.

—

Measure the flour, butter and icing sugar into a food processor and whiz until the mixture resembles fine breadcrumbs. Add the egg yolk and water and whiz again until it forms a ball.

—

Roll the pastry out thinly on a lightly floured work surface. Stamp out 18 rounds using a 6.5cm (2½in) round cutter. Line the mini muffin tin(s) with the pastry and prick the bases with a fork.

—

Spoon 1 heaped teaspoon of jam or lemon curd into each of the cases. Bake in the preheated oven for about 15 minutes, or until the pastry is pale golden. Leave for a few minutes, then transfer to a wire rack to cool.

Once made, keep these in a cool place in warm weather. When I was small, my mother made them on the waxed paper from inside the cornflake packet!

CHOCOLATE CRISPIES

MAKES 18 SMALL OR 12 LARGE CRISPIES

225g (8oz) dark chocolate,
   broken into pieces
1 tablespoon golden syrup
55g (2oz) butter
75g (3oz) cornflakes

Place the chocolate in a large saucepan with the golden syrup and butter. Melt over a low heat, stirring occasionally. Meanwhile, place 18 paper cake cases on a large baking tray.

—

Add the cornflakes to the pan and stir gently until they are evenly coated. Spoon the mixture into the paper cases and chill in the fridge to set.

TIP
If you haven't any paper cases, you can spoon the mixture on to non-stick baking paper in mounds and leave to set.

Young children can easily make these – under supervision, of course.
They're fun for Bonfire Night.

CHOCOLATE AND VANILLA

MAKES ABOUT 20 BISCUITS

PINWHEEL BISCUITS

For the vanilla
biscuit mixture
55g (2oz) butter, softened
30g (1oz) caster sugar
30g (1oz) cornflour
55g (2oz) plain flour
½ large beaten egg
a few drops of vanilla extract

For the chocolate
biscuit mixture
55g (2oz) butter, softened
30g (1oz) caster sugar
30g (1oz) cornflour
40g (1½oz) plain flour
½ large beaten egg
1 tablespoon cocoa powder

Measure all the ingredients for the vanilla biscuit mixture into a bowl and mix to form a soft dough. Wrap in clingfilm and chill in the fridge for about 30 minutes until firm. Meanwhile, make the chocolate biscuit mixture in the same way, then wrap and chill.

—

Roll out both pieces of dough on a lightly floured work surface to oblongs about 25 x 18cm (10 x 7in). Place the vanilla biscuit dough on top of the chocolate dough, then roll up the two together from a narrow edge. Wrap in clingfilm and chill again for about 30 minutes.

—

Preheat the oven to 180°C/Fan 160°C/Gas 4 and lightly grease two baking trays.

—

Using a sharp knife, cut the roll into about 20 slices and place on the prepared baking trays.

—

Bake in the preheated oven for about 20 minutes, or until the vanilla biscuit is golden in colour. Lift on to a wire rack and leave to cool.

This is a popular traybake for parties, and children particularly enjoy the fun of making marble cakes.

CHOCOLATE CHIP AND VANILLA MARBLE CAKE

CUTS INTO 21 SMALL PIECES

225g (8oz) baking spread, straight from the fridge
225g (8oz) caster sugar
275g (10oz) self-raising flour
1 level teaspoon baking powder
4 large eggs
2 tablespoons milk
½ teaspoon vanilla extract
1½ level tablespoons cocoa powder
2 tablespoons boiling water
55g (2oz) dark chocolate chips

For the icing
55g (2oz) dark chocolate, broken into pieces
55g (2oz) Belgian white chocolate, broken into pieces

Preheat the oven to 180°C/Fan 160°C/Gas 4. Grease a 30 x 23cm (12 x 9in) traybake or roasting tin and line the base with non-stick baking paper.

—

Measure the baking spread, sugar, flour, baking powder, eggs, milk and vanilla extract into a large bowl and beat well for about 2 minutes until well blended. Spoon half the mixture into the prepared tin, dotting the spoonfuls apart.

—

In a small bowl, blend the cocoa and boiling water. Cool slightly, then stir into the remaining cake mixture along with the chocolate chips. Spoon this chocolate mixture in between the plain cake mixture in the tin to fill the gaps.

—

Bake in the preheated oven for about 35–40 minutes, or until the cake has shrunk from the sides of the tin and springs back when pressed in the centre with your fingertips. Leave to cool in the tin, then turn out and peel off the baking paper.

—

To make the icing, melt the plain and white chocolate separately in small heatproof bowls set over pans of simmering water, making sure the base of the bowls are not touching the water, stirring occasionally. Spoon into two separate small plastic bags, snip off a corner of each bag and drizzle the chocolates all over the top of the cake to decorate.

—

Leave to set for about 30 minutes before cutting into pieces.

Excellent for hungry teenagers, these are best eaten as fresh as possible.

DOUGHNUTS

MAKES 16 DOUGHNUTS

550g (1¼lb) plain flour,
   plus extra for dusting
7g sachet fast-action yeast
30g (1oz) butter
75g (3oz) caster sugar
2 large eggs, beaten
6 tablespoons tepid milk
6 tablespoons tepid water
light vegetable oil,
   for deep-frying

For the filling
raspberry jam

For the coating
115g (4oz) caster sugar
2 level teaspoons
   ground cinnamon

Lightly grease and flour three baking trays.

Measure the flour into a large bowl and stir in the yeast. Rub in the butter with your fingertips until the mixture resembles fine breadcrumbs, then stir in the sugar. Make a well in the centre of the dry ingredients and pour in the eggs, milk and water. Mix to a smooth dough.

Turn out on to a lightly floured work surface and knead for about 5 minutes until the dough is smooth and elastic. Return it to the bowl, cover with oiled clingfilm and leave to rise until doubled in size, about 1–1½ hours in a warm room.

Turn the dough out and knead to knock out the air until the dough is smooth and elastic once more. Divide into 16 equal pieces and shape each into a ball. Flatten each ball, then place a small teaspoon of jam in the centre of each piece. Gather the edges together over the jam and pinch firmly to seal. Place well apart on the prepared baking trays, then cover with oiled clingfilm or put the trays inside large polythene bags and leave to prove for about 30 minutes, until they have doubled in size.

Heat 5cm (2in) oil in a deep-fat fryer or heavy saucepan until a cube of bread dropped into the fat browns in 30 seconds. Fry the doughnuts a few at a time, turning them once, until they are golden brown all over. This will take about 5 minutes. Lift out with a slotted spoon and drain well on kitchen paper.

Measure the sugar and cinnamon into a large polythene bag and shake to mix. Then toss the doughnuts, a few at a time, in the sugar mixture until each is well coated. Serve freshly made.

Let the children ice the animals themselves with their favourite colours.
Animal cutters are available from good cook shops.

ICED ANIMAL BISCUITS

MAKES ABOUT 50 BISCUITS

115g (4oz) butter, softened
225g (8oz) self-raising flour
a few drops of vanilla extract
115g (4oz) caster sugar
1 large egg, beaten

For the icing
115g (4oz) icing sugar, sifted
about 1 tablespoon fresh
   lemon juice
food colouring (red, green,
   blue, yellow)
silver balls, for eyes

Preheat the oven to 190°C/Fan 170°C/Gas 5. Lightly grease two baking trays.

—

Rub the butter into the flour with your fingertips until the mixture resembles fine breadcrumbs. Add the vanilla extract, sugar, beaten egg and mix to form a fairly stiff dough. Roll out thinly on a lightly floured work surface and cut into animal shapes using cutters. Place on the prepared baking trays.

—

Bake in the preheated oven for 10–15 minutes until golden brown. Cool on a wire rack.

—

To make the icing, measure the icing sugar into a bowl and add enough lemon juice to give a spreading consistency. Divide the icing between 2–3 small bowls (cups would do) and add a drop of different food colouring to each bowl, mixing well.

—

Spoon a little icing on to each of the biscuits and spread out with the back of the teaspoon. Finish by adding silver balls for eyes.

It is usual to shape this mixture into 'S' shapes, but you can shape it into any letter or number of your choice.

JUMBLES

MAKES ABOUT 32 JUMBLES

150g (5oz) butter, softened
150g (5oz) caster sugar
a few drops of vanilla extract
finely grated zest of 1 lemon
1 large egg
350g (12oz) plain flour
clear honey, to glaze
demerara sugar, for dusting

Lightly grease and line three baking trays with non-stick baking paper.

—

Measure all the ingredients, except the honey and demerara sugar, into a bowl and work together by hand until a dough is formed. This can also be done in a food processor or with an electric mixer.

—

Divide the dough into 32 pieces. Roll each piece of dough into a strip about 10cm (4in) long, then twist into an 'S' shape. Place them on the prepared baking trays and chill for about 30 minutes.

—

Preheat the oven to 190°C/Fan 170°C/Gas 5.

—

Bake the jumbles in the preheated oven for 10–15 minutes until they are a pale golden colour, then remove from the oven. Increase the oven temperature to 220°C/Fan 200°C/Gas 7 and, while the jumbles are still warm, brush them well with the honey and sprinkle with the demerara sugar. Return to the oven for 2–3 minutes. Cool slightly, then lift on to a wire rack and leave to cool completely.

Children love to cut out and decorate these biscuits. The dough is easy to handle and can be rerolled successfully.

GINGERBREAD MEN

MAKES ABOUT 20 GINGERBREAD MEN

350g (12oz) plain flour
1 level teaspoon
    bicarbonate of soda
2 level teaspoons
    ground ginger
115g (4oz) butter
175g (6oz) light
    muscovado sugar
4 tablespoons golden syrup
1 large egg, beaten
currants, to decorate

Preheat the oven to 190°C/Fan 170°C/Gas 5. Lightly grease three baking trays.

—

Measure the flour, bicarbonate of soda and ginger into a bowl. Rub in the butter with your fingertips until the mixture resembles fine breadcrumbs, then stir in the sugar. Add the golden syrup and beaten egg and mix to form a smooth dough, kneading lightly towards the end.

—

Divide the dough in half and lightly flour a work surface. Roll out one half to a thickness of about 5mm (¼in). Cut out gingerbread men using a cutter and place them on the prepared baking trays. (I used a 13.5cm/5½in cutter to get 20 gingerbread men.) Place the currants for eyes and buttons. Repeat with the remaining dough. Reroll as necessary.

—

Bake in the preheated oven for 10–12 minutes until they become a slightly darker shade. Cool slightly, then lift on to a wire rack and leave to cool completely.

You can use dariole moulds or egg cups for these easy-to-make little cakes, or you can buy pyramid moulds for a more pointed shape.

COCONUT PYRAMIDS

MAKES 12 PYRAMIDS

225g (8oz) desiccated
  coconut
115g (4oz) caster sugar
2 large eggs, beaten
a little pink food
  colouring (optional)

Preheat the oven to 180°C/Fan 160°C/Gas 4. Line two baking trays with non-stick baking paper.

—

Measure the coconut and sugar into a bowl and mix together. Beat in enough egg to bind the mixture together and add a few drops of pink colouring, if you like.

—

Dip each mould or egg cup into cold water and drain well.

—

Fill the moulds with the coconut mixture and press down lightly. Turn the moulded coconut out on to a prepared baking tray and continue with the remaining mixture.

—

Bake in the preheated oven for about 20 minutes, or until the pyramids are tinged pale golden brown. Lift off the baking trays and leave to cool on a wire rack.

*These are not oversweet, so a slightly healthier option than flapjacks.
Great to add to a lunch box.*

OAT AND SUNFLOWER SQUARES

MAKES 16 SQUARES

75g (3oz) butter
75g (3oz) golden syrup
150g (5oz) porridge oats
55g (2oz) sunflower seeds

Preheat the oven to 180°C/Fan 160°C/Gas 4. Lightly grease an 18cm (7in) shallow square cake tin.

———

Heat the butter and syrup together gently until evenly blended.

———

Add the oats and sunflower seeds to the pan with the syrup mixture and stir thoroughly to mix. Spoon into the prepared tin and press the mixture down well with the back of a spoon.

———

Bake in the preheated oven for 20–25 minutes, or until set in the middle and golden brown around the edges. Cut into 16 squares, then leave to cool in the tin before carefully lifting out.

This is the perfect birthday cake for any child – a chocolate castle, which you can make for a Prince or a Princess depending on how you decorate it.

CASTLE BIRTHDAY CAKE
SERVES 20

For the chocolate cake
80g (3¼oz) cocoa powder
240ml (8½fl oz) boiling
   water
700g (1lb 9oz) caster sugar
700g (1lb 9oz) baking
   spread, from the fridge
4 teaspoons baking powder
750g (1lb 10oz) self-raising
   flour
12 large eggs
4 tablespoons milk

For the chocolate icing
250g (9oz) butter, softened
2 tablespoons milk
350g (12oz) icing sugar
5 tablespoons cocoa
   powder
4 tablespoons boiling water

To decorate
2 wafer biscuits
1 tube edible glue
1 small packet jelly beans
8 x 4-finger KitKats or
   chocolate fingers
2 x 105g packets Smarties
5 waffle ice cream cones

Preheat the oven to 180°C/160°C Fan/Gas 4. Grease and base line two 20cm (8in) square loose-bottomed cake tins with non-stick baking paper.

Measure half of the cocoa and boiling water into a large bowl. Mix until smooth. Add half the remaining cake ingredients to the bowl and whisk with an electric hand whisk for 2 minutes until light and fluffy.

Divide between two tins and level the surfaces. Bake for 35–40 minutes, or until well risen and springing back when pressed in the centre with your fingertips. Remove from the tins and leave to cool on a wire rack.

Wash, grease and reline the tins with non-stick baking paper. Repeat the cake method with the remaining ingredients and divide between the tins. Bake for 35–40 minutes, as before, and leave to cool on a wire rack.

To make the chocolate icing, beat the butter, milk and half of the icing sugar together until smooth, using an electric hand whisk. Add the remaining icing sugar and beat again. Mix the cocoa and boiling water together in a small bowl to make a smooth paste. Add to the icing and beat until well incorporated.

Recipe continued overleaf

To assemble the cake, remove the baking paper from all four cakes. Place one cake on a cake board, spread with icing and sandwich together with another cake. This will be the castle's base. Make a 11cm (4½in) square template out of paper and place on top of the remaining two whole cakes on one corner. Slice around the template to make two 11cm (4½in) squares. Sandwich them together with icing and place in the centre on top of the castle's base.

—

Using a 5cm (2in) round cutter, stamp 10 rounds out of the leftover cakes. Sandwich them together with icing to make 5 rounds (these will be the turrets).

—

Place 4 of the cake turrets on top of the base cake and one on top of the centre tier. Cover the whole cake with chocolate icing.

—

Stick the wafer biscuits on to the front of the cake to make the door. Glue halved jelly beans on for the door knobs. Trim the KitKats or chocolate fingers to size and arrange in neat rows around the base and second tier of the cake to make walls. Cover the tops of the turrets with Smarties. Glue halved jelly beans on to one of the ice cream cones and place in the middle on the very top. Sit the remaining cones on the four turrets.

—

Add a flag, soldiers, princesses and glitter, as liked!

Children love to help by putting their favourite sweets on top of these tiny cakes.

LITTLE GEMS

MAKES 40 GEMS

75g (3oz) butter, softened
2 large eggs
115g (4oz) self-raising flour
1 level teaspoon baking
    powder
75g (3oz) caster sugar
1 tablespoon milk

For the decoration
115g (4oz) icing sugar, sifted
about 1 tablespoon fresh
    lemon juice
small sweets, to decorate

Preheat the oven to 180°C/Fan 160°C/Gas 4. Arrange about 40 petit four cases on baking trays.

—

Measure all the cake ingredients into a bowl and beat well until thoroughly blended.

—

Spoon scant teaspoonfuls of the mixture into the cases, being careful not to overfill. Bake in the preheated oven for 15–20 minutes, or until well risen and pale golden brown. Cool on a wire rack.

—

To make the icing, measure the icing sugar into a bowl and add enough lemon juice to give a spreading consistency. Spoon a little on top of each cooled gem and spread out with the back of a teaspoon. When the icing has almost set, top with a sweet.

You can use this basic shape to make other animals, such as a cat, teddy bear, koala or an owl. Chocolate sprinkles can be used in place of the coconut, if preferred.

BUNNY RABBIT BIRTHDAY CAKE

SERVES 20

For the cake
275g (10oz) butter, softened
275g (10oz) caster sugar
5 large eggs
275g (10oz) self-raising flour
1 level teaspoon baking
    powder

For the butter cream
225g (8oz) butter, softened
450g (1lb) icing sugar, sifted
juice of ½ lemon

For the decoration
about 250g (9oz)
    desiccated coconut
sweets for the eyes,
    nose and whiskers

Preheat the oven to 180°C/Fan 160°C/Gas 4. Grease one 15cm (6in), one 18cm (7in) and one 20cm (8in) shallow sandwich tin and line the bases with non-stick baking paper.

—

Measure all the cake ingredients into a large bowl and beat well for about 2 minutes until blended and smooth.

—

Divide the mixture between the tins and level the surfaces. Bake in the preheated oven for 20–25 minutes (15cm/6in cake), 25–30 minutes (18cm/7in cake) and 30–35 minutes (20cm/8in cake), until well risen. Leave to cool in the tins for a few minutes, then turn out, peel off the baking paper and finish cooling on a wire rack.

—

Meanwhile, make the butter cream by mixing the butter, icing sugar and lemon juice in a bowl until thoroughly blended.

—

Toast two-thirds of the coconut until golden brown.

—

To make the rabbit shape, cut the 18cm (7in) cake to form the ears, paw and tail. For the ears, cut 2 oval pieces from each side of the cake and then 1 smaller oval to form the hind paw and a circle for the tail. The 20cm (8in) cake becomes the body and the 15cm (6in) cake becomes the head. Assemble the rabbit on a large cake board or a foil-covered baking sheet, positioning the ears, paw and tail.

—

Cover the cakes with the butter cream, then sprinkle over the toasted coconut, leaving the tail, inner ear and tummy clear to be covered by the untoasted coconut. Finish by adding the sweets to make the eyes, nose and whiskers. (I use thinly sliced liquorice sweets to create the whiskers.)

A fun cake for a special occasion. From the outside, it looks like any other cake, but once you cut into it, it reveals itself to be as colourful as a rainbow.

RAINBOW CAKE

SERVES 20

6 eggs
375g (13oz) caster sugar
375g (13oz) baking spread,
    straight from the fridge
375g (13oz) self-raising flour
3 teaspoons baking powder
3 teaspoons vanilla extract
3 tablespoons milk
food colouring paste or gel
    (in 6 different colours)

For the cream cheese icing
375g (13oz) butter, softened
3 tablespoons milk
750g (1lb 10oz) icing sugar,
    sifted
1½ teaspoons vanilla extract
275g (10oz) full-fat cream
    cheese
hundreds and thousands,
    to decorate

Preheat the oven to 180°C/160°C Fan/Gas 4. Grease and base line two 20cm (8in) round loose-bottomed cake tins with non-stick baking paper.

—

Measure one-third of the cake ingredients into a large bowl and whisk using an electric hand whisk for 2 minutes. Divide the mixture into 2 bowls and add some food colouring to each bowl (two different colours) and mix well.

—

Spoon into the tins and bake in the preheated oven for 15 minutes, or until well risen and springing back when pressed in the centre with your fingertips. Remove from the tins and leave to cool on a wire rack.

—

Wash, grease and reline the tins. Repeat the method to make four more cakes, all in different colours.

—

To make the cream cheese icing, beat the butter and milk with half of the icing sugar in a large bowl, using an electric hand whisk, until smooth. Add the remaining icing sugar, the vanilla extract and the cream cheese and beat until light and fluffy.

—

To assemble the cake, remove the baking paper from all six cakes. Place the violet cake on to a cake board and spread with a little icing. Continue to layer the cakes with icing until you have all six cakes stacked neatly with the red cake on top. Cover the whole surface of the cake with a thin layer of icing, then place in the fridge for 20 minutes. This will help to seal the crumbs.

—

Once the icing is firm, cover with a final layer and spread to make a smooth finish. Sprinkle the top with hundreds and thousands.

CHAPTER NINE

BISCUITS
AND
COOKIES

Buy a pretty tin and fill it with a variety of homemade biscuits. Vary the recipe by using caster sugar in place of the light muscovado sugar, if you like.

SPECIAL SHORTBREAD BISCUITS

MAKES ABOUT 20 BISCUITS

175g (6oz) plain flour
75g (3oz) light
   muscovado sugar
125g (4½oz) butter
a little demerara sugar,
   for sprinkling

Preheat the oven to 160°C/Fan 140°C/Gas 3. Lightly grease two baking trays.

—

Measure the flour and sugar into a large bowl or food processor. Add the butter and rub together with your fingertips or whiz in the processor until the mixture is just beginning to bind together. Knead gently to bring together to form a dough.

—

Roll out the dough on a lightly floured work surface to a thickness of about 5mm (¼in). Cut into circles using a 5cm (2in) fluted cutter and transfer the biscuits to the prepared baking trays. Prick the biscuits all over with a fork and sprinkle with demerara sugar.

—

Bake in the preheated oven for 20–25 minutes, or until pale golden. Leave to cool on the baking trays for a few minutes, then lift on to a wire rack to cool completely.

To make Cherry Shortbread Biscuits, follow the recipe above and then press 30g (1oz) of chopped red or natural glacé cherries into the top of each biscuit before baking. Do not sprinkle with demerara sugar as the cherries sweeten the biscuits.

To make Walnut Shortbread Biscuits, follow the recipe above, adding 55g (2oz) roughly chopped walnuts after rubbing in the butter before kneading the mixture into a dough. Dust generously with sifted icing sugar when cooled.

For really good shortbread it is essential to use butter. I like to use semolina as well as flour to give crunch, but you can use cornflour or ground rice instead.

THE VERY BEST SHORTBREAD

MAKES 30 FINGERS

225g (8oz) plain flour
115g (4oz) semolina
225g (8oz) butter
115g (4oz) caster sugar
2 tablespoons demerara
    sugar, for dusting

Lightly grease a 30 x 23cm (12 x 9in) traybake or roasting tin.

—

Mix together the flour and semolina in a bowl or food processor. Add the butter and caster sugar and rub together with your fingertips or whiz in the processor until the mixture is just beginning to bind together. Knead lightly until the mixture forms a smooth dough.

—

Press the dough into the prepared tin and level it with a spatula or palette knife, making sure the mixture is evenly spread. Prick all over with a fork and chill until firm.

—

Preheat the oven to 160°C/Fan 140°C/Gas 3.

—

Bake in the preheated oven for about 50 minutes, or until a very pale golden brown. Sprinkle with the demerara sugar and leave to cool on the baking tray for a few minutes, then cut into 30 fingers. Carefully lift the fingers out of the tin with a palette knife and finish cooling on a wire rack. Store in an airtight tin.

To make Orange Shortbread, add the finely grated zest of one large orange to the mixture.

TIP
Glacé cherries, dried apricots and sultanas make delicious additions to shortbread, but the biscuits then need to be eaten on the day of making, as they soon become soggy with the moisture from the fruit.

These old-fashioned biscuits are very short in texture. They are best eaten within a couple of days of making.

MELTING MOMENTS

MAKES ABOUT 40 BISCUITS

225g (8oz) butter, softened
175g (6oz) caster sugar
2 large egg yolks
a few drops of vanilla extract
275g (10oz) self-raising flour
55g (2oz) old-fashioned oats
20 red or natural glacé
　　cherries, halved (optional)

Preheat the oven to 180°C/Fan 160°C/Gas 4 and line two baking trays with non-stick baking paper.

—

Measure the butter, sugar, egg yolks, vanilla extract and flour into a mixing bowl and beat together to form a soft dough.

—

Divide the mixture into about 40 pieces. Form each one into a ball and roll in the oats to cover. Place on the prepared baking trays, leaving space between them. Flatten each ball slightly and top each one with a halved glacé cherry, if using.

—

Bake in the preheated oven for about 20 minutes or until golden. Leave to cool on the baking trays for a few minutes, then lift on to a wire rack to finish cooling.

These are neither fork biscuits nor shortbread, but a combination of the two! You could use any flavoured chocolate and omit the orange zest, if you like. Be creative!

ORANGE AND CHOCOLATE FORK SHORTBREAD BISCUITS

MAKES 25 BISCUITS

175g (6oz) butter, softened
75g (3oz) caster sugar
175g (6oz) plain flour
75g (3oz) cornflour
finely grated zest of
    1 small orange
115g (4oz) orange chocolate,
    chopped into pieces

Preheat the oven to 180°C/Fan 160°C/Gas 4. Line two baking trays with non-stick baking paper.

—

Measure the butter and sugar into a food processor and whiz until soft. Add the flours and orange zest and whiz again until the mixture comes together. Stir in the chocolate pieces.

—

Knead lightly until the mixture forms a smooth dough. Divide into 25 balls and place well apart on the prepared baking trays. Dip a fork in a little water and use this to flatten the biscuits.

—

Bake in the preheated oven for 25 minutes until pale golden. Leave to cool on the baking trays for a few minutes, then lift on to a wire rack to cool completely.

*Don't expect these cookies to be as crisp as traditional biscuits –
they should be slightly chewy. They will keep in an airtight tin for a week.*

CHOCOLATE CHIP COOKIES

MAKES 20 COOKIES

115g (4oz) butter, softened
75g (3oz) caster sugar
55g (2oz) light
  muscovado sugar
½ teaspoon vanilla extract
1 large egg, beaten
150g (5oz) self-raising flour
115g (4oz) plain
  chocolate chips

Preheat the oven to 190°C/Fan 170°C/Gas 5 and line two large baking trays with non-stick baking paper.

—

Measure the butter and sugars into a large bowl and beat thoroughly until evenly blended.

—

Add the vanilla extract to the beaten egg, then add this a little at a time to the butter and sugar mixture in the bowl, beating well between each addition.

—

Mix in the flour, and lastly stir in the chocolate chips. Spoon tablespoons of the mixture on to the prepared baking trays, leaving room for the cookies to spread.

—

Bake on the top shelf of the oven for 10–12 minutes, or until the cookies are golden. Watch them like a hawk, as they will turn dark brown very quickly. Leave the cookies on the baking trays for a few minutes, then lift off with a palette knife and place on a wire rack to cool completely. Store in an airtight tin.

To make Chocolate and Orange Cookies, follow the recipe above, but chop a bar of plain orange chocolate into small pieces and use instead of the chocolate chips.

Dead easy to make, these are wonderful cookies. Expect an irregular shape. They are very soft when they come out of the oven but will harden up considerably on cooling.

DOUBLE CHOCOLATE COOKIES

MAKES ABOUT 36 COOKIES

180g (6¼oz) dark chocolate, broken into pieces
55g (2oz) butter
1 × 397g can full-fat condensed milk
225g (8oz) self-raising flour
115g (4oz) white chocolate chips

Melt the chocolate with the butter in a heatproof bowl set over a pan of simmering water, stirring occasionally.

—

Remove from the heat, stir in the condensed milk and cool.

—

Mix in the flour and the chocolate chips and chill the mixture in the fridge for about 30 minutes, until firm enough to handle.

—

Preheat the oven to 180°C/Fan 160°C/Gas 4 and line two baking trays with non-stick baking paper.

—

Roll the mixture into 36 balls and place well apart on the prepared baking trays. Press down to flatten.

—

Bake in the preheated oven for about 15 minutes. The cookies should still look soft and will glisten. Don't overcook them as they soon become very hard. Leave to cool on the baking trays for a few minutes, then remove the cookies carefully with a palette knife and place on a wire rack to cool completely.

Both the flowers and the leaves of lavender can be used, although it is best to use only young leaves. If you are using fresh lavender, make sure it is unsprayed. Dried lavender is stronger in flavour, so use half the quantity.

LAVENDER BISCUITS

MAKES ABOUT 36 BISCUITS

175g (6oz) butter, softened
2 tablespoons fresh,
    finely chopped lavender
    flowers and leaves
    (pick the flowerlets
    and the leaves off the
    stems to measure),
    or 1 tablespoon
    dried lavender
115g (4oz) caster sugar
225g (8oz) plain flour
30g (1oz) demerara sugar

Place the softened butter and lavender in a mixing bowl and beat together (this will obtain the maximum flavour from the lavender).

—

Beat the caster sugar into the butter and lavender, then stir in the flour, bringing the mixture together with your hands and kneading lightly until smooth.

—

Divide the mixture in half and roll out to form 2 sausage shapes 15cm (6in) long. Roll the biscuit 'sausages' in the demerara sugar until evenly coated. Wrap in non-stick baking paper or foil and chill until firm.

—

Preheat the oven to 180°C/Fan 160°C/Gas 4 and line two large baking trays with non-stick baking paper.

—

Cut each 'sausage' into about 18 slices and place on the prepared baking trays, allowing a little room for them to spread.

—

Bake in the preheated oven for 15–20 minutes, until the biscuits are pale golden brown at the edges. Leave to cool on the baking trays for a few minutes, then lift them off with a fish slice or palette knife and place on a wire rack to cool completely.

These biscuits first made their appearance in an old red Cordon Bleu cookery book, and I've been making them for years.

FORK BISCUITS

MAKES ABOUT 16 BISCUITS

115g (4oz) butter, softened
55g (2oz) caster sugar
finely grated zest of 1 lemon
150g (5oz) self-raising flour

Preheat the oven to 190°C/Fan 170°C/Gas 5 and line two baking trays with non-stick baking paper.

—

Measure the butter into a bowl and beat to soften further. Gradually beat in the sugar and lemon zest, then the flour. Bring the mixture together with your hands to form a dough.

—

Form the dough into 16 balls about the size of a walnut and place well apart on the prepared baking trays. Dip a fork in a little water and use this to flatten the biscuits.

—

Bake in the preheated oven for 15 minutes until a very pale golden. Leave to cool on the baking trays for a few minutes, then lift on to a wire rack to cool completely.

To make Chocolate Fork Biscuits, follow the recipe above, but omit the lemon zest and use only 120g (4½oz) self-raising flour along with 15g (½oz) cocoa powder. Bake until browned.

These biscuits have a delicate lemony flavour.

SHREWSBURY BISCUITS

MAKES ABOUT 24 BISCUITS

115g (4oz) butter, softened
75g (3oz) caster sugar,
   plus extra for sprinkling
1 large egg, separated
200g (7oz) plain flour
finely grated zest of 1 lemon
55g (2oz) currants
1–2 tablespoons milk

Preheat the oven to 200°C/Fan 180°C/Gas 6 and line two large baking trays with non-stick baking paper.

—

Measure the butter and sugar into a bowl and cream together until light and fluffy. Beat in the egg yolk.

—

Sift in the flour and add the grated lemon zest. Mix well. Add the currants and enough milk to give a fairly soft dough.

—

Knead the mixture gently on a lightly floured surface and roll out to a thickness of 5mm (¼in). Cut into about 24 rounds, using a 6cm (2½in) fluted cutter. Place on the prepared baking trays.

—

Bake in the preheated oven for 10 minutes.

—

Meanwhile, lightly beat the egg whites. Remove the biscuits from the oven, brush with the beaten egg white, sprinkle with a little caster sugar and return the biscuits to the oven for a further 4–5 minutes, or until pale golden brown. Leave to cool on the baking trays for a few minutes, then lift on to a wire rack to cool completely.

Take care not to bake these biscuits too long as they become hard and crisp.

CORNISH FAIRINGS

MAKES ABOUT 24 BISCUITS

115g (4oz) plain flour
¼ level teaspoon
   ground ginger
¼ level teaspoon
   ground mixed spice
¼ level teaspoon
   ground cinnamon
½ level teaspoon
   bicarbonate of soda
55g (2oz) butter, softened
55g (2oz) caster sugar
75g (3oz) golden syrup

Preheat the oven to 180°C/Fan 160°C/Gas 4 and line a large baking tray with non-stick baking paper.

—

Measure the flour, spices and bicarbonate of soda into a bowl. Rub the butter into the flour with your fingertips until the mixture resembles fine breadcrumbs, then mix in the sugar.

—

Gently heat the golden syrup, then stir into the mixture to make a soft dough.

—

Roll the dough into 24 balls roughly the size of a cherry and place on the prepared baking tray, allowing room for them to spread.

—

Bake in the preheated oven for about 10 minutes, then take the baking tray out of the oven and carefully hit it on a solid surface to make the biscuits crack and spread. Bake for a further 5 minutes, until they are a good even brown. Leave to cool on the baking tray for a few minutes, then lift on to a wire rack to cool completely.

TIP
Banging the baking tray part-way through cooking makes the mixture crack and flatten.

These flapjacks are crunchy and traditional. Take care not to overbake them, as they can become hard and dark.

FAST FLAPJACKS

MAKES 24 FLAPJACKS

225g (8oz) butter
225g (8oz) demerara sugar
75g (3oz) golden syrup
275g (10oz) old-fashioned
    porridge oats

Preheat the oven to 160°C/Fan 140°C/Gas 3. Line a 30 x 23cm (12 x 9in) traybake or roasting tin with non-stick baking paper.

———

Measure the butter, demerara sugar and golden syrup into a saucepan. Slowly melt over a low heat until the sugar has dissolved. Remove from the heat and stir in the oats. Mix well then turn into the prepared tin and press flat, using the back of a spoon.

———

Bake in the preheated oven for 30–35 minutes until evenly pale golden brown. Make sure you don't overcook them or they will become hard. If you don't cook them for long enough the middle will be soft. Remove from the oven and leave to cool in the tin for 10 minutes. Score the flapjack into 24 squares, using a small sharp knife, and leave to finish cooling in the tin.

———

Once completely cool, transfer the squares on to kitchen paper to absorb any excess grease. Store in an airtight container with non-stick baking paper in between the flapjacks so they don't stick together.

To make Chocolate Chip Flapjacks, leave the mixture to cool after stirring in the oats. Stir in 115g (4oz) dark chocolate chips, then turn into the prepared tin and cook as above.

To make Muesli Flapjacks, replace 175g (6oz) of the porridge oats with your favourite muesli, then turn into the prepared tin and cook as above. If you like a lot of raisins, add an extra 30-55g (1-2oz) to the flapjack mixture.

A variation of a flapjack jammed full of dried fruits and seeds. You could use chia and sunflower seeds instead of pumpkin and sesame, and swap the cranberries and sultanas for apricots and raisins. A flexible recipe that is great for a picnic or a packed lunch.

FRUITY GRANOLA BARS

MAKES 12 BARS

150g (5oz) old-fashioned porridge oats
30g (1oz) pumpkin seeds
30g (1oz) sesame seeds
115g (4oz) butter
2 tablespoons honey
115g (4oz) light muscovado sugar
55g (2oz) cranberries, chopped
55g (2oz) sultanas
a pinch of sea salt (optional)

Preheat the oven to 180°C/Fan 160°C/Gas 4. Grease an 18cm (7in) square cake tin and line the base and sides with a piece of non-stick baking paper.

—

Place the oats and seeds on a baking tray and toast in the oven for 10–15 minutes until the oats are lightly golden. Leave to cool.

—

Melt the butter, honey and sugar together in a large saucepan. Add the toasted oats, seeds and dried fruits and mix well. Add a pinch of sea salt, if using. Spoon into the prepared tin and smooth the surface with the back of a spoon.

—

Bake for 25 minutes until pale golden and the mixture is firm to touch in the centre. Leave to cool in the tin for 15 minutes, then turn out carefully and slice into 12 bars. Leave to cool completely on a wire rack.

The flavour and consistency will depend on the muesli used. These are good for a lunch box, for a snack at school or work, or to take on a picnic.

MUESLI COOKIES

MAKES ABOUT 24 COOKIES

175g (6oz) butter, softened
115g (4oz) caster sugar
1 large egg
175g (6oz) self-raising flour
200g (7oz) muesli
demerara sugar,
   for sprinkling

Preheat the oven to 180°C/Fan 160°C/Gas 4 and line two large baking trays with non-stick baking paper.

—

Measure all the ingredients, except the muesli and demerara sugar, into a large bowl and beat together until well blended and smooth. Stir in 175g (6oz) of the muesli.

—

Spoon 24 teaspoonfuls of the mixture on to the prepared baking trays, leaving room for the cookies to spread. Sprinkle the top of each one with a little extra muesli and demerara sugar.

—

Bake in the preheated oven for 15–20 minutes, or until golden brown at the edges. Leave to cool on the baking trays for a few minutes, then lift on to a wire rack to cool completely.

Cheesy biscuits always go well with drinks. If you make these ahead of time, they are best heated again in the oven before serving.

RICH CHEESY BISCUITS

MAKES ABOUT 60 BISCUITS

175g (6oz) plain flour
½ teaspoon fine sea salt
1 teaspoon mustard powder
75g (3oz) butter
175g (6oz) mature
    Cheddar, grated
2 large eggs
sesame or poppy seeds,
    for sprinkling

Sift the flour, salt and mustard powder into a bowl and rub in the butter with your fingertips until the mixture resembles fine breadcrumbs. Stir in the grated cheese.

—

Beat the eggs, then stir just enough egg into the flour mixture to form a soft dough (there will be some egg left over for glazing). Wrap the dough in clingfilm and chill for about 15 minutes.

—

Preheat the oven to 200°C/Fan 180°C/Gas 6 and line two baking trays with non-stick baking paper.

—

Roll the dough out on a lightly floured work surface to a thickness of about 5mm (¼in) and cut into 5cm (2in) rounds or triangles. Place on the prepared baking trays and brush with the remaining beaten egg. Sprinkle lightly with sesame or poppy seeds. Re-roll the trimmings once only.

—

Bake in the preheated oven for 15–18 minutes, or until crisp and golden. Leave to cool on the baking trays for a few minutes, then lift on to a wire rack to cool completely.

Savoury biscuits are great with drinks and these cheesy, nutty ones are delicious. Children like to roll these little balls, and they could give them as a present to a relative.

DORCHESTER BISCUITS

MAKES ABOUT 20 BISCUITS

115g (4oz) mature
    Cheddar, grated
115g (4oz) plain flour
a little salt
115g (4oz) butter, softened
½ teaspoon mustard powder
20 pistachio nuts, shelled

Preheat the oven to 190°C/Fan 170°C/Gas 5 and line two large baking trays with non-stick baking paper.

—

Measure all the ingredients, except the nuts, into a large bowl and work together with a knife, then with your hand, to form a dough.

—

Roll into 20 balls about the size of a walnut and place well apart on the prepared baking trays. Top each biscuit with a pistachio nut, then just slightly flatten each one with your hand.

—

Bake in the preheated oven for 15 minutes, or until golden brown. Leave to cool on the baking trays for a few minutes, then lift on to a wire rack to cool completely.

—

Serve warm or cold.

TIP
Try whole or halved cashew nuts, instead of pistachios.

With flecks of rosemary and a slight chewiness from the sun-dried tomatoes, these are delicious savoury biscuits that capture the best Mediterranean flavours and look as lovely as they taste.

SUN-DRIED TOMATO AND ROSEMARY BISCUITS

MAKES 48 BISCUITS

115g (4oz) Parmesan, grated
55g (2oz) sun-dried
  tomatoes, chopped
2 tablespoons chopped
  fresh rosemary, plus
  extra for rolling
125g (4½oz) plain flour
115g (4oz) butter, cubed

Measure the Parmesan, tomatoes and rosemary into a food processor. Whiz until finely chopped. Add the flour and butter and whiz again until the mixture comes together and forms a dough.

—

Divide the dough in half and roll each half into a tube measuring about 15cm (6in) long and 3cm (1¼in) diameter. Roll the tube in the extra rosemary, then wrap in clingfilm and chill in the fridge for 30 minutes.

—

Preheat the oven to 200°C/Fan 180°C/Gas 6. Line two large baking trays with non-stick baking paper.

—

Slice each tube into 24 thin rounds and arrange on the baking trays. Bake in the preheated oven for about 10–15 minutes until lightly golden. Leave to cool on the baking trays for a few minutes, then lift on to a wire rack to cool completely.

These make a lovely gift when beautifully presented in a box. They can be made in advance, but do not keep them in the larder, as they can quickly go off. Freeze them once cold.

PUFF PASTRY CHEESE STRAWS

MAKES 32 STRAWS

1 × 320g packet of
    ready-rolled puff pastry
plain flour, for dusting
3 tablespoons black
    olive tapenade
1 large egg, beaten
55g (2oz) Parmesan, grated
55g (2oz) mature
    Cheddar, grated
2 tablespoons poppy seeds

Preheat the oven to 220°C/Fan 200°C/Gas 7 and line two large baking trays with non-stick baking paper.

—

Unroll the pastry sheet on a floured work surface with the long side nearest to you. Spread the tapenade over the bottom half of the pastry. Brush the top half with the beaten egg. Sprinkle both cheeses on top of the tapenade in an even layer. Fold the top half of the pastry over the cheese covered section. Using a rolling pin, carefully re-roll the pastry back to its original rectangle size (about 38 x 23cm/15 x 9in).

—

Slice the pastry in half horizontally, then slice each half into 16 strips, 2cm (¾in) wide. Twist the strips and place on the prepared baking trays, leaving space between them. Brush with the remaining beaten egg and sprinkle with the poppy seeds.

—

Bake in the preheated oven for 15–18 minutes, then turn the straws over and continue to bake for another 5 minutes, until golden brown and crisp. Leave to cool on the baking trays for a few minutes, then lift on to a wire rack to cool completely.

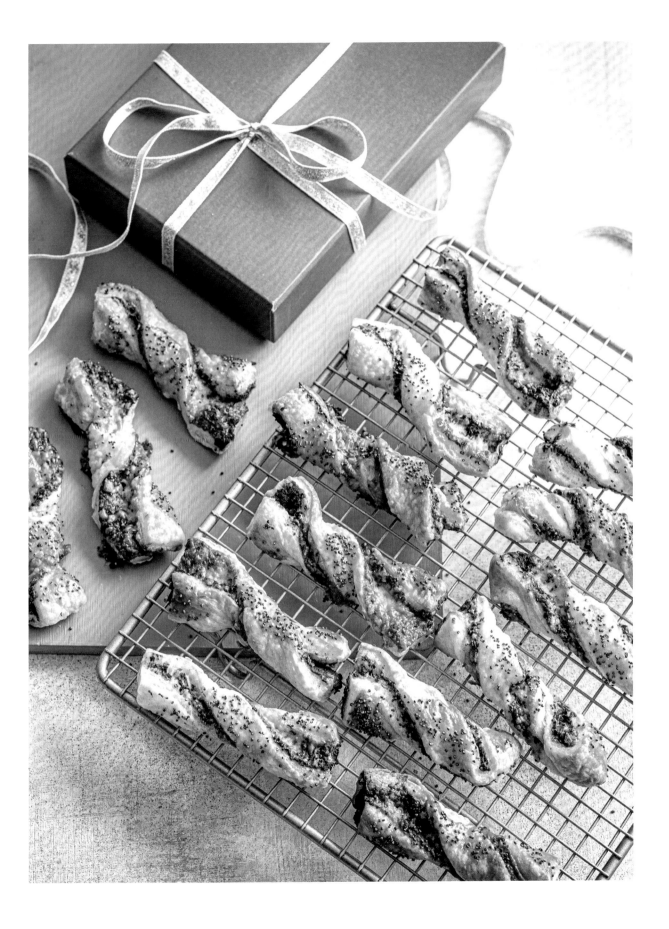

CHAPTER TEN

FANCY BISCUITS

These biscuits must be made with butter. The mixture holds its shape beautifully for piping, so use it for all shapes of piped biscuits.

VIENNESE FINGERS

MAKES ABOUT 20 BISCUITS

115g (4oz) butter, softened
30g (1oz) icing sugar
150g (5oz) plain flour
75g (3oz) dark chocolate,
  broken into pieces

Preheat the oven to 190°C/Fan 170°C/Gas 5. Lightly grease two baking trays. Fit a piping bag with a medium star nozzle.

Measure the butter and icing sugar into a bowl and beat well until pale and fluffy. Sift the flour into the bowl and beat well until thoroughly mixed.

Spoon into the piping bag and pipe out finger shapes about 7.5cm (3in) long, spacing them well apart.

Bake in the preheated oven for 10–15 minutes, or until a pale golden brown. Leave to cool on the baking trays for a few minutes, then lift on to a wire rack to cool completely.

Melt the chocolate gently in a heatproof bowl set over a pan of hot water, making sure the base of the bowl doesn't touch the water, stirring occasionally. Dip both ends of the biscuits into the chocolate and leave to set on the wire rack.

Using non-stick baking paper makes it so much simpler to get these biscuits off the baking trays. You can simply use a well-greased baking tray, but be careful not to leave them for too long or they will harden before you have a chance to lift them off.

FLORENTINES

MAKES ABOUT 20 FLORENTINES

55g (2oz) butter
55g (2oz) demerara sugar
55g (2oz) golden syrup
55g (2oz) plain flour
4 red or natural glacé cherries, finely chopped
55g (2oz) candied peel, finely chopped
55g (2oz) mixed almonds and walnuts, finely chopped
175g (6oz) dark chocolate, broken into pieces

Preheat the oven to 180°C/Fan 160°C/Gas 4. Line three baking trays with non-stick baking paper.

Measure the butter, sugar and syrup into a small pan and heat gently until the butter has melted. Remove from the heat and add the flour, chopped cherries, candied peel and nuts to the pan and stir well to mix.

Spoon teaspoonfuls of the mixture on to the prepared baking trays, leaving plenty of room for them to spread. Bake in the preheated oven for 8–10 minutes, or until golden brown. Leave the Florentines to cool before lifting on to a wire rack with a palette knife (if they have been baked on greased baking trays, then allow them to harden for a few moments only before lifting on to cooling racks to cool completely). If the Florentines become too hard to remove, pop them back into the oven for a few moments to allow them to soften.

Melt the chocolate in a heatproof bowl set over a pan of hot water, making sure the base of the bowl doesn't touch the water, stirring occasionally. Spread a little melted chocolate over the flat base of each Florentine, mark a zigzag in the chocolate with a fork and leave to set, chocolate side up, on the wire rack. Store in an airtight container.

TIP

These are luxurious biscuits, but you do need patience and accurate scales to make them.

These make a very special present! Look out for a pretty or unusual plate in an antique shop or car boot sale, and arrange the petits fours on this. Cover with clear cellophane and decorate with a ribbon. The milk and sugar glaze is optional for these petits fours, but it does give a nice shine.

PETITS FOURS AUX AMANDES

MAKES 24 PETITS FOURS

2 large egg whites
115g (4oz) ground almonds
75g (3oz) caster sugar
a little almond extract

To decorate
red or natural glacé
   cherries, chopped

To finish (optional)
1 tablespoon caster sugar
2 tablespoons milk

Preheat the oven to 180°C/Fan 160°C/Gas 4. Line two baking trays with non-stick baking paper. Fit a piping bag with a large star nozzle.

Whisk the egg whites until stiff. Fold in the ground almonds, sugar and almond extract. Spoon the mixture into the prepared piping bag and pipe the mixture into small rosettes. Decorate each rosette with a small piece of glacé cherry.

Bake in the preheated oven for about 15 minutes, or until golden. Leave to cool on the baking trays for a few minutes, then lift on to a wire rack to cool completely.

To finish, mix the caster sugar and milk together and lightly brush over the petits fours.

These are irresistible, but keep them in a cool place or they'll become very soft.

CHOCOLATE GANACHE PETITS FOURS

MAKES 24 PETITS FOURS

For the casings
175g (6oz) dark chocolate,
    broken into pieces
1 teaspoon sunflower oil

For the chocolate ganache
150ml (¼ pint) double cream
100g (4oz) dark chocolate,
    broken into pieces
a little rum or brandy,
    to flavour

To decorate
pistachio nuts, chopped
edible gold leaf (optional)

First make the chocolate casings. Melt the chocolate gently with the oil in a heatproof bowl set over a pan of hot water, making sure the base of the bowl doesn't touch the water, stirring occasionally. Allow to cool slightly then brush the inside of about 24 petit four paper cases with a thin layer of chocolate (you can use a fine brush to do this, or even just a fingertip). Leave to set in a cool place. Give the cases three or four coats of chocolate, leaving them to set each time.

To make the ganache, pour the cream into a small saucepan and bring to the boil. Remove from the heat and add the chocolate pieces and a little rum or brandy. Stir until the chocolate has melted.

Return the pan to the heat, bring to the boil, then take off the heat and leave to cool. When firm, spoon the chocolate ganache into a piping bag fitted with a medium star nozzle and pipe rosettes of the ganache into the chocolate cases.

Carefully peel off the paper cases. Decorate the top of each petit four with a small piece of pistachio nut or a touch of gold leaf (optional), and chill until required.

Traditionally macaroons were always made on rice paper but, as this is not always easy to get hold of, I've used baking paper.

MACAROONS

MAKES 16 MACAROONS

2 large egg whites
8 blanched almonds, halved
100g (4oz) ground almonds
175g (6oz) caster sugar
30g (1oz) semolina
a few drops of almond
    extract

Preheat the oven to 150°C/Fan 130°C/Gas 2. Line two baking trays with non-stick baking paper.

Put the egg whites into a bowl, dip in the halved almonds and set them aside. Whisk the egg whites until they form soft peaks. Gently fold in the ground almonds, sugar, semolina and almond extract.

Spoon the mixture in teaspoonfuls on to the prepared baking trays and smooth out with the back of a spoon to form circles. Place an almond half in the centre of each.

Bake in the preheated oven for 20–25 minutes, or until a pale golden brown. Leave to cool on the trays for a few minutes, then lift on to a wire rack to cool completely.

I use a quick method for making the pastry here rather than the classic way.

SUGARED PRETZELS

MAKES 10 PRETZELS

150g (5oz) plain flour,
    plus extra for dusting
65g (2½oz) butter
35g (1¼oz) caster sugar
1 large egg, beaten
a few drops of vanilla extract

To finish
1 large egg, beaten
1 tablespoon nibbed
    or pearled sugar
a little icing sugar,
    for dusting

Measure the flour into a large bowl, add the butter and rub in with your fingertips until the mixture resembles fine breadcrumbs. Stir in the sugar, then the egg and vanilla extract and mix until the pastry comes together. Knead very gently on a lightly floured work surface until smooth, then wrap in clingfilm and chill for about 30 minutes, or until firm enough to roll.

Preheat the oven to 200°C/Fan 180°C/Gas 6. Lightly grease two baking trays.

Divide the dough equally into 10 pieces and roll each into a ball. Roll each ball into a thin sausage measuring approximately 30cm (12in), then twist into the traditional pretzel shape, like a loose knot. Place on the prepared baking trays and brush gently with the beaten egg.

Scatter the nibbed or pearled sugar over the top of the pretzels and bake in the preheated oven for 15 minutes, or until barely changing colour. Lift on to a wire rack and dust thickly with icing sugar while still hot.

Also known as 'Diggers', these traditional Australian biscuits are really easy to make and taste delicious.

ANZAC BISCUITS

150g (5oz) butter, softened
1 tablespoon golden syrup
175g (6oz) granulated sugar
75g (3oz) self-raising flour
75g (3oz) desiccated
   coconut
115g (4oz) porridge oats

Preheat the oven to 180°C/Fan 160°C/Gas 4. Lightly grease two baking trays.

Measure the butter, golden syrup and sugar into a medium saucepan and heat gently until the butter has melted and the sugar has dissolved. Stir in the flour, coconut and oats and mix well until evenly blended.

Place large teaspoonfuls of the mixture well apart on the prepared baking trays and flatten slightly with the back of the spoon. You should have enough mixture for about 45 mounds, and you will need to bake them in batches.

Bake in the preheated oven for 8–10 minutes, or until they have spread out flat and are lightly browned at the edges. Leave to cool on the trays for a few minutes, then carefully lift off with a palette knife and place on a wire rack to cool completely. If the biscuits harden too much to lift off the tray, pop them back in the oven for a few minutes to soften.

Store in an airtight container.

These slim, crisp, curled biscuits are wonderful with light mousses, ice cream and fruit salads.

ALMOND TUILES

MAKES ABOUT 20 BISCUITS

75g (3oz) butter, softened
75g (3oz) caster sugar
1 large egg white
55g (2oz) plain flour
75g (3oz) blanched almonds, finely chopped

To finish
a little icing sugar, for dusting

Preheat the oven to 200°C/Fan 180°C/Gas 6. Lightly grease two baking trays.

Measure the butter and sugar into a bowl and beat well until pale and fluffy.

Place the egg white in a separate bowl and sift the flour over the top. Mix well then stir into the butter mixture, along with the finely chopped almonds.

Place teaspoonfuls of the mixture on the prepared baking trays, leaving ample room for the biscuits to spread (bake about 4 at a time).

Bake in batches in the preheated oven for 6–8 minutes, or until they are browned around the edge but not in the middle. Remove from the oven and leave to stand for a second or two then remove from the tray with a palette knife and curl over a rolling pin until set.

When cool, store in an airtight container. Serve with a dusting of icing sugar.

These keep well in an airtight tin or, if made a long time in advance, in the freezer. Store them in a rigid box or tin so they cannot be broken.

Bought Easter biscuits are usually larger than this. If you like them that way, simply use a larger cutter.

EASTER BISCUITS

115g (4oz) butter, softened
75g (3oz) caster sugar
1 large egg, separated
200g (7oz) plain flour,
    plus extra for dusting
½ level teaspoon ground
    mixed spice
½ level teaspoon
    ground cinnamon
55g (2oz) currants
30g (1oz) candied
    peel, chopped
1–2 tablespoons milk
a little caster sugar,
    for sprinkling

Preheat the oven to 200°C/Fan 180°C/Gas 6. Lightly grease three baking trays.

Measure the butter and sugar into a bowl and beat together until light and fluffy. Beat in the egg yolk. Sift in the flour and spices and mix well. Add the currants and chopped peel and enough milk to give a fairly soft dough.

Knead the mixture lightly on a lightly floured work surface and roll out to a thickness of 5mm (¼in). Cut into rounds using a 6cm (2½in) fluted cutter.

Place on the prepared baking trays and bake in the preheated oven for 8–10 minutes.

Meanwhile, lightly beat the egg white. Remove the biscuits from the oven, brush them with the beaten egg white, sprinkle with a little caster sugar and return to the oven for a further 4–5 minutes, or until pale golden brown. Lift on to a wire rack to cool.

Store in an airtight container.

If bought or homemade biscuits have gone a little soft, place them on a baking tray and crisp them in a moderate oven for a few minutes.

I must confess that I rarely make these as it is so easy to buy good ones! Serve plain with ice cream or mousses, or fill with whipped cream and serve with fruit.

BRANDY SNAPS

55g (2oz) butter
55g (2oz) demerara sugar
55g (2oz) golden syrup
55g (2oz) plain flour
½ level teaspoon
    ground ginger
½ teaspoon fresh
    lemon juice

Preheat the oven to 180°C/Fan 160°C/Gas 4. Line two baking trays with non-stick baking paper and oil the handles of four wooden spoons.

Measure the butter, sugar and syrup into a small pan and heat gently until the butter has melted and the sugar has dissolved. Leave the mixture to cool slightly, then sift in the flour and the ginger. Add the lemon juice and stir well to mix thoroughly.

Place teaspoons of the mixture on the prepared baking trays, at least 10cm (4in) apart and only 4 teaspoons at a time. Bake in the preheated oven for about 8 minutes, or until the mixture is well spread out and a dark golden colour.

Remove from the oven and leave for a few minutes to firm, then lift from the baking paper using a fish slice. Turn over and roll around the handle of the wooden spoons. Leave to set on a wire rack, then slip out the spoons. Repeat until all the mixture has been used.

When cold, store in an airtight tin.

To make Brandy Snap Baskets, mould the cooked mixture around the base of a greased cup or an orange and use your fingers to flute the top. You don't need to grease the orange, as its natural oils will prevent the brandy snap mixture from sticking.

If you notice that the underside of the shortbread is not pale gold, return the tray to the oven for a further 5–10 minutes.

BISHOP'S FINGERS

115g (4oz) plain flour
30g (1oz) ground almonds
30g (1oz) semolina
115g (4oz) butter
55g (2oz) caster sugar
a few drops of almond
    extract
30g (1oz) flaked almonds
a little caster sugar,
    for dusting

Preheat the oven to 160°C/Fan 140°C/Gas 3. Lightly grease an 18cm (7in) shallow square tin.

Mix together the flour, ground almonds and semolina in a bowl or food processor. Add the butter, sugar and almond extract and rub together with your fingertips until the mixture is just beginning to bind together. Knead lightly until smooth.

Press the dough into the prepared tin and level the surface with the back of a metal spoon or a palette knife. Sprinkle over the flaked almonds.

Bake in the preheated oven for 30–35 minutes, or until a very pale golden brown. Mark the shortbread into 12 fingers with a knife, sprinkle with caster sugar and leave to cool in the tin.

When completely cold, cut into fingers, lift out carefully and store in an airtight tin.

This shortbread is always popular. The different textures are the principal appeal – the crunch of the shortbread base, the caramel in the middle, and the chunky chocolate on top.

MILLIONAIRES' SHORTBREAD

MAKES 24 SQUARES

For the shortbread
250g (9oz) plain flour
75g (3oz) caster sugar
175g (6oz) butter, softened

For the caramel
115g (4oz) butter
115g (4oz) light
    muscovado sugar
2 × 397g cans full-fat
    condensed milk

For the topping
200g (7oz) dark
    or milk chocolate,
    broken into pieces

TIP

A marbled chocolate top looks stunning. Simply melt just over 55g (2oz) each of plain, milk and white chocolate in separate bowls. Place the chocolate in spoonfuls over the set caramel, alternating the 3 types. Use a skewer to marble the edges of the chocolates together, then leave to set.

Preheat the oven to 180°C/Fan 160°C/Gas 4. Lightly grease a 33 x 23cm (13 x 9in) Swiss roll tin.

To make the shortbread, mix the flour and caster sugar in a bowl. Rub in the butter with your fingertips until the mixture resembles fine breadcrumbs. Knead until it forms a dough, then press into the base of the prepared tin. Prick the shortbread lightly with a fork and bake in the preheated oven for about 20 minutes or until firm to the touch and very lightly browned. Cool in the tin.

To make the caramel, measure the butter and sugar into a large non-stick pan. Heat gently until the butter has melted and the sugar has dissolved. Add the condensed milk and stir continuously and evenly with a flat-ended wooden spoon for about 5 minutes, or until the mixture is thick and has turned a golden toffee colour – take care, as it burns easily.

Pour the caramel over the shortbread and leave to cool.

To make the topping, melt the chocolate gently in a bowl set over a pan of hot water, making sure the base of the bowl doesn't touch the water, stirring occasionally. Pour over the cold caramel and leave to set.

Cut into squares or bars.

Be generous with the raspberry jam, it makes all the difference. As the shortcrust pastry contains a lot of fat and no sugar, there is no need to line the tin with baking paper.

BAKEWELL SLICES

MAKES 24 SLICES

For the shortcrust pastry
175g (6oz) plain flour,
    plus extra for dusting
75g (3oz) butter

For the sponge
100g (4oz) butter, softened
100g (4oz) caster sugar
175g (6oz) self-raising flour
1 level teaspoon baking
    powder
2 large eggs
2 tablespoons milk
½ teaspoon almond extract

To finish
about 4 tablespoons
    raspberry jam
flaked almonds,
    for sprinkling

To make the pastry, measure the flour into a bowl and rub in the butter with your fingertips until the mixture resembles fine breadcrumbs. Add 2–3 tablespoons cold water gradually, mixing to form a soft dough.

Roll out the dough on a lightly floured work surface and use to line a 30 x 23cm (12 x 9in) traybake or roasting tin.

Preheat the oven to 180°C/Fan 160°C/Gas 4.

Measure all the sponge ingredients into a bowl and beat until well blended.

Spread the pastry with raspberry jam, then top with the sponge mixture.

Sprinkle with the flaked almonds and bake in the preheated oven for about 25 minutes, or until the sponge has shrunk from the sides of the tin and springs back when pressed in the centre with your fingertips. Leave to cool in the tin, then cut into slices.

CHAPTER ELEVEN

TARTS
AND
PASTRIES

This classic 'upside-down' French tart is usually served warm, as a pudding, rather than as a cold cake.

TARTE TATIN

SERVES 6

175g (6oz) granulated sugar
butter, for greasing
200g (7oz) peeled and
　cored Bramley apples,
　cut into 2cm (¾in) chunks
2 tbsp caster sugar
4 large eating apples
plain flour, for dusting
1 x 375g packet of all-butter
　puff pastry

You will need a 23cm (9in) fixed-base cake tin with deep sides.

First make the caramel. Measure the granulated sugar and 6 tablespoons of water into a stainless-steel saucepan. Stir gently over a low heat until the sugar has fully dissolved, then remove the spoon and increase the heat. Boil until a golden straw colour and immediately pour into the cake tin, letting it spread evenly over the base, then set aside. After about 30 minutes when the caramel has set, butter the sides of the tin above the caramel line.

Meanwhile, place the Bramley apples, caster sugar and 2 tablespoons of water in another saucepan. Stir over a medium heat, then cover with a lid and simmer for about 5–10 minutes until the apples are soft. Remove from the heat, then use a fork to mash the apples to a purée and leave to cool.

Preheat the oven to 220°C/Fan 200°C/Gas 7.

Peel and core the eating apples, then thinly slice so they are about 5mm (¼in) thick. Arrange a layer over the caramel in the tin in a circular pattern. Start from the outside of the tin and work inwards. Scatter the remaining apples on top and press down. Add the cooled apple purée in spoonfuls over the sliced apples and carefully spread out in an even layer.

Lightly dust a work surface in flour, then roll out the pastry to a circle 2–3cm (¾–1¼in) bigger than the tin. Cover the apples with the pastry and tuck in the edges. Make a small cross in the top of the pastry with a sharp knife, to let the steam out. Bake in the oven for 35–40 minutes, until the pastry is crisp and golden and the apples are soft.

Carefully turn the tarte tatin out on to a plate and spoon the syrup over the apples. Serve with cream or crème fraîche.

Another lovely tart with a crisp sweet pastry case and a sharp lemon filling.

LEMON TART WITH LEMON PASSION FRUIT CURD

For the pâte sucrée
175g (6oz) plain flour,
    plus extra for dusting
75g (3oz) butter, softened
75g (3oz) caster sugar
3 large egg yolks

For the filling
5 large eggs
225g (8oz) caster sugar
125ml (4fl oz) pouring
    double cream
3 large lemons

To finish
6 tablespoons lemon curd
2 passion fruits

First make the pâte sucrée (sweet pastry). Measure the flour and butter into a bowl. Rub in the butter with your fingertips until the mixture resembles fine breadcrumbs. Stir in the sugar, then add the egg yolks. Mix until the ingredients come together to form a firm dough. Roll out the pastry on a lightly floured work surface and use to line a 23cm (9in) loose-bottomed flan tin. Prick the pastry all over with a fork. Chill in the fridge for 30 minutes.

Preheat the oven to 200°C/Fan 180°C/Gas 6.

Line the flan tin with non-stick baking paper and baking beans. Bake blind in the preheated oven for 15 minutes, then remove the paper and beans and bake for another 5 minutes until golden and crisp.

Reduce the oven temperature to 160°C/Fan 140°C/Gas 2.

To make the filling, mix the eggs, sugar and cream together in a large bowl. Zest the lemons and add to the mixture. Squeeze the juice from the lemons and add 150ml (¼ pint) to the bowl.

Pour the mixture into the tin and carefully slide back into the oven. Bake for about 30–35 minutes until the filling is set, but with a slight wobble. Leave to cool.

Meanwhile, mix the lemon curd and passion fruit pulp together in a bowl. Serve alongside the tart, or drizzle over the top.

These little tarts look best if each one is filled with a single type of fruit. Use redcurrant glaze for red fruits, and apricot glaze for orange or green fruits, such as green grapes and kiwi fruit. Fill the pastry cases at the last moment as they soften quickly.

GLAZED FRUIT TARTLETS

MAKES 12 TARTLETS

For the pâte sucrée
115g (4oz) plain flour,
    plus extra for dusting
55g (2oz) butter, softened
55g (2oz) caster sugar
2 large egg yolks

For the filling and glaze
150ml (¼ pint) pouring
    double cream
225g (8oz) fresh fruits
    (such as raspberries
    and blueberries)
about 4 tablespoons
    redcurrant jelly
    (or apricot jam)

You will need twelve 9cm (3½in) patty tins.

First make the pâte sucrée (sweet pastry). Measure the flour into a bowl. Rub in the butter with your fingertips until the mixture resembles fine breadcrumbs. Stir in the sugar, then add the egg yolks and mix until the ingredients come together to form a dough. Knead the mixture gently until smooth. Wrap the dough in clingfilm and leave to rest in the fridge for about 30 minutes.

Preheat the oven to 200°C/Fan 180°C/Gas 6.

Roll out the pastry on a lightly floured work surface and cut out about 12 rounds using a 9cm (3½in) fluted pastry cutter. Re-roll the trimmings once only. Ease the pastry rounds into the patty tins and prick lightly with a fork. Place a small piece of baking paper or foil in each pastry case and fill with baking beans.

Bake the pastry cases in the preheated oven for about 15 minutes or until golden brown. Turn out on to a wire rack, remove the paper and baking beans, and leave to cool.

To make the filling, whip the cream until it forms soft peaks and spoon a little into each tartlet case. Arrange the fruits on top.

Warm the redcurrant jelly or apricot jam in a small pan and brush liberally over the fruits to glaze.

These lovely little shortbread cases can actually be filled with anything you like – they are a good way of spinning out a small amount of fruit.

LEMON AND STRAWBERRY CREAM TARTLETS

For the shortbread
115g (4oz) butter, softened
55g (2oz) caster sugar
55g (2oz) semolina
115g (4oz) plain flour

For the filling
about 3 tablespoons
    good lemon curd
150ml (¼ pint) pouring
    double cream, whipped
a few sliced strawberries

You will need a 12-hole bun tin.

First make the shortbread. Measure the butter, sugar, semolina and flour into a bowl and work together to form a smooth dough. Wrap in clingfilm and chill in the fridge for about 15 minutes.

Preheat the oven to 150°C/Fan 130°C/Gas 2.

On a lightly floured work surface, roll out the shortbread to just under 5mm (¼in) in thickness. Cut out 10 circles using a 7.5cm (3in) fluted cutter, then press the circles gently into the bun tin. Prick the bases well.

Bake in the preheated oven for about 20–25 minutes or until firm and golden. Leave the shortbread in the tins to harden slightly, then ease out of the tins and leave to cool completely on a wire rack.

To make the filling, mix together the lemon curd and whipped cream.

Just before serving, spoon a little of the filling into each shortbread case and top with sliced strawberries.

TIP
The shortbread cases can be made ahead, and they can be frozen for up to 2 months. Once filled, however, they go soft very quickly, so serve and eat straight away.

I've used ready-made filo pastry in this recipe, for ease. Try to find the shorter packets of filo pastry as then you won't need to trim the pastry to size.

FILO APPLE STRUDELS

For the filling
350g (12oz) cooking
   apples, peeled, cored
   and roughly chopped
   (prepared weight)
juice of ½ lemon
75g (3oz) demerara sugar
30g (1oz) fresh breadcrumbs
55g (2oz) sultanas
1 level teaspoon
   ground cinnamon
8 sheets filo pastry
   18 x 33cm (7 x 13in)
115g (4oz) butter, melted

For the topping
2 tablespoons caster sugar
2 tablespoons water
icing sugar, for dusting

Preheat the oven to 200°C/Fan 180°C/Gas 6. Lightly grease two baking trays.

First prepare the filling. Mix the apples, lemon juice, sugar, breadcrumbs, sultanas and cinnamon together in a bowl.

Unfold 1 sheet of filo pastry and brush liberally with melted butter. Spoon one-eighth of the apple mixture to cover the middle third of the longest edge of the pastry, leaving a small border. Fold in this border, then bring the two short sides over the apple to cover it. Roll the filled pastry over and over to form a neat strudel. Put it on one of the prepared baking trays, then repeat the process with the remaining 7 pastry sheets and apple mixture.

Brush the strudels with melted butter and bake in the preheated oven for about 15–20 minutes, or until golden brown and crisp.

Meanwhile, mix the caster sugar and water together in a small pan and heat gently until all the sugar has dissolved. Spoon the syrup over the warm strudels and dust with icing sugar to serve.

Any leftover filo will keep in the fridge for 2 days. Alternatively, you can wrap it carefully, put it into the freezer straight away and use within 1 month.

This delicious tart is an economical choice in the autumn, when you can use your own free apples or get them cheaply from elsewhere. You will need a 20cm (8in) loose-bottomed fluted flan tin.

FRENCH APPLE TART

SERVES 6–8

For the pastry
175g (6oz) plain flour,
    plus extra for dusting
75g (3oz) butter, cubed
1 large egg yolk

For the filling
900g (2lb) cooking apples
55g (2oz) butter
4 tablespoons apricot jam
55g (2oz) caster sugar,
    plus extra for sprinkling
finely grated zest of ½ lemon
225g (8oz) dessert apples
1–2 tablespoons fresh
    lemon juice

For the glaze
4 tablespoons apricot jam

To make the pastry, measure the flour into a large bowl, add the butter and rub in with your fingertips until the mixture resembles fine breadcrumbs. Add the egg yolk, stir into the flour mixture with a round-bladed knife, and bring the mixture to a dough, adding a little water if necessary. Knead the pastry very lightly, then wrap in clingfilm and chill in the fridge for about 30 minutes.

Preheat the oven to 200°C/Fan 180°C/Gas 6.

To make the apple filling, cut the cooking apples into quarters, remove the core and chop the apple into chunks (no need to peel).

Melt the butter in a large pan and then add the prepared apples and 2 tablespoons water. Cover and cook very gently for 10–15 minutes until the apples have become soft and mushy.

Rub the apple through a sieve into a clean pan, add the apricot jam, sugar and lemon zest. Cook over a high heat for 10–15 minutes, stirring continuously, until all the excess liquid has evaporated and the apple mixture is thick. Set aside to cool.

Roll out the pastry thinly on a lightly floured work surface and use to line a deep 20cm (8in) loose-bottomed fluted flan tin. Cover with baking paper and fill with baking beans. Bake blind in the preheated oven for 10–15 minutes.

Recipe continued overleaf

Remove the paper and beans and bake for a further 5 minutes until the pastry at the base of the flan has dried out. Remove from the oven but do not turn off the oven.

Spoon the cooled apple purée into the tart case and level the surface. Peel, quarter and core the dessert apples, then slice them very thinly. Arrange in neat overlapping circles over the apple purée, brush with the lemon juice and sprinkle with 1 teaspoon caster sugar. Return the tart to the oven and bake for 25 minutes or until the pastry and the edges of the apples are lightly browned.

To make the glaze, sieve the apricot jam into a small pan and heat gently until runny. Brush all over the top of the apples and pastry.

Serve warm or cold.

This tart looks wonderful cooked because the top layer of pastry moulds itself around the apricot halves. I use canned apricots as I find them more reliable and a readily obtainable alternative to fresh. You will need a 25cm (10in) deep loose-bottomed fluted flan tin.

AUSTRIAN APRICOT AND ALMOND TART

For the pastry
275g (10oz) plain flour, plus extra for dusting
150g (5oz) icing sugar, sifted
150g (5oz) chilled butter, cubed
1 large egg, beaten

For the filling
175g (6oz) almond paste or marzipan, grated (see page 398 for almond paste recipe)
800g (1¾lb) canned apricot halves in natural juice, drained and dried on kitchen paper

TIP
You can prepare the tart ahead of time. Cover the uncooked tart in clingfilm and keep in the fridge for up to 24 hours before baking. Remove the tart from the fridge and leave at room temperature for about 20 minutes before baking.

First make the pastry. Measure the flour and icing sugar into a large bowl and rub in the butter with your fingertips until the mixture resembles breadcrumbs. Stir in the beaten egg and bring together to form a dough. Form into a smooth ball, wrap in clingfilm and chill in the fridge for 30 minutes.

Preheat the oven to 180°C/Fan 160°C/Gas 4 and put a heavy baking tray in the oven to heat.

Cut off a little less than half the pastry, wrap it in clingfilm and return it to the fridge. Take the larger piece and roll out on a lightly floured work surface to a circle about 30cm (11½in). Line the base and sides of a 25cm (10in) deep loose-bottomed fluted flan tin with the pastry, then trim the excess from the top edge with a knife. Use the trimmings to patch the pastry if necessary.

Spread the grated almond paste or marzipan evenly over the base. Place the apricots on top of the almond paste, evenly spaced, rounded side up.

Roll out any trimmings along with the remaining pastry to a circle large enough to fit the top of the flan tin. Use a little water to dampen the rim of the pastry in the tin then, with the aid of the rolling pin, lift the top circle of pastry into position. Trim off any excess pastry, then press the edges together so no juices can escape. Again, use the pastry trimmings to patch if necessary.

Transfer to the preheated oven to bake on the hot tray for 30–35 minutes, or until pale golden. Watch the pastry carefully: if it is browning too quickly, protect the edge with strips of foil.

A familiar option on pub dessert menus, and a popular choice with adults and children alike. Delicious served with cream, ice cream or custard.

DEEP TREACLE TART

SERVES 6

For the pastry
150g (5oz) plain flour,
   plus extra for dusting
1 tablespoon icing sugar
75g (3oz) butter
1 medium egg

For the filling
450g (1lb) golden syrup
about 150g (5oz) fresh white
   or brown breadcrumbs
finely grated zest and juice
   of ½ large lemon

First make the pastry. Measure the flour and icing sugar into a large bowl and rub in the butter with your fingertips until the mixture resembles fine breadcrumbs. Add the egg and mix to a firm dough.

Roll the pastry out thinly on a lightly floured work surface and use to line an 23cm (9in) deep loose-bottomed fluted flan tin. Chill in the fridge for 30 minutes.

Preheat the oven to 200°C/Fan 180°C/Gas 6 and put a heavy baking tray in the oven to heat.

To make the filling, heat the syrup in a large pan and stir in the breadcrumbs and lemon zest and juice. If the mixture looks runny, add a few more breadcrumbs (it depends whether you use white or brown bread). Pour the syrup mixture into the pastry case and level the surface.

Bake in the preheated oven, on the hot baking tray, for 15 minutes, then reduce the oven temperature to 180°C/Fan 160°C/Gas 4 and bake for a further 25–30 minutes until the pastry is golden and the filling set. Leave to cool in the tin.

Serve warm or cold.

It's fiddly and time-consuming to make these pastries in their various traditional shapes, but they'll be better than any you can buy! They are best eaten on the day they are made. The basic recipe filling is almond paste, but do try the alternative fillings, too.

DANISH PASTRIES

For the pastry dough
450g (1lb) strong plain flour
½ level teaspoon salt
350g (12oz) butter, softened
7g sachet fast-action yeast
55g (2oz) caster sugar
150ml (¼ pint) warm milk
2 large eggs, beaten, plus
  a little extra, to glaze

For the filling and topping
225g (8oz) almond paste or
  marzipan (see page 398
  for almond paste recipe)
1–2 tablespoons warm water
115g (4oz) icing sugar
55g (2oz) flaked almonds,
  toasted
55g (2oz) red or natural
  glacé cherries, chopped

Lightly grease three baking trays.

Measure the flour and salt into a bowl and rub in 55g (2oz) of the butter with your fingertips. Add the yeast and sugar and stir to mix. Make a well in the centre, add the warm milk and beaten eggs, and mix to a soft dough. Knead the dough until smooth. Place it in a clean bowl, cover with clingfilm and leave to rise in a warm place for about 1 hour or until the dough has doubled in bulk.

Punch down the dough, knead until smooth, then roll out to an oblong about 35 x 20cm (14 x 8in). Cover the top two-thirds of the oblong with half the remaining butter, dotting pieces of butter over the dough. Fold the bottom third of dough up and the top third down to form a parcel. Seal the edges then give the dough a quarter turn so that the folded side is to the left. Roll out to the same sized oblong as before. Dot over the remaining butter in the same way and fold the dough as before. Wrap the dough in clingfilm and leave to rest in the fridge for about 15 minutes.

Set the dough so that the fold is on the left again and roll and fold the dough, with no butter, twice more. Wrap the dough in clingfilm and return to the fridge for 15 minutes.

To make crescents, divide the dough into quarters and roll out one section to a 23cm (9in) circle. Divide the circle into four equal wedges. Place a small sausage of almond paste at the wide end of each wedge and roll up loosely towards the point. Bend them round to form a crescent. Repeat with the remaining dough or try a different shape.

Recipe continued overleaf

To make pinwheels, roll out a quarter of dough to form a 20cm (8in) square. Cut into four squares. Place a small amount of almond paste in the centre of each square. Make cuts from each corner almost to the centre and fold four alternate points to the centre, pressing them down firmly.

To make kite shapes, roll out a quarter of dough to form a 20cm (8in) square. Cut into four squares. Place a small amount of almond paste in the centre of each square. Make cuts at opposite corners to create two L shaped strips. Lift the strips, crossing them over the almond paste in the centre.

To make envelopes, roll out a quarter of dough to form a 40cm (16in) square. Cut this into four squares. In the centre of each square, place a piece of almond paste or some other filling (vanilla cream or apple mixture are especially good here). Fold two opposite corners or all four corners into the middle. Press the edges down lightly.

Arrange the pastries on the prepared baking trays, cover with oiled clingfilm or put the trays inside oiled polythene bags, and leave to prove for about 20 minutes in a warm place, until they are beginning to look puffy.

Preheat the oven to 220°C/Fan 200°C/Gas 7.

Brush each pastry with beaten egg and bake in the preheated oven for about 15 minutes until golden brown. Lift on to a wire rack to cool.

Make up some glacé icing by gradually mixing the warm water into the icing sugar. Spoon a little icing over the pastries while they are still warm. Sprinkle with toasted flaked almonds or small pieces of glacé cherry.

ALTERNATIVE DANISH PASTRY FILLINGS

ALMOND FILLING

This is softer and moister than almond paste. Use it in any of the pastry shapes.

115g (4oz) ground almonds
115g (4oz) caster sugar
a little beaten egg

Mix the almonds and sugar together and bind with enough egg to form a soft paste.

VANILLA CREAM

This is particularly good in the 'envelopes'.

1 tablespoon plain flour
1 teaspoon cornflour
1 large egg yolk
1 tablespoon caster sugar
150ml (¼ pint) milk
2–3 drops of vanilla extract

Mix together the flours, egg yolk and sugar, and blend with a little of the milk. Bring the remaining milk to the boil, pour on to the flour mixture, blend and then return to the pan. Heat gently, stirring, until the mixture comes to the boil. Allow to cool then flavour with a few drops of vanilla extract.

APPLE FILLING

Use this filling in any of the pastry shapes.

450g (1lb) cooking apples, quartered and cored (no need to peel)
15g (½oz) butter
finely grated zest and juice of ½ lemon
4 tablespoons light muscovado sugar
75g (3oz) sultanas (optional)

Place the apples in a pan with the butter and the lemon zest and juice. Cover and cook until soft. Rub the apples through a sieve, return to the rinsed-out pan and add the sugar. Cook until the sugar has dissolved and the apple mixture is thick. Add the sultanas, if using, and leave until cold before using.

Pâte sucrée is the classic French sweet pastry. I make mine in the food processor, which is easier than the traditional way, on a work surface.

FRANGIPANE TARTLETS

MAKES 12 TARTLETS

For the pâte sucrée
115g (4oz) plain flour
55g (2oz) butter, softened
55g (2oz) caster sugar
2 large egg yolks

For the frangipane
55g (2oz) butter, softened
55g (2oz) caster sugar
1 large egg, beaten
65g (2½oz) ground almonds
a few drops of
　　almond extract
55g (2oz) flaked almonds

To finish
3 tablespoons apricot jam
2 tablespoons
　　ground almonds

You will need twelve 7.5cm (3in) patty tins.

First make the pâte sucrée (sweet pastry). Measure the flour into a bowl. Rub in the butter with your fingertips until the mixture resembles fine breadcrumbs. Stir in the sugar, then add the egg yolks and mix until the ingredients come together to form a dough. Knead the mixture gently until smooth. Wrap the dough in clingfilm and leave to rest in the fridge for about 30 minutes.

Roll out the pastry on a lightly floured work surface and cut out about 12 rounds using a 7.5cm (3in) plain pastry cutter. Re-roll the trimmings once only. Ease the pastry rounds into the patty tins and prick lightly with a fork. Chill while you are making the frangipane.

Preheat the oven to 190°C/Fan 170°C/Gas 5.

To make the frangipane, measure the butter and sugar into a bowl and beat well together until light and fluffy. Gradually beat in the egg, then stir in the ground almonds and almond extract. Divide the frangipane between the chilled tartlet cases and scatter the flaked almonds on top.

Bake in the preheated oven for about 15 minutes, until the frangipane is golden and firm to the touch. Ease the tartlets out of the tin and on to a wire rack to cool.

Sieve the apricot jam into a small pan and warm gently. Brush the tartlets with the apricot jam to glaze and decorate the outside edge with a thin line of ground almonds. Leave the tartlets to cool completely before serving.

Choux pastry must be well cooked until it is really firm and has turned a good straw colour. The profiteroles look wonderful piled up in a pyramid.

PROFITEROLES

MAKES 12 PROFITEROLES

For the choux pastry
55g (2oz) butter
150ml (¼ pint) water
75g (3oz) plain flour, sifted
2 large eggs, beaten,
   plus 1 extra egg, beaten,
   to glaze

For the chocolate sauce
75ml (2½fl oz) double cream
75g (3oz) dark chocolate,
   broken into pieces

For the filling
200ml (⅓ pint) pouring
   double cream

TIP

These can be made and assembled up to 4 hours ahead. Unfilled buns can be made up to a day ahead. Not for freezing.

Preheat the oven to 220°C/Fan 200°C/Gas 7 and line a baking tray with non-stick baking paper.

To make the pastry, place the butter and water in a small pan until the water is boiling and the butter has melted. Remove from the heat and immediately add the flour, all at once. Quickly beat with a wooden spoon until the mixture comes together and makes a smooth, thick dough. Add the beaten egg, a little at a time, beating after each addition, until the egg is incorporated and the dough is thick and smooth.

Spoon 12 domes of pastry on to the prepared baking tray. Brush with the extra beaten egg and bake in the preheated oven for 10 minutes. Reduce the oven temperature to 190°C/170°C fan/Gas 5 and bake for another 20 minutes.

Remove the buns from the oven and turn the oven off. Slice each bun in half and put the buns cut side up back on to the baking tray. Return to the cooling oven for 15–20 minutes to dry out.

Meanwhile, to make the chocolate sauce, pour the cream into a pan and heat until hot. Add the chocolate and stir until melted. Remove from the heat and set aside in a cool place to thicken up.

Once the buns have dried out and are crisp, dip one half into the chocolate sauce and place on a wire rack to set. Repeat with the remaining 11 bun tops.

Pour the cream into a large bowl and whisk until it forms soft peaks. Place a generous dollop of cream on each of the bun bases, then sandwich a chocolate half on top. Repeat to make 12.

These are sheer luxury and well worth making. Serve for tea or as a dessert.

CHOCOLATE ÉCLAIRS

MAKES ABOUT 12 ÉCLAIRS

For the choux pastry
55g (2oz) butter, cubed
150ml (¼ pint) water
65g (2½oz) plain flour, sifted
2 large eggs, beaten

For the filling
300ml (½ pint) pouring
    double cream

For the icing
55g (2oz) dark chocolate,
    broken into pieces
15g (½oz) butter
2 tablespoons water
75g (3oz) icing sugar, sifted

TIP

Do not fill choux pastry
items too long before
serving, as the pastry
tends to go soggy.

Preheat the oven to 220°C/Fan 200°C/Gas 7. Lightly grease two baking trays.

To make the choux pastry, put the butter and water into a small pan and place over a low heat. Allow the butter to melt, then bring slowly to the boil. Remove the pan from the heat, add the flour all at once and beat until the mixture forms a soft ball and leaves the side of the pan. Allow to cool slightly.

Add the eggs to the mixture a little at a time, beating really well between each addition to give a smooth, shiny paste. It is easiest to use a hand-held electric mixer for this.

Spoon the mixture into a large piping bag fitted with a 1cm (½in) plain nozzle. Pipe on to the prepared baking trays into shapes about 13–15cm (5–6in) long, leaving room to spread. Bake in the preheated oven for 10 minutes, then reduce the temperature to 190°C/Fan 170°C/Gas 5 and bake for a further 20 minutes. (It is important that the éclairs are golden brown all over. Any pale, undercooked parts will become soggy once they have cooled.) Remove them from the oven and split down the side to allow the steam to escape. Leave to cool completely on a wire rack.

Whip the cream until it is just firm enough to pipe. Fill the éclairs with whipped cream, using a piping bag fitted with a plain nozzle.

To make the icing, place the chocolate in a bowl set over a pan of hot water, making sure the base of the bowl doesn't touch the water. Add the butter and water to the chocolate and place the pan over a low heat until the chocolate and butter have melted, stirring occasionally. Remove from the heat and add the sifted icing sugar, beating well until smooth.

Spoon the icing over the top of each éclair, then leave to set.

CHAPTER TWELVE

BREADS

These old-fashioned English muffins are traditionally pulled apart through the middle, not cut, and eaten warm with lashings of butter. Any left over will store for 2–3 days in an airtight container and are then best split in half and eaten toasted.

ENGLISH MUFFINS

MAKES ABOUT 14 MUFFINS

675g (1½lb) strong white
    flour, plus extra for dusting
2 teaspoons caster sugar
7g sachet fast-action yeast
1½ level teaspoons salt
450ml (¾ pint) tepid milk
1 level teaspoon fine
    semolina, for dusting

Measure the dry ingredients into a bowl or electric mixer then pour in the milk in a continuous stream while mixing the ingredients, to form a dough. Knead the dough with your hands or with a mixer fitted with a dough hook until smooth and elastic.

—

Turn the dough out on to a lightly floured work surface and roll to a thickness of about 1cm (½in) with a floured rolling pin.

—

Cut the dough into rounds using a 7.5cm (3in) plain cutter and place on a well-floured baking tray. Dust the tops with the semolina, cover loosely and leave in a warm place until doubled in size (approximately 1 hour).

—

Lightly oil a griddle or heavy-based frying pan and place on the hob to heat. Cook the muffins, in 2–3 batches, for about 7 minutes on each side, turning the heat down once the muffins go into the pan. When cooked they should be well risen and brown on both sides.

—

Cool slightly on a wire rack before splitting and buttering to serve.

This is a good, everyday loaf. You can make it in other shapes if you prefer. Individual rolls will take less time to prove and bake.

WHITE COTTAGE LOAF

MAKES 1 STANDARD ROUND LOAF

450g (1lb) strong white flour
7g sachet fast-action yeast
40g (1½oz) butter, melted
1 level teaspoon salt
300ml (½ pint) warm water

To glaze
1 tablespoon milk

Measure all the ingredients into a bowl and mix together by hand or with an electric mixer fitted with a dough hook until combined to a fairly sticky, soft dough. Knead on a floured work surface, adding a little extra flour if needed, for about 4–5 minutes.

—

Transfer to a large oiled bowl, cover tightly with clingfilm (make sure no air can escape) and leave to rise in a warm place for 1–1½ hours, or until the dough has doubled in size.

—

Line a baking tray with non-stick baking paper. Tip the dough out on to a floured work surface and knock back by hand until smooth. Cut off a quarter of the dough and shape into a round ball. Shape the remaining dough into a large ball and place on the prepared tray. Sit the small ball on top of the large ball.

—

Flour the handle of a wooden spoon and push the handle vertically through the centre of the two balls until you hit the baking tray, then remove the handle carefully. Slide the baking tray into a large plastic bag so the dough and baking tray are completely covered. Seal the end of the bag completely. Leave to prove in a warm place for 35–45 minutes, or until doubled in size.

—

Preheat the oven to 220°C/Fan 200°C/Gas 7.

—

Brush the loaf with the milk and bake in the preheated oven for 20–25 minutes, or until golden and the bread sounds hollow when tapped on the base. Leave to cool on a wire rack.

To make a close-textured, more substantial roll you could use all granary flour instead of the mix given here.

QUICK GRANARY ROLLS

MAKES 12 ROLLS

350g (12oz) strong white
    flour, plus extra for dusting
350g (12oz) granary flour
1½ level teaspoons salt
1½ level teaspoons sugar
7g sachet fast-action yeast
40g (1½oz) butter
about 450ml (¾ pint) tepid
    milk and water, mixed

Lightly grease two baking trays.

—

Measure the dry ingredients and the butter into a bowl or electric mixer. If mixing by hand, rub in the butter with your fingertips. If using a mixer, briefly mix in the butter.

—

Add the milk and water mixture in a continuous stream while mixing the ingredients to a dough. Knead thoroughly until smooth and elastic. Alternatively, use a mixer fitted with a dough hook to knead the dough for a further 2 minutes.

—

Turn the dough out on to a floured work surface and divide into 12 even pieces. Shape the pieces into rounds and place on the prepared baking trays, allowing room for expansion. Cover the rolls with oiled clingfilm and leave in a warm place to prove until doubled in size.

—

Preheat the oven to 220°C/Fan 200°C/Gas 7.

—

Uncover the rolls and bake in the preheated oven for 10–15 minutes, or until they have browned on top and sound hollow when the base is tapped. Lift on to a wire rack to cool.

TIP
To glaze the rolls, brush the dough with a little milk and sprinkle with cracked wheat just before baking them.

This loaf is made in a 20cm (8in) sandwich tin and breaks off into
12 individual rolls – perfect for a picnic or special meal.

CROWN LOAF

MAKES 1 CROWN

350g (12oz) strong white
    flour, plus extra for dusting
2 level teaspoons fast-action
    dried yeast
1 level teaspoon salt
20g (¾oz) butter, melted
225ml (8fl oz) warm water
a little milk, to glaze

Lightly grease a 20cm (8in) sandwich tin.

Measure all the ingredients, except the milk, into a bowl and mix together by hand or with an electric mixer fitted with a dough hook until combined to a fairly sticky dough.

Remove from the bowl and tip on to a floured work surface. Knead by hand for about 4–5 minutes, adding a little extra flour if needed.

Transfer to a large oiled bowl, cover tightly with clingfilm (make sure no air can escape) and leave to rise in a warm place for 1–1½ hours, or until the dough has doubled in size.

Tip on to a lightly floured work surface and knock back by hand for about 5 minutes. Divide the dough into 12 evenly sized balls. Arrange the balls in the tin so they are snug and touching. Cover the tin with clingfilm and leave to prove in a warm place for about 30 minutes, or until doubled in size.

Preheat the oven to 220°C/Fan 200°C/Gas 7.

Glaze the loaf with a little milk, then bake in the preheated oven for 20–25 minutes, until lightly golden on top and well risen. Leave to cool in the tin for a few minutes then remove from the tin and leave to cool on a wire rack.

This is good with soup or a cheeseboard and best eaten on the day of making.

CHEESE AND OLIVE CROWN LOAF

MAKES 1 CROWN

250g (9oz) strong
    white flour
1½ teaspoons fast-action
    dried yeast
½ level teaspoon salt
1½ tablespoons olive oil
175ml (6fl oz) slightly
    warm water
55g (2oz) black olives,
    pitted and chopped
55g (2oz) Parmesan,
    finely grated
1 large egg, beaten
30g (1 oz) mature
    Cheddar, grated

Measure the flour, yeast, salt, olive oil and water into a bowl. Mix using a wooden spoon until you have a wettish dough.

Tip the dough on to a lightly floured work surface. Knead by hand for 5–8 minutes until the dough is smooth and shiny. Place in an oiled bowl, cover with clingfilm and leave to rise for about 1½ hours, or until doubled in size.

Lightly grease a 20cm (8in) springform or deep round cake tin.

Knock back the dough by hand for a few minutes, then scatter over the olives and Parmesan and knead again. Divide the dough into 12 balls and arrange them in a circle in the prepared tin, starting from the outside. Cover with clingfilm and leave to prove for 30 minutes, or until doubled in size.

Preheat the oven to 220°C/Fan 200°C/Gas 7.

Brush the tops with beaten egg and sprinkle with the Cheddar. Bake in the preheated oven for 25–30 minutes, or until well risen and golden brown on the top and underneath. Cool on a wire rack.

This recipe makes very good bread, very quickly! It needs mixing, shaping and rising only once before baking, which takes about 1¼ hours altogether. Use walnut oil instead of olive oil, if you wish. This bread makes the best toast ever!

HONEY-GLAZED WALNUT BREAD

MAKES 2 STANDARD ROUND LOAVES

115g (4oz) walnut pieces
350g (12oz) granary flour
350g (12oz) strong white
　flour, plus extra for dusting
7g sachet fast-action yeast
2 level teaspoons salt
1 tablespoon black treacle
500ml (18fl oz) warm milk
　(1 part boiling to 2
　parts cold)
2 tablespoons olive oil
115g (4oz) sunflower seeds

To glaze
1 tablespoon beaten egg
1 tablespoon clear honey

TIPS
You could make 16 rolls with the dough instead. Just remember, they will need less time in the oven.

To freeze the bread, seal in freezer-proof bags, label and freeze for up to 6 months. To defrost, thaw in the plastic bag for 5–6 hours at room temperature. The bread is best served warm, so refresh in a preheated oven at 160°C/Fan 140°C/ Gas 3 for about 15 minutes or until warmed through.

Grease two baking trays. Briefly process the walnuts, or coarsely chop by hand, taking care to keep the pieces quite large. Set aside until ready to use.

Combine the flours, yeast and salt together in a large bowl. Add the treacle, milk and olive oil and mix to form a dough, either with your hands or an electric mixer. Add a little more milk, if necessary, to make the dough slightly sticky.

Turn the dough out on to a lightly floured work surface and knead for about 10 minutes. Alternatively, use a mixer fitted with a dough hook and leave running for about 5 minutes. When ready, the dough should be smooth and elastic and leave the bowl and your hands clean.

Reserve about 2 tablespoons of sunflower seeds, then work the rest of the seeds and the chopped walnuts into the dough. Divide the dough in half, then shape each piece into a smooth round and set in the centre of the prepared baking trays. Enclose each tray inside a large plastic bag, sealing a little air inside so that the plastic is not in contact with the bread. Leave to rise in a warm place for 30–45 minutes, or until doubled in size. If your kitchen is cool this may take as long as 1–1½ hours.

Preheat the oven to 200°C/Fan 180°C/Gas 6.

To glaze the loaves, mix together the egg and honey and brush gently over the surface of the dough. Sprinkle the loaves with the reserved seeds and bake in the preheated oven for about 20–25 minutes, or until the loaves are a good conker brown and sound hollow when tapped on the base. Cool on a wire rack.

This textured loaf is packed with flavour and keeps well.

FARMHOUSE BROWN SEEDED LOAVES

MAKES 2 STANDARD ROUND LOAVES

40g (1½oz) linseed
150g (5oz) porridge oats
300ml (½ pint) boiling water
450g (1lb) strong white
    flour, plus extra for dusting
115g (4oz) strong
    wholemeal flour
55g (2oz) sunflower seeds
1 level teaspoon salt
7g sachet fast-action yeast
about 350ml (12fl oz)
    warm water

To finish
a little milk, to glaze
a few porridge oats,
    to decorate

Measure the linseed and porridge oats into a bowl, pour over the boiling water and mix. This can be done by hand or with an electric mixer. Leave to absorb for about 10 minutes and cool slightly.

Add all the remaining ingredients and mix to form a soft dough. Tip out on to a floured work surface and knead by hand for about 5 minutes, or in a mixer fitted with a dough hook. Put into an oiled bowl, cover with clingfilm and leave to rise in a warm place for about 1–1½ hours.

Knock back by hand for a few minutes, then divide and shape into 2 rounds.

Line a baking tray with non-stick baking paper. Place the rounds on the prepared tray. Slip the tray into a large plastic bag and leave to prove in a warm place for about 30 minutes or until doubled in size.

Preheat the oven to 220°C/Fan 200°C/Gas 7.

Brush the rounds with milk and scatter with oats. Bake in the preheated oven for 20–25 minutes, or until golden brown and the loaves sound hollow when tapped on the bottom. Cool on a wire rack.

TIP
This can be made into one large loaf but it will take a little longer to bake.

This generously fruited savoury loaf with added walnuts is delicious with cheese.

WALNUT AND RAISIN LOAF

MAKES 1 LARGE OR 2 SMALLER LOAVES

225g (8oz) strong white
flour, plus extra for dusting
225g (8oz) strong
wholemeal flour
1 level teaspoon salt
1 level tablespoon light
muscovado sugar
1 level teaspoon ground
cinnamon
40g (1½oz) butter, melted
300ml (½ pint) warm water
7g sachet fast-action yeast
115g (4oz) walnuts,
finely chopped
115g (4oz) raisins

To glaze
1 large egg, beaten

Measure the flours, salt, sugar, cinnamon, butter, water and yeast into a bowl and mix together by hand or with an electric mixer fitted with a dough hook, until combined to a fairly sticky dough.

Knead for about 4–5 minutes on a lightly floured work surface or in the mixer, adding a little extra flour, if needed.

Transfer to a large oiled bowl, cover tightly with clingfilm (make sure no air can escape) and leave to rise in a warm place for 1–1½ hours, or until the dough has doubled in size.

Tip the dough on to a lightly floured work surface and flatten the ball slightly. Add the chopped walnuts and raisins and knead into the dough. Shape into a long thick sausage shape about 40 x 10cm (16 x 4in) or two smaller sausage shapes.

Line a baking tray with non-stick baking paper. Place the dough on the prepared tray and slide into a large plastic bag, so the dough and baking tray are completely covered. Seal the end of the bag. Leave to prove in a warm place for 35–45 minutes, or until doubled in size.

Preheat the oven to 220°C/Fan 200°C/Gas 7.

Brush the dough with beaten egg and bake in the preheated oven for 20–25 minutes (a little less for two smaller loaves), or until golden brown and the bread sounds hollow when tapped on the bottom. Cool on a wire rack.

Perfect with cheese or smoked salmon. Use a selection of different seeds, such as pumpkin, sunflower, flax and chia.

SEEDED NUT LOAF

MAKES 1 LOAF

4 large eggs
3 tablespoons olive oil
115g (4oz) dried cranberries, finely chopped
5g sea salt
115g (4oz) mixed seeds (these are readily available as mixed bags)
150g (5oz) pistachio nuts, chopped
75g (3oz) walnuts, chopped
75g (3oz) skin-on whole almonds, chopped

Preheat the oven to 180°C/160°C Fan/Gas 4. Grease and line the base and sides of a 900g (2lb) loaf tin with non-stick baking paper.

—

Break the eggs into a large bowl and beat with a fork until combined. Add all the remaining ingredients and mix well.

—

Pour into the prepared tin and bake in the preheated oven for 45–50 minutes until golden brown and firm in the centre. Cool on a wire rack.

Sourdough is a delicious crisp loaf and makes wonderful toast, too.
A starter dough is needed and there are various ways to make your bread.
We have used a quick starter dough for home baking.

QUICK SOURDOUGH LOAF

MAKES 1 STANDARD LOAF

For the starter
125g (4½oz) dark rye flour
125g (4½oz) strong
    white flour
1 teaspoon fast-action
    dried yeast
300ml (½ pint) slightly
    warm water

For the loaf
350g (12oz) strong white
    flour, plus extra for dusting
1 teaspoon fast-action
    dried yeast
2 teaspoons salt
150ml (¼ pint) slightly
    warm water

Mix all the starter ingredients together in a large bowl. Cover with clingfilm and leave at room temperature for 24 hours.

The next day, add the loaf ingredients to the starter and mix well to form a dough.

Tip the dough out on to a lightly floured work surface and knead for 10 minutes, adding a little more flour if it is very sticky.

Transfer to a large oiled bowl, cover tightly with clingfilm and leave to rise until doubled in size – this will take about an hour.

Tip the dough out on to a lightly floured work surface and gently shape into a round or oblong, whichever you prefer. Line a large baking tray with non-stick baking paper and dust with flour. Carefully transfer the dough on to the prepared baking tray, cover with a tea towel and leave to rise for another hour, or until doubled in size.

Preheat the oven to 220°C/200°C Fan/Gas 7.

Dust the bread with a little flour and, using a sharp knife, slash a cross in the centre (this will stop the loaf from bursting). Place the tray in the oven with a second lipped baking tray on the shelf below. Drop 4–5 ice cubes into the lipped tray (this will create steam and give the loaf a lovely crust) and bake in the preheated oven for 30–35 minutes, or until the loaf sounds hollow when the underside is tapped. Cool on a wire rack.

Naan breads are rustic fluffy breads baked in the oven. They are easy to shape into different sizes and are good for adding different flavours.

GARLIC AND CORIANDER NAAN BREADS

MAKES 6 NAAN BREADS

300g (10½oz) strong white flour, plus extra for dusting
7g sachet fast-action yeast
30g (1oz) butter, melted
1 teaspoon salt
2 garlic cloves, crushed
225ml (8fl oz) warm milk
1 small bunch of coriander, finely chopped
olive oil, for brushing

Measure the flour, yeast, melted butter and salt into a large bowl. Mix the garlic into the milk, then pour into the dry ingredients and mix well into a dough.

Tip out on to a lightly floured work surface and knead for 10 minutes until smooth.

Place in a large oiled bowl, cover and leave to rise for 1½ hours, or until doubled in size.

Preheat the grill to high and lightly grease a baking tray.

Tip the dough out onto a lightly floured work surface. Add the coriander and knead until smooth. Divide into 6 equal pieces. Using a rolling pin, roll each piece into a tear shape about the size of your hand.

Place three naans on the prepared tray and brush the tops with oil. Grill for 2–4 minutes on each side until cooked and golden brown. Repeat with the remaining three naans.

The quickest of flatbreads, this is like a pizza base with herbs and garlic. The very best garlic bread for sharing!

HERB AND GARLIC FLATBREAD

MAKES 1 LARGE ROUND FLATBREAD

For the flatbread
175g (6oz) self-raising flour, plus extra for dusting
a pinch of salt
1 medium egg
70ml (2½fl oz) milk

For the topping
115g (4oz) butter, softened
1 large garlic clove, crushed
1 tablespoon chopped parsley
1 tablespoon snipped chives
1 teaspoon chopped thyme leaves
a pinch of sea salt

Preheat the oven to 200°C/220°C Fan/Gas 6. Slide a large flat baking tray into the oven to get hot.

—

To make the flatbread, measure the flour into a bowl. Add the salt. Combine the egg and milk in a small jug and beat to mix. Pour into the flour and mix to form a soft dough.

—

Tip out on to a floured work surface and knead gently. Shape into a ball and place on a large piece of non-stick baking paper. Using a rolling pin, roll out the dough to a large round measuring about 30cm (12in) diameter.

—

To make the topping, mix the butter, garlic, parsley, chives, thyme and sea salt together in a bowl. Spread the herb butter over the dough base. Carefully transfer the flatbread, on the baking paper, to the hot baking tray and bake in the preheated oven for about 12 minutes, until golden and crisp underneath.

—

Slice into wedges and serve at once.

CHAPTER THIRTEEN

FRUIT LOAVES

These can be made in advance as they keep very well and can also be frozen. Malt extract is a thick syrup and can be bought in a jar.

SULTANA MALT LOAVES

MAKES 2 LOAVES

225g (8oz) plain flour
½ level teaspoon
    bicarbonate of soda
1 level teaspoon
    baking powder
225g (8oz) sultanas
55g (2oz) demerara sugar
175g (6oz) malt extract
1 tablespoon black treacle
2 large eggs, beaten
150ml (5fl oz) cold black tea

Preheat the oven to 150°C/Fan 130°C/Gas 2. Grease two 450g (1lb) loaf tins then line the base of each tin with non-stick baking paper.

—

Measure the flour, bicarbonate of soda and baking powder into a bowl and stir in the sultanas.

—

Gently heat the sugar, malt extract and black treacle together. Pour on to the dry ingredients, along with the beaten eggs and the tea. Beat well until smooth.

—

Pour into the prepared tins and level the surfaces. Bake in the preheated oven for about 1 hour or until well risen and firm to the touch. Leave to cool in the tins for 10 minutes, then turn out, peel off the baking paper and finish cooling on a wire rack.

—

These loaves are best kept for 2 days before eating.

TIP
Freeze the loaves as soon as they are cold.

This teabread has quite a pale colour even when cooked, because of the thick pale honey used. It is a very good way of using up over-ripe bananas.

BANANA AND HONEY TEABREAD

MAKES 1 LOAF

225g (8oz) self-raising flour
¼ level teaspoon freshly
    grated nutmeg
115g (4oz) butter
225g (8oz) bananas
115g (4oz) caster sugar
finely grated zest of 1 lemon
2 large eggs
6 tablespoons thick
    pale honey

For the topping
2 tablespoons honey
nibbed sugar or crushed
    sugar cubes, for sprinkling

Preheat the oven to 160°C/Fan 140°C/Gas 3. Lightly grease a 900g (2lb) loaf tin then line the base with non-stick baking paper.

——

Measure the flour and nutmeg into a large bowl and rub in the butter using your fingertips until the mixture resembles fine breadcrumbs.

——

Peel and mash the bananas and stir into the flour mixture, along with the sugar, lemon zest, eggs and honey. Beat well until evenly mixed.

——

Turn into the prepared tin and level the surface. Bake in the preheated oven for about 1¼ hours or until a fine skewer inserted into the centre comes out clean. Cover the teabread loosely with foil during the end of the cooking time if it is browning too much. Leave to cool in the tin for a few minutes then turn out, peel off the baking paper and finish cooling on a wire rack.

——

To make the topping, gently warm the honey in a small pan then brush over the top of the cold teabread. Sprinkle with the nibbed sugar.

Like any fruit loaf, this is easy to make. I've found this to be a popular choice at fêtes and charity events, sold in slices or whole.

ICED APRICOT FRUIT LOAF

MAKES 1 LOAF

75g (3oz) red or natural
   glacé cherries, quartered
3 large eggs
175g (6oz) self-raising flour
115g (4oz) butter, softened
115g (4oz) light
   muscovado sugar
115g (4oz) ready-to-eat
   dried apricots, chopped
150g (5oz) sultanas

For the icing
115g (4oz) icing sugar, sifted
1 tablespoon apricot jam
1 tablespoon water
2 ready-to-eat dried
   apricots, chopped

Preheat the oven to 160°C/Fan 140°C/Gas 3. Lightly grease a 900g (2lb) loaf tin then line the base with non-stick baking paper.

—

Place the cherries in a sieve and rinse under running water. Drain well then dry thoroughly on kitchen paper.

—

Break the eggs into a large bowl, then measure in the remaining loaf ingredients including the cherries. Beat well until the mixture is smooth.

—

Turn into the prepared tin and level the surface. Bake in the preheated oven for about 1 hour 10 minutes or until the loaf is golden brown, firm to the touch and shrinking away from the sides of the tin. A fine skewer inserted into the centre of the loaf should come out clean. Leave to cool in the tin for 10 minutes then turn out, peel off the baking paper and finish cooling on a wire rack.

—

To make the icing, measure the icing sugar into a bowl. Heat the apricot jam and water together until the jam melts then pour on to the icing sugar. Mix to a smooth spreading consistency, then spoon over the top of the cold loaf. Decorate the loaf by sprinkling the chopped apricots down the centre.

I've seen loaves similar to these for sale in Wycombe market. They may not look madly exciting, but they are very popular, and delicious.

CRUNCHY ORANGE SYRUP LOAVES

MAKES 2 LOAVES

115g (4oz) butter, softened
175g (6oz) self-raising flour
1 level teaspoon baking
 powder
175g (6oz) caster sugar
2 large eggs
4 tablespoons milk
finely grated zest of 1 orange

For the topping
juice of 1 orange
115g (4oz) granulated sugar

Preheat the oven to 180°C/Fan 160°C/Gas 4. Lightly grease two 450g (1lb) loaf tins then line the base of each tin with non-stick baking paper.

—

Measure all the loaf ingredients into a large bowl and beat well for about 2 minutes.

—

Divide the mixture evenly between the tins and level the surface of each. Bake in the preheated oven for about 30 minutes or until the loaves spring back when the surface is lightly pressed.

—

While the loaves are baking, make the crunchy topping. Measure the orange juice and sugar into a small bowl and stir to mix. Spread the mixture over the baked loaves while they are still hot, then leave to cool completely in the tins. Turn out and remove the baking paper once cold.

This teabread freezes well. It's delicious spread with good butter, and I like coming across the walnuts in the bread – they give an interesting texture.

WALNUT AND CRANBERRY TEABREAD

MAKES 1 LOAF

115g (4oz) caster sugar
175g (6oz) golden syrup
200ml (7fl oz) milk
55g (2oz) sultanas
55g (2oz) dried cranberries
225g (8oz) self-raising flour
1 level teaspoon baking
   powder
55g (2oz) walnuts,
   roughly chopped
1 large egg, beaten

Preheat the oven to 180°C/Fan 160°C/Gas 4. Lightly grease a 900g (2lb) loaf tin then line the base with non-stick baking paper.

—

Measure the sugar, syrup, milk, sultanas and cranberries into a pan and heat gently until the sugar has dissolved. Set aside to cool.

—

Measure the flour and baking powder into a bowl and add the roughly chopped walnuts. Add the cooled syrup mixture to the dry ingredients along with the beaten egg and stir well until the mixture is smooth.

—

Pour into the prepared tin and level the surface. Bake in the preheated oven for 1 hour, until firm to the touch and a skewer inserted into the centre comes out clean. Cover the top of the teabread loosely with foil towards the end of the cooking time if it is becoming too brown. Leave to cool in the tin for 10 minutes then turn out, peel off the baking paper and finish cooling on a wire rack.

—

Serve buttered.

TIP
To break up walnuts, or pulverise biscuits or cornflakes, put them in a strong polythene bag and crush with a rolling pin.

Expect this cake to have a sugary top, which is quite normal. Freeze one of the loaves and store the second one in the fridge. Serve sliced and buttered, or spread with low-fat cream cheese. Use small courgettes as they will not produce as much liquid as the large ones.

COURGETTE LOAVES

MAKES 2 LOAVES

3 large eggs
250ml (9fl oz) sunflower oil
350g (12oz) caster sugar
350g (12oz) small and thin courgettes, grated
165g (5½oz) plain flour
165g (5½oz) buckwheat flour
1 level teaspoon baking powder
2 level teaspoons bicarbonate of soda
1 level tablespoon ground cinnamon
175g (6oz) raisins
150g (5oz) walnuts, chopped

Preheat the oven to 180°C/Fan 160°C/Gas 4. Grease two 900g (2lb) loaf tins then line the base of each tin with non-stick baking paper.

—

Measure all the ingredients into a large bowl and mix well to make a thick batter.

—

Pour into the prepared tins. Bake in the preheated oven for about 1 hour or until the loaves are firm and a skewer inserted into the centre comes out clean. Leave to cool in the tin for 10 minutes then turn out, peel off the baking paper and finish cooling on a wire rack.

—

Store in the fridge and use within 3 weeks.

A wonderful moist teabread to serve buttered. The fruit is soaked in tea overnight. You can make two 450g (1lb) loaves from this recipe instead of one large loaf, but shorten the cooking time to 30–40 minutes.

BORROWDALE TEABREAD

MAKES 1 LOAF

115g (4oz) sultanas
115g (4oz) currants
115g (4oz) raisins
475ml (16fl oz) strong
  black tea
225g (8oz) light
  muscovado sugar
2 large eggs
450g (1lb) wholemeal
  self-raising flour

Put the sultanas, currants and raisins in a bowl along with the tea, cover and leave to soak overnight.

—

Preheat the oven to 180°C/Fan 160°C/Gas 4. Grease a 900g (2lb) loaf tin then line the base with non-stick baking paper.

—

Mix the sugar and eggs together until light and fluffy. Add the flour along with the soaked fruits and any remaining liquid, and mix thoroughly together.

—

Spoon the mixture into the prepared loaf tin and level the surface. Bake in the preheated oven for about 1 hour or until a skewer inserted into the centre comes out clean. Leave to cool in the tin, then turn out and peel off the baking paper.

—

Serve sliced and spread with butter.

Don't overdo the marmalade or the fruit will sink to the bottom of the loaf. Too much marmalade alters the sugar proportion of the recipe, slackening the mixture, which causes the fruit to drop.

MARMALADE LOAF

MAKES 1 LOAF

40g (1½oz) red or natural glacé cherries, quartered
115g (4oz) butter, softened
115g (4oz) caster sugar
115g (4oz) sultanas
115g (4oz) currants
2 large eggs
175g (6oz) self-raising flour
1 rounded tablespoon chunky marmalade

To finish
1 tablespoon chunky marmalade, or a little caster sugar for sprinkling

Preheat the oven to 160°C/Fan 140°C/Gas 3. Grease a 900g (2lb) loaf tin and line the base with non-stick baking paper.

—

Place the cherries in a sieve and rinse under running water. Drain well then dry thoroughly on kitchen paper.

—

Measure all the remaining ingredients into a large bowl, add the cherries and mix well until blended.

—

Turn into the prepared tin and level the top. Bake in the preheated oven for about 1½ hours or until a skewer inserted into the centre of the loaf comes out clean. Leave to cool in the tin for 10 minutes then turn out, peel off the baking paper and finish cooling on a wire rack.

—

To finish, warm the marmalade in a small pan and then spoon over the top of the loaf and leave to set. Or simply sprinkle the top of the loaf with caster sugar before serving.

TIP
Store dried fruits in the freezer, well wrapped, and use within 2 years.

CHAPTER FOURTEEN

BUNS

AND

SCONES

The secret to making good scones is not to handle them too much before baking, and to make the mixture on the sticky side. Either eat the scones fresh or leave them to cool completely then freeze them. Thaw them at room temperature and then refresh in a moderate oven for about 10 minutes.

VERY BEST SCONES

MAKES 20 SCONES

450g (1lb) self-raising flour, plus extra for dusting
2 rounded teaspoons baking powder
75g (3oz) butter, softened
55g (2oz) caster sugar
2 large eggs
about 225ml (8fl oz) milk

TIP

Make Wholemeal Scones by using 450g (1lb) wholemeal self-raising flour instead of white. You may need to add a little more liquid to make the dough.

You could make 8–10 large scones using a 9cm/3½in cutter.

Preheat the oven to 220°C/Fan 200°C/Gas 7. Lightly grease two baking trays.

—

Measure the flour and baking powder into a large bowl. Add the butter and rub it in with your fingertips until the mixture resembles fine breadcrumbs. Stir in the sugar.

—

Beat the eggs together and make up to a generous 300ml (½ pint) with the milk. Place about 2 tablespoons of the mixture aside in a cup for glazing the scones later. Gradually add the egg mixture to the dry ingredients, stirring until you have a soft dough. The scone mixture should be on the wet side, sticking to your fingers, as the scones will rise better.

—

Turn the dough on to a lightly floured surface and flatten it out with your hand or a rolling pin to a thickness of 1–2cm (½–¾in). Use a 5cm (2in) fluted cutter to stamp out the scones by pushing the cutter straight down into the dough (as opposed to twisting it), then lifting it straight out. This will ensure that the scones rise evenly and keep their shape. Gently push the remaining dough together, knead lightly then re-roll and cut more scones.

—

Arrange the scones on the prepared baking trays and brush the tops with the reserved beaten egg mixture to glaze. Bake in the preheated oven for about 10–15 minutes, until well risen and golden. Transfer to a wire rack and leave to cool, covered with a clean tea towel to keep them moist.

—

Serve cut in half and spread generously with strawberry jam. Top with a good spoonful of clotted or whipped cream, if you like.

Making good scones is so easy if the mixture is not too dry and the dough is not overhandled. Wrap them in a clean tea towel after baking to keep them moist.

SPECIAL FRUIT SCONES

MAKES 14 SCONES

225g (8oz) self-raising flour, plus extra for dusting
1 level teaspoon baking powder
55g (2oz) butter, softened
30g (1oz) caster sugar
20g (¾oz) sultanas
20g (¾oz) ready-to-eat dried apricots, snipped into pieces
15g (½oz) dried cranberries, roughly chopped
1 large egg
a little milk

Preheat the oven to 220°C/Fan 200°C/Gas 7. Lightly grease two baking trays.

Measure the flour and baking powder into a large bowl, add the butter and rub in with your fingertips until the mixture resembles fine breadcrumbs. Stir in the sugar and the dried fruit.

Break the egg into a measuring jug, then make up to 150ml (¼ pint) with milk. Stir the egg and milk into the flour and mix to a soft but not sticky dough.

Turn out on to a lightly floured work surface, knead lightly and roll out to a 1cm (½in) thickness. Cut into rounds with a fluted 5cm (2in) cutter and place them on the prepared baking trays. Brush the tops with a little milk.

Bake in the preheated oven for about 10 minutes or until pale golden brown. Lift the scones on to a wire rack to cool.

Eat as fresh as possible.

Serve these warm with cold meats, soup or a cheese board – and with butter, of course!

CHEESE SCONE ROUND

SERVES 6

225g (8oz) self-raising flour, plus extra for dusting
½ level teaspoon salt
½ level teaspoon mustard powder
¼ level teaspoon cayenne pepper
1 level teaspoon baking powder
30g (1oz) butter, softened
150g (5oz) mature Cheddar, grated
1 large egg
a little milk

Preheat the oven to 220°C/Fan 200°C/Gas 7. Lightly grease a baking tray.

—

Measure the flour, salt, mustard powder, cayenne pepper and baking powder into a large bowl. Add the butter and rub in with your fingertips until the mixture resembles fine breadcrumbs. Stir in 115g (4oz) of the grated cheese.

—

Break the egg into a measuring jug then make up to 150ml (¼ pint) with milk. Stir the egg and milk into the dry ingredients and mix to a soft but not sticky dough.

—

Turn out on to a lightly floured work surface and knead lightly. Roll out to a 15cm (6in) circle and place on the prepared baking tray.

—

Mark into 6 wedges, then brush with a little milk. Sprinkle with the remaining grated cheese and bake in the preheated oven for about 15 minutes, or until golden brown and firm to the touch. Slide on to a wire rack to cool.

—

Eat as fresh as possible.

Making one large scone is fastest of all, as you don't have to roll and cut out the mixture. If you don't have a traybake or roasting tin, shape the dough into an oblong on a baking tray.

GRUYÈRE AND OLIVE SCONE BAKE

MAKES 12 SQUARES

450g (1lb) self-raising flour,
  plus extra for dusting
2 level teaspoons
  baking powder
1 level teaspoon salt
115g (4oz) butter, softened
225g (8oz) mature
  Gruyère, coarsely grated
115g (4oz) pitted black
  olives, roughly chopped
2 large eggs
a little milk

Preheat the oven to 230°C/Fan 210°C/Gas 8. Lightly grease a 30 x 23cm (12 x 9in) traybake or roasting tin.

—

Measure the flour, baking powder and salt into a large bowl. Add the butter and rub in with your fingertips until the mixture resembles fine breadcrumbs. Stir in 200g (7oz) of the grated Gruyère and the roughly chopped olives.

—

Break the eggs into a measuring jug and make up to 300ml (½ pint) with milk. Add to the flour mixture, mixing to form a soft dough.

—

Knead the dough quickly and lightly until smooth, then roll out on a lightly floured work surface to an oblong to fit the tin. Transfer to the prepared tin and mark into 12 squares, then brush the top with a little milk.

—

Bake in the preheated oven for about 15 minutes. Sprinkle the top with the remaining Gruyère and bake for a further 5 minutes or until the scone is well risen and golden. Turn out on to a wire rack to cool.

These scones are particularly moist, excellent if you want to keep them a day or two. They can be made sweet or savoury: for savoury potato scones, omit the sugar and add ½ teaspoon of salt to the flour.

POTATO SCONES

MAKES 6 SCONES

175g (6oz) self-raising flour,
    plus extra for dusting
2 level teaspoons
    baking powder
55g (2oz) butter, softened
40g (1½oz) caster sugar
115g (4oz) fresh
    mashed potato
1 egg, beaten

Preheat the oven to 220°C/Fan 200°C/Gas 7. Lightly grease two baking trays.

—

Measure the flour and baking powder into a large bowl, add the butter and rub in with your fingertips until the mixture resembles fine breadcrumbs.

—

Stir in the sugar and mashed potato, mixing with a fork to prevent the potato from forming lumps. Add enough egg to form a soft but not sticky dough.

—

Turn the mixture out on to a lightly floured work surface and knead very lightly. Roll out to a thickness of about 2cm (¾in) and cut into rounds using a 7cm (2¾in) fluted cutter (use a plain cutter for savoury scones).

—

Transfer to the prepared baking tray and bake in the preheated oven for 12–15 minutes, or until well risen and golden brown.

—

Serve warm and buttered.

These are also known as Scotch pancakes. In the old days, they were made on a solid metal griddle over an open fire. Now it is more practical to use a large, non-stick frying pan.

DROP SCONES

MAKES ABOUT 24 DROP SCONES

175g (6oz) self-raising flour
1 level teaspoon
    baking powder
40g (1½oz) caster sugar
1 large egg
about 200ml (7fl oz) milk

Prepare a griddle or heavy-based frying pan (preferably non-stick) by heating and greasing with oil or white vegetable fat.

—

Measure the flour, baking powder and sugar into a large bowl. Make a well in the centre and add the egg and 100ml (3½fl oz) milk. Beat to a smooth, thick batter, then beat in enough of the remaining milk to make the batter the consistency of thick cream.

—

Drop the mixture in tablespoonfuls on to the hot griddle or pan, spacing them well apart. When bubbles rise to the surface, turn the scones over with a palette knife and cook on the other side for a further 30 seconds–1 minute, until golden brown. Lift off on to a wire rack and cover them with a clean tea towel to keep them soft.

—

Cook the remaining mixture in the same way.

—

Serve warm with butter and golden syrup.

Serve as soon as they are made, with butter and syrup. If you do make them in advance and need to reheat them, arrange them in a single layer on an ovenproof plate, cover tightly with foil and reheat in a moderate oven for about 10 minutes.

ORANGE DROP SCONES

MAKES ABOUT 24 DROP SCONES

2 oranges
a little milk
175g (6oz) self-raising flour
1 level teaspoon
 baking powder
40g (1½oz) caster sugar
1 large egg

Finely grate the zest from the oranges and set aside, and then squeeze the juice. Pour the juice into a measuring jug and make it up to 200ml (7fl oz) with milk.

Measure the flour, baking powder, sugar and orange zest into a mixing bowl. Make a well in the centre and add the egg and half the orange juice and milk mixture. Beat well to make a smooth, thick batter, then beat in enough of the remaining orange juice and milk to give a batter the consistency of thick cream.

Heat a large, non-stick frying pan over a medium heat and grease with a little oil or white vegetable fat.

Drop the mixture in dessert spoonfuls on to the hot pan, spacing them well apart to allow the mixture to spread. When bubbles appear on the surface, turn the drop scones over with a palette knife and cook on the other side for 30 seconds–1 minute, until golden brown. Transfer to a wire rack and cover with a clean tea towel.

Cook the remaining mixture in the same way.

Serve warm with butter and golden or maple syrup, and a little extra grated orange zest, if liked.

This Northumberland griddle cake 'sings' or sizzles as it cooks on the griddle, hence its name. 'Hinny' is northern slang for honey, a term of endearment applied especially to children and young women. Traditionally the Singin' Hinny is made in one large round, but you can make two or three smaller ones in the same way.

SINGIN' HINNY

SERVES 4-6

350g (12oz) plain flour,
   plus extra for dusting
½ level teaspoon
   bicarbonate of soda
1 level teaspoon cream
   of tartar
75g (3oz) lard or white
   vegetable fat (not butter)
115g (4oz) currants
about 200ml (7fl oz) milk
butter, to serve

Prepare a griddle or large heavy-based frying pan (preferably non-stick) by heating and lightly greasing it with oil or white vegetable fat.

—

Measure the flour, bicarbonate of soda and cream of tartar into a large bowl, add the lard or white vegetable fat and rub in with your fingertips until the mixture resembles fine breadcrumbs. Stir in the currants.

—

Gradually add the milk, mixing to form a soft but not sticky dough. Turn out on to a lightly floured work surface. Knead lightly then roll out to a large round about 5mm (¼in) thick.

—

Lift the scone round on to the prepared hot griddle and cook on a gentle heat for about 5 minutes on one side, then carefully turn over and cook on the other side for a further 5 minutes or until both sides are a good brown.

—

Slide the Singin' Hinny on to a wire rack to cool slightly.

—

Split in half and butter, then sandwich back together and serve hot.

Make these with white or wholemeal flour and eat them really fresh spread with butter. If you use wholemeal flour, the mixture will need a little more milk. It is traditional to use bicarbonate of soda and cream of tartar, but you can use self-raising flour and two teaspoons of baking powder instead.

GRIDDLE SCONES

MAKES 12 SCONES

225g (8oz) plain flour,
  plus extra for dusting
1 level teaspoon bicarbonate
  of soda
2 level teaspoons cream
  of tartar
30g (1oz) butter
30g (1oz) caster sugar
about 150ml (¼ pint) milk

Prepare a griddle or heavy-based frying pan (preferably non-stick) by heating and lightly greasing with oil or white vegetable fat.

Measure the flour, bicarbonate of soda and cream of tartar into a large bowl. Add the butter and rub in with your fingertips until the mixture resembles fine breadcrumbs. Stir in the sugar.

Gradually add the milk, mixing with a round-bladed knife to a soft but not sticky dough.

Divide the dough in half and knead each piece very lightly on a lightly floured work surface. Roll out each piece into a round about 1cm (½in) thick, then cut each round into 6 equal wedges. Cook the wedges in batches on the prepared hot griddle for about 5 minutes on each side until evenly brown. Lift on to a wire rack to cool.

Eat as fresh as possible.

The spa town of Bath is famous for its buns, distinguished by the coarse sugar topping. They are said to have been created in the eighteenth century.

BATH BUNS

MAKES 12 BUNS

450g (1lb) strong white
   flour, plus extra for dusting
7g sachet fast-action yeast
1 level teaspoon salt
55g (2oz) caster sugar
55g (2oz) butter, melted
   and cooled
2 large eggs, beaten
150ml (¼ pint) tepid milk
175g (6oz) sultanas
55g (2oz) candied peel,
   chopped

To finish
1 large egg, beaten, to glaze
nibbed sugar or coarsely
   crushed sugar cubes

Measure the flour, yeast, salt and caster sugar into a large bowl and mix well.

Make a well in the centre and pour in the melted and cooled butter, the eggs and milk. Add the sultanas and chopped peel and mix to a smooth, soft dough.

Turn the dough out on to a lightly floured work surface and knead for about 5 minutes or until smooth and elastic. Place in an oiled bowl and cover with oiled clingfilm, or put the bowl inside a large polythene bag. Leave to rise until doubled in size, about 1 hour in a warm room.

Lightly grease two baking trays.

Turn the risen dough out of the bowl and knead well until the dough is again smooth and elastic. Divide into 12 equal pieces. Shape each piece of dough into a bun and place on the prepared baking trays. Cover again with oiled clingfilm and leave in a warm place until doubled in size, about 30 minutes.

Preheat the oven to 200°C/Fan 180°C/Gas 6.

Brush the buns with beaten egg and sprinkle with nibbed sugar. Bake in the preheated oven for about 15 minutes, or until golden brown and they sound hollow when the base is tapped. Lift on to a wire rack to cool.

Serve buttered.

For sweet cakes it is traditional to use a fluted cutter, but you may find a plain cutter easier for these as it will cut through the fruit in the dough more easily.

WELSH CAKES

MAKES 10 CAKES

350g (12oz) self-raising
    flour, plus extra for dusting
2 level teaspoons
    baking powder
175g (6oz) butter
115g (4oz) caster sugar
115g (4oz) currants
¾ level teaspoon
    ground mixed spice
1 large egg
about 2 tablespoons milk

To finish
caster sugar, for sprinkling

Prepare a griddle or heavy-based frying pan by heating and lightly greasing with oil.

Measure the flour and baking powder into a large bowl and rub in the butter with your fingertips until the mixture resembles fine breadcrumbs. Add the sugar, currants and spice.

Beat the egg with the milk, then pour into the flour mixture. Mix to form a firm dough, adding a little more milk if necessary.

Roll out the dough on a lightly floured work surface to a thickness of 5mm (¼in), then cut into rounds with a 7.5cm (3in) plain round cutter.

Cook the Welsh Cakes on the hot griddle over a low heat for about 3 minutes on each side, or until golden brown (be careful not to cook them too fast, otherwise the centres will not be fully cooked).

Cool on a wire rack then sprinkle with caster sugar.

Eat on the day of making, spread with butter, if liked.

These are very traditional English cakes, probably the first things most of us made at school. They're inexpensive, can be large or tiny, and need no special equipment. They are best eaten on the day of making.

ROCK CAKES

MAKES 12 CAKES

225g (8oz) self-raising flour
2 level teaspoons
    baking powder
115g (4oz) butter, softened
55g (2oz) caster sugar
55g (2oz) currants
75g (3oz) sultanas
52g (2oz) apricots, chopped
1 large egg
3 tablespoons milk
a little demerara sugar,
    for sprinkling

Preheat the oven to 200°C/Fan 180°C/Gas 6. Lightly grease two baking trays.

—

Measure the flour and baking powder into a large bowl. Add the butter and rub in with your fingertips until the mixture resembles fine breadcrumbs. Stir in the sugar and dried fruit.

—

Beat the egg and milk together and add to the fruity mixture. If the mixture is too dry, add a little more milk.

—

Using 2 teaspoons, shape the mixture into about 12 rough mounds on the prepared baking trays. Sprinkle generously with demerara sugar. Bake in the preheated oven for about 15 minutes, or until a pale golden brown at the edges. Cool on a wire rack.

TIP
Use wholemeal self-raising flour, if you like, although you may need a little more milk to mix.

These 'upside-down' buns should be eaten very fresh, on the day of making. You need 12 mini brioche tins to give the buns their pretty shape, but you can make them plain using a 12-hole bun tin, if you like.

COBURG BUNS

MAKES 12 BUNS

about 55g (2oz) flaked
  almonds
150g (5oz) self-raising flour
1 level teaspoon
  baking powder
½ level teaspoon
  ground mixed spice
½ level teaspoon
  ground ginger
½ level teaspoon
  ground cinnamon
55g (2oz) butter, softened
55g (2oz) caster sugar
1 large egg
1 tablespoon golden syrup
4 tablespoons milk

Preheat the oven to 180°C/Fan 160°C/Gas 4. Lightly grease 12 mini brioche tins or use a 12-hole bun tin.

—

Place a few almond flakes in the base of each tin.

—

Measure all the ingredients into a large bowl and beat for about 2 minutes until the mixture is well blended and smooth.

—

Divide the mixture between the tins and bake in the preheated oven for about 15 minutes, until well risen, golden and firm to the touch. Leave to cool for a few minutes then turn out so that the almond flakes are on top, and finish cooling on a wire rack.

This used to be baked as one large bun, but now it is usual to have individual buns. For a more definite cross on the top of the buns, make up 55g (2oz) of shortcrust pastry (using 55g/2oz plain flour and 30g/1oz butter and a little water), cut it into thin strips and lay it over the top of the buns before baking.

HOT CROSS BUNS

MAKES 12 BUNS

450g (1lb) strong white flour, plus extra for dusting
1 level teaspoon salt
1 level teaspoon ground mixed spice
1 level teaspoon ground cinnamon
½ level teaspoon freshly grated nutmeg
7g sachet fast-action yeast
55g (2oz) caster sugar
55g (2oz) butter, melted and cooled
150ml (¼ pint) tepid milk
5 tablespoons tepid water
1 large egg, beaten
75g (3oz) currants
55g (2oz) candied peel, chopped

To finish
55g (2oz) plain flour
2 tablespoons granulated sugar

Lightly grease two baking trays.

Measure the flour, salt, spices, yeast and caster sugar into a large bowl and stir to mix.

Make a well in the centre and pour in the melted and cooled butter, the milk, water and egg. Add the currants and chopped peel and mix to a soft dough.

Turn out on to a lightly floured work surface and knead for about 10 minutes until smooth and elastic. Transfer to an oiled bowl, cover with oiled clingfilm and leave to rise until the dough has doubled in size, about 1½ hours in a warm room. (Because this is an enriched dough, it will take longer to rise than a plain dough.)

Turn the risen dough out on to a lightly floured work surface again and knead for 2–3 minutes. Divide the dough into 12 equal pieces and shape each one into a round bun. Place on to the prepared baking trays and cover with oiled clingfilm. Leave to rise again in a warm place until doubled in size, about 30 minutes.

Preheat the oven to 220°C/Fan 200°C/Gas 7.

Mix the plain flour with 4 tablespoons of water to make a paste and pipe or drizzle over the buns to make the crosses. Bake in the preheated oven for about 15 minutes, until brown and hollow-sounding when the base is tapped.

While the buns are baking, dissolve the granulated sugar in 2 tablespoons of water over a gentle heat. As soon as the buns come out of the oven, brush them with the syrup to give a sticky glaze.

CHAPTER FIFTEEN

HOT PUDDINGS AND PIES

One of my favourite desserts. I always decorate my sweet pies with lots of pastry leaves, so that they look more inviting.

CLASSIC APPLE PIE
SERVES 6

675g (1½lb) cooking apples,
    peeled, cored and cut
    into thick slices
75g (3oz) caster sugar
4 whole cloves
3 tablespoons cold water

For the pastry
175g (6oz) plain flour,
    plus extra for dusting
55g (2oz) butter, cubed
55g (2oz) white baking
    vegetable fat, cubed
milk, to glaze
granulated sugar,
    for sprinkling

TIP
You can freeze the pie after cooking and when completely cool. Leave to defrost almost completely before reheating and serving. Uncooked homemade pastry is an excellent standby for the freezer. Pack it in separate quantities of 225g (8oz) and 450g (1lb), labelling it clearly. Defrost in the fridge or kitchen until pliable enough to roll and use.

Use an 900ml (1½ pint) shallow pie dish.

Arrange half the apple slices in the bottom of the dish. Sprinkle with the caster sugar and arrange the cloves evenly among the apples. Cover with the remaining apple slices and add the cold water.

To make the pastry, measure the flour, butter and white vegetable fat into a food processor. Whiz until breadcrumb stage. Add about 2 tablespoons cold water and whiz again until it comes together to form a stiff dough. Tip out onto a floured work surface and gently knead into a ball.

Roll out the dough on a lightly floured work surface to a size that will cover the top of the pie dish. Lift the dough on to the dish and trim the edges. If you like, cut the trimmings into decorative shapes and lightly press on to the dough. Chill in the fridge for 30 minutes.

Preheat the oven to 200°C/Fan 180°C/Gas 6.

Brush the pie with a little milk, then sprinkle the top with granulated sugar. Make a small slit in the centre of the pie for the steam to escape. Bake in the preheated oven for about 40–45 minutes, until the apples are tender and the pastry is crisp and pale golden. Cover the pie loosely with foil towards the end of the cooking time if the pastry starts to brown before the apples are cooked.

Serve warm with cream or custard.

A great family favourite as a pudding to follow a weekend lunch. You can use semi-skimmed milk for a healthier pudding, or slices of brioche instead of sliced white bread to make it even richer! Use a rectangular dish as the bread will fit better.

MY MOTHER'S BREAD
SERVES 6-8 AND BUTTER PUDDING

115g (4oz) butter, melted
250g (9oz) currants
    and sultanas
75g (3oz) caster sugar
finely grated zest of 1 lemon
½ level teaspoon ground
    mixed spice
about 8–12 thin slices white
    bread, crusts removed
    and each cut into 3 strips
3 large eggs
300ml (½ pint) milk
150ml (¼ pint) double cream
2 tablespoons demerara
    sugar, for sprinkling

Grease an 18 x 23cm (7 x 9in) deep ovenproof dish with a little of the melted butter. Measure the dried fruit, caster sugar, lemon zest and spice into a bowl and toss to mix well.

Take enough bread strips to cover the base of the dish and dip one side of each strip in melted butter. Lay them in the prepared dish, buttered side down. Sprinkle with half the dried fruit mixture. Repeat the bread layer, placing the bread buttered side up, and sprinkle with the remaining dried fruit mixture. Place a third and final layer of bread strips on top, buttered side up.

Beat together the eggs, milk and cream until combined. Pour over the pudding. Sprinkle with demerara sugar, then leave to stand for about 1 hour if time allows.

Preheat the oven to 180°C/Fan 160°C/Gas 4.

Bake in the preheated oven for about 40 minutes, or until the top is golden brown and crisp and the pudding is slightly puffed up.

Serve hot with cream, though there are some who insist that it is just as delicious cold!

TIP
You can prepare the pudding ahead of time and keep it covered in the fridge for up to 6 hours before baking. Don't sprinkle over the demerara sugar topping until 1 hour before you are ready to bake.

Something like the old-fashioned Eve's pudding, but this one makes its own creamy lemon sauce. If buying lemon curd, check that it contains butter, sugar and lemons. It may be labelled lemon cheese or luxury lemon curd.

BAKED APPLE LEMON SPONGE

SERVES 6-8

For the base
300ml (½ pint) single cream
6 tablespoons lemon curd
2 level tablespoons
    caster sugar
1 heaped teaspoon
    plain flour
750g (1¾lb) cooking apples,
    peeled, cored and very
    thinly sliced

For the topping
2 large eggs
175g (6oz) self-raising flour
115g (4oz) caster sugar
115g (4oz) butter, softened
1 level teaspoon baking
    powder
2 tablespoons milk
1-1½ tablespoons
    demerara sugar

Preheat the oven to 160°C/Fan 140°C/Gas 3. Place a heavy baking tray to heat in the oven. You will need a 27 x 18cm (10½ x 7in) deep ovenproof dish.

To prepare the base, measure the cream, lemon curd, sugar and flour into a bowl and beat until smooth. Mix the sliced apples into the cream mixture, then spoon into the baking dish and level with the back of a spoon.

To make the topping, measure all the ingredients except the demerara sugar into a mixing bowl. Beat until smooth, then spread gently over the fruit in the baking dish.

Sprinkle with demerara sugar. Bake in the preheated oven on the hot baking tray for about 30 minutes, or until perfect golden brown.

Cover the pudding with foil then continue to bake for a further 45 minutes or until the sponge springs back when lightly pressed in the centre with a fingertip.

Serve warm with cream or crème fraîche.

TIPS

The unbaked pudding can be kept covered in the fridge for up to 6 hours. Bring up to room temperature before baking in the oven on the hot baking tray.

I find it easiest to use a mandolin cutter for the apples, or the thin slicing disc in the food processor.

A great family favourite for a cold winter's day.

TREACLE SPONGES

MAKES 4 INDIVIDUAL SPONGES

8 tablespoons golden syrup,
    plus extra to serve
1 tablespoon fresh
    lemon juice
finely grated zest of 1 lemon
115g (4oz) butter, softened
115g (4oz) caster sugar
2 large eggs
115g (4oz) self-raising flour
1 level teaspoon
    baking powder

Grease four 175ml (6fl oz) pudding basins and line the base of each one with a square of non-stick baking paper.

Mix the syrup with the lemon juice and divide between the basins.

Measure all the remaining ingredients into a mixing bowl and beat well for 2 minutes or until well blended.

Divide the mixture between the basins and smooth the tops. Cover each basin with a pleated lid of non-stick baking paper and then foil, to allow for the steam and expanding pudding.

Steam in a steamer, or place in a large pan with enough boiling water to come halfway up each basin, for about 45 minutes (see Tip).

Turn out and serve with extra, warm golden syrup.

TIP

Keep the water boiling in the pan, topping up when needed with more boiling water. Stand the pudding basins on an old, upturned saucer to keep them off the pan bottom.

This is a very adaptable recipe and one of my family's favourites. You can use a variety of different fruits, either fresh or canned. It's a good dessert to serve for Sunday lunch. Just place the pudding on the top oven shelf, above the roast, and let it cook there. It couldn't be easier.

STICKY APRICOT PUDDING

SERVES 6-8

175g (6oz) self-raising flour
1 level teaspoon baking
    powder
55g (2oz) caster sugar
55g (2oz) butter, softened
1 large egg
finely grated zest of 1 lemon
150ml (¼ pint) milk
1 × 410g can apricot halves
    (or other canned fruit),
    drained

For the topping
55g (2oz) butter, melted
55g (2oz) demerara sugar

Preheat the oven to 180°C/Fan 160°C/Gas 8. Grease a 28cm (11in) shallow ovenproof baking dish.

Measure the flour, baking powder, sugar, butter, egg, lemon zest and milk in a large bowl. Beat together until the mixture forms a soft, cake batter consistency.

Spread the mixture into the prepared baking dish and arrange the apricots, cut side down, over the top.

Brush or drizzle the melted butter for the topping over the apricots, then sprinkle with the demerara sugar.

Bake in the preheated oven for about 35 minutes, or until the top has caramelised to a deep golden brown.

Serve warm, with crème fraîche, whipped cream, ice cream or even hot custard on a cold winter day.

TIP
You can replace the apricots with whatever fruit you have to hand. Both sliced dessert and cooking apples work well. Arrange the apple slices evenly over the top of the sponge mixture. Other good alternatives are rhubarb and plums. Cut the plums in half and remove the stones, then arrange them cut side down.

*This baked creamy 'custard' tastes like sheer luxury but is not difficult to make.
Choose a shallow dish or individual dishes that will withstand being put under
the grill, and be careful not to overcook the mixture, or it will form bubbles.
Use the surplus egg whites to make a meringue dessert (see pages 362–8).*

CRÈME BRÛLÉE

SERVES 6–8

4 large egg yolks
30g (1oz) caster sugar
a few drops of vanilla extract
300ml (½ pint) single cream
300ml (½ pint) double cream
about 55g (2oz)
    demerara sugar

TIP

You could replace the
caster sugar and vanilla
extract with vanilla sugar.
Simply store two or three
vanilla pods in a jar of
caster sugar. After about
two weeks, the sugar is
imbued with the pungency
of the vanilla.

Preheat the oven to 160°C/Fan 140°C/Gas 3. Grease a
900ml (1½ pint) shallow ovenproof dish or 6–8 small ramekins.

—

Beat the egg yolks with the caster sugar and vanilla extract.

—

Heat the creams to scalding (just too hot to put your finger in!),
leave to cool slightly, then pour into the egg yolks in a steady
stream, beating all the time.

—

Pour into the dish or ramekins. Stand the dish or ramekins in
a roasting tin half-filled with hot water. Bake in the preheated
oven for 45 minutes (for the single dish) or about 25–30 minutes
(for the ramekins), or until set.

—

Remove from the oven and leave to cool. Cover then chill in
the fridge overnight. These can be made 2 days ahead.

—

Preheat the grill to hot.

—

Sprinkle the top of the custard with the demerara sugar to
about a 5mm (¼in) thickness and place under the grill, on a high
shelf, until the sugar melts then caramelises to a golden brown.
This takes 3–4 minutes. Keep a careful watch to make sure the
sugar does not burn. Alternatively, use a cook's blowtorch to
caramelise the sugar.

—

Leave to cool, then chill for 2–3 hours before serving. Chilling
again after caramelising the sugar gives time for the hard topping
to become slightly less hard, easier to crack and serve. If you
leave it considerably longer, the caramel will melt and soften,
which is not nearly so attractive and does not taste as good.

The combination of toffee, bananas and cream makes this one of the most popular desserts around. Make sure you use a non-stick pan for the toffee and watch it very closely as you are making it, as it can burn easily.

BANOFFEE PIE
SERVES 6

For the base
175g (6oz) digestive biscuits
65g (2½oz) butter

For the toffee filling
115g (4oz) butter
115g (4oz) light
    muscovado sugar
2 x 397g cans full-fat
    condensed milk

For the topping
3 bananas, sliced
a little fresh lemon juice
300ml (½ pint) double
    cream
a little grated Belgian
    milk or dark chocolate,
    for sprinkling

You will need a 23cm (9in) deep loose-bottomed fluted flan tin.

To make the base, put the biscuits into a polythene bag and crush them to crumbs with a rolling pin. Melt the butter in a small pan, remove from the heat and stir in the crushed biscuits. Mix well.

Spread the mixture over the base and sides of the flan tin. Press the mixture with the back of a metal spoon.

To make the toffee filling, measure the butter and sugar into a large non-stick pan. Heat gently until the butter has melted and the sugar has dissolved. Add the condensed milk and stir continuously and evenly with a flat-ended wooden spoon for about 5 minutes, or until the mixture is thick and has turned a golden toffee colour – take care, as it burns easily. Turn it into the prepared crumb crust and leave to cool and set.

To make the topping, toss the bananas in lemon juice and arrange the slices over the toffee in a neat layer. Lightly whip the double cream until it forms soft peaks and spread evenly over the bananas. Sprinkle the whole pie with grated chocolate.

Remove the ring and transfer to a flat plate.

Serve well chilled.

TIP
Most condensed milk cans now have ring pulls, so the old method of simmering the can in a pan of water for 4 hours to caramelise the condensed milk is not advised.

This is an all-American creation that is delicious served with coffee, or as a dessert served with cream or ice cream.

PECAN PIE

SERVES 6

For the rich
   shortcrust pastry
175g (6oz) plain flour,
   plus extra for dusting
15g (½oz) icing sugar
75g (3oz) butter, cubed
1 large egg yolk
about 1 tablespoon
   cold water

For the filling
30g (1oz) butter, softened
175g (6oz) light
   muscovado sugar
3 large eggs
200ml (7fl oz) maple syrup
1 teaspoon vanilla extract
150g (5oz) pecan halves

You will need a 23cm (9in) loose-bottomed fluted flan tin.

To make the pastry, measure the flour, icing sugar and butter into a food processor and whiz until the mixture resembles fine breadcrumbs. Add the egg yolk and water and whiz again until it comes together to form a firm dough. Wrap in clingfilm and leave to rest in the fridge for about 30 minutes.

Preheat the oven to 200°C/Fan 180°C/Gas 6.

Roll out the dough on a lightly floured work surface and use to line the flan tin. Prick the pastry all over with a fork, line with non-stick baking paper or foil and fill with baking beans. Bake blind in the preheated oven for about 15 minutes.

Remove the baking beans and paper and return the pastry case to the oven for 5 minutes or until it is pale golden and dried out.

Remove from the oven and reduce the temperature to 180°C/Fan 160°C/Gas 4.

To make the filling, beat the butter with the sugar. Add the eggs, maple syrup and vanilla extract and beat well.

Place the flan tin on a baking tray and layer the pecan halves flat-side-down over the pastry base. Pour in the filling. Bake in the oven at the reduced temperature for about 30–35 minutes until set. The filling will rise up in the oven but will fall back on cooling. Leave to cool slightly.

Serve warm with cream or ice cream.

CHAPTER SIXTEEN

SOUFFLÉS

AND

MERINGUES

Meringues are easily broken, so store them in a rigid airtight tin or plastic container, with kitchen paper in between them. If you use golden caster sugar, expect darker meringues but they will taste just as good!

BASIC WHITE MERINGUES

MAKES 18 MERINGUES

3 large egg whites
175g (6oz) caster sugar

For the filling
300ml (½ pint) pouring
    double cream, whipped
icing sugar, for dusting
    (optional)

Preheat the oven to 120°C/Fan 100°C/Gas ½. Line two baking trays with non-stick baking paper.

Place the egg whites in a large bowl and whisk until stiff but not dry. Add the sugar, a teaspoonful at a time, whisking well after each addition, until all the sugar has been added. The meringue should be stiff and glossy.

Fit a 1cm (½in) plain nozzle into a large nylon piping bag and stand, nozzle down, in a large measuring jug. Spoon the meringue into the bag. Squeeze the meringue mixture towards the nozzle and twist the top of the piping bag to seal. Pipe the meringue into 18 'shells' 5cm (2in) in diameter on the prepared baking trays. Alternatively, use 2 dessertspoons to shape the mixture into 18 mini meringues.

Bake in the preheated oven for about 1–1½ hours, or until they are a creamy colour and can be lifted easily from the baking paper without sticking. Turn off the oven, leave the door ajar and leave the meringues until cold.

Serve them sandwiched with whipped cream and dusted with icing sugar, if liked.

To make Brown Sugar Meringues, follow the recipe above but instead of 175g (6oz) caster sugar use half light muscovado sugar and half caster sugar.

A favourite with all ages. Traditionally the inside of the meringue is soft and marshmallow-like and the outside is crisp. Don't worry if the pavlova cracks on the top – this is all part of its charm.

MANGO AND PASSION FRUIT PAVLOVA

SERVES 8

4 large egg whites
225g (8oz) caster sugar
2 level teaspoons cornflour
2 teaspoons white
    wine vinegar

For the filling
4 tablespoons lemon curd
2 mangoes, sliced into
    thin strips
4 passion fruit, halved
    and pulp and seeds
    scooped out
300ml (½ pint) pouring
    double cream, whipped

Preheat the oven to 160°C/Fan 140°C/Gas 3. Place a sheet of non-stick baking paper on a baking tray and mark a 23cm (9in) circle on it.

Place the egg whites in a large bowl and whisk until stiff and cloud-like. Add the sugar a teaspoonful at a time, whisking well after each addition, until all the sugar has been added.

Blend the cornflour and vinegar together and whisk into the meringue mixture.

Spread the meringue out to cover the circle on the baking paper, building up the sides so they are higher than the middle. Place in the oven but immediately reduce the temperature to 150°C/Fan 130°C/Gas 2. Bake for about 1 hour until firm to the touch and a pale beige colour.

Turn the oven off and allow the pavlova to cool while still in the oven. If you keep the oven door closed you will encourage a more marshmallowy meringue.

Remove the cold pavlova from the baking tray and baking paper and slide on to a serving plate.

Stir the lemon curd and half the fruit through the whipped cream and spread into the centre of the meringue. Top with the remaining mango slices and passion fruit, then chill in the fridge for 1 hour before serving.

This is rather an unusual idea, and it makes a generous roulade, an excellent size for a party. It also freezes extremely well. Simply wrap it in foil to freeze, then allow about 8 hours to thaw before serving.

RASPBERRY MERINGUE ROULADE

SERVES 8-10

5 large egg whites
275g (10oz) caster sugar
55g (2oz) flaked almonds

For the filling
300ml (½ pint) pouring
    double cream
350g (12oz) raspberries

Preheat the oven to 220°C/Fan 200°C/Gas 7. Line a 33 x 23cm (13 x 9in) Swiss roll tin with non-stick baking paper.

Place the egg whites in a large bowl and whisk until very stiff. Gradually add the sugar, a teaspoonful at a time, whisking well between each addition. Whisk until very, very stiff and all the sugar has been added.

Spread the meringue mixture into the prepared tin and sprinkle with the almonds. Place the tin fairly near the top of the preheated oven and bake for about 8 minutes until pale golden. Reduce the oven temperature to 160°C/Fan 140°C/Gas 3 and bake for a further 15 minutes until firm to the touch.

Remove the meringue from the oven and turn it almond side down on to a sheet of non-stick baking paper. Remove the paper from the base of the cooked meringue and allow to cool for about 10 minutes.

Meanwhile, whisk the cream until it stands in stiff peaks, and gently mix in the raspberries. Spread the cream and raspberries evenly over the meringue.

Start to roll the meringue from a long end fairly tightly until rolled up like a roulade. Wrap in baking paper and chill before serving.

TIP
Leftover egg yolks should be stored in the fridge in a small container. Pour a tablespoon of cold water over the top, and then cover with clingfilm. Use within a week.

This has become a classic, the raspberries and hazelnuts being a particularly good combination. Fill the meringue about 3 hours before serving; it will then cut into portions without splintering.

HAZELNUT MERINGUE CAKE

SERVES 6-8

125g (4½oz) hazelnuts
4 large egg whites
250g (9oz) caster sugar
a few drops of vanilla extract
½ teaspoon white
    wine vinegar

For the filling
300ml (½ pint) pouring
    double cream
225g (8oz) raspberries
icing sugar, for dusting

TIPS

If you don't have sandwich tins, you can cook the mixture on two flat baking trays, spread out into two circles. It won't look quite so neat, but it tastes the same! Walnuts can be used in place of the hazelnuts in the meringue. Choose a fruit to complement the walnuts, such as strawberries or ripe peaches in season

Preheat the oven to 190°C/Fan 170°C/Gas 5. Lightly brush two 20cm (8in) sandwich tins with oil then line the base of each tin with non-stick baking paper.

Place the hazelnuts on a baking tray and roast in the oven for about 10 minutes, then tip on to a clean tea towel and rub well together to remove the skins. (Some stubborn ones may need to go back into the oven but don't worry about getting every last bit of skin off, it's not necessary.) Grind the nuts in a food processor.

Place the egg whites in a large bowl and whisk until stiff. Add the sugar, a teaspoonful at a time, whisking well between each addition. Whisk until the mixture is very stiff, stands in peaks, and all the sugar has been added.

Whisk in the vanilla extract and wine vinegar then fold in the prepared nuts. Divide the mixture between the prepared tins and smooth the top with a palette knife.

Bake in the preheated oven for about 30–40 minutes, but no longer. The top of the meringue will be crisp and the inside soft and marshmallow-like. Turn out of the tins and leave to cool on a wire rack.

Whip the cream until thick and use about two-thirds to sandwich the meringues together along with two-thirds of the raspberries. Spread the remaining cream over the top, scatter on the remaining raspberries and dust with icing sugar.

Ordinary meringue could be used for these nests, but they won't be quite so firm, nor will they store so well. Meringue cuite is traditional because it holds its shape so well and is drier. Vary the fruit in these nests depending on the season.

SUMMER FRUIT MERINGUE NESTS

MAKES 6 NESTS

For the meringue cuite
4 large egg whites
225g (8oz) icing sugar
a few drops of vanilla
    extract (optional)

For the filling
115g (4oz) strawberries,
    halved if large
115g (4oz) raspberries
115g (4oz) blueberries
about 2 tablespoons
    redcurrant jelly

TIP

To fill a piping bag, stand the bag and nozzle point down in a jug and then fold the top edges of the bag over the top of the jug. That way it is much easier to spoon the meringue (or cream or icing) into the bag without getting it all over yourself!

Preheat the oven to 140°C/Fan 120°C/Gas 1. Line a baking tray with non-stick baking paper.

Place the egg whites in a large bowl and whisk until foaming. Sift the icing sugar through a fine sieve into the egg whites. Set the bowl over a pan of gently simmering water and whisk the whites and sugar together until very thick and holding its shape. Add the vanilla extract, if using, and whisk again to mix. Be careful not to let the bowl get too hot or the meringue mixture will crust around the edges.

Spoon the mixture into a piping bag fitted with a large star nozzle. Pipe into 6 basket shapes on the prepared baking tray, starting at the centre of each nest and lastly building up the sides.

Bake in the preheated oven for about 45 minutes until crisp and dry. Carefully lift off the baking tray and allow to cool on a wire rack.

Use the summer fruits to fill the cold 'nests'.

Warm the redcurrant jelly in a small pan and gently spoon over the fruit to glaze.

To make Baby Meringues, follow the ingredients and recipe above then pipe the mixture into 30 tiny shapes such as baskets, shells, spiral oblongs and fingers. Bake in the preheated oven until crisp and dry, then carefully lift off the baking trays on to a wire rack to cool.

To make different fillings, whip 300ml (½ pint) double cream with 1 tablespoon brandy or liqueur of your choice until it holds its shape. Divide between 2 bowls. Stir 30g (1oz) chopped nuts into one bowl, and leave the other cream plain. Sandwich the spiral oblongs and tiny shells together with the nutty cream mixture, pipe a little plain cream into the baskets and use it to sandwich the fingers together. Top the baskets and the sandwiched fingers with a small single piece of fruit, if you like. These are perfect for a party; the different shapes and fillings make a wonderful centrepiece for the dessert table.

Lemon meringue pie is a classic popular dessert, with a crisp pastry base and sharp lemon filling. The meringue topping adds sweetness and crunch.

LEMON MERINGUE PIE

SERVES 6-8

For the pastry
175g (6oz) plain flour,
    plus extra for dusting
2 tablespoons icing sugar
75g (3oz) butter, cubed
1 large egg, beaten

For the filling
30g (1oz) cornflour
finely grated zest and juice
    of 2 lemons
55g (2oz) caster sugar
3 large egg yolks

For the topping
3 large egg whites
175g (6oz) caster sugar

TIP

You can make a cheat's version of the lemon filling by pouring a 397g can of condensed milk into a bowl, then beating in 3 large egg yolks and the finely grated zest and strained juice of 3 lemons. The mixture will seem to thicken on standing, then loosen again as soon as it is stirred. This is caused by the combination of condensed milk and lemon juice and is nothing to worry about. Pour the mixture into the biscuit-lined dish.

You will need a 23cm (9in) deep fluted flan dish.

To make the pastry, measure the flour and icing sugar into a food processor. Add the butter and whiz until the mixture resembles fine breadcrumbs. Add the egg and mix to a firm dough.

Roll out the dough on a lightly floured work surface and use to line the base and sides of the dish. Prick the pastry all over with a fork and chill in the fridge for 30 minutes.

Preheat the oven to 200°C/Fan 180°C/Gas 6. Line the pastry with non-stick baking paper, add baking beans and bake blind in the preheated oven for about 15 minutes. Remove the beans and paper and return to the oven for another 5 minutes until the pastry is lightly golden. Leave to cool.

Reduce the oven temperature to 150°C/Fan 130°C/Gas 1.

Measure the cornflour and 200ml water into a pan and whisk to combine. Add the lemon zest and juice and place the pan over a medium heat. Whisk continuously until the mixture has boiled and thickened. Remove from the heat, add the caster sugar and yolks and whisk again. Pour into the pastry case.

To make the topping, place the egg whites in a large bowl and whisk until stiff. Gradually add the sugar, a teaspoonful at a time, whisking well between each addition, until shiny and glossy. Spoon into a piping bag and pipe blobs over the surface in a neat pattern or use two dessert spoons. Bake in the preheated oven for about 35–40 minutes until pale golden on top and firm to touch. Leave to cool for about 15 minutes before removing from the tin.

Serve slightly warm with cream.

A vacherin meringue, which is rather grand, is piped in a spiral pattern.

GINGER AND PEAR VACHERIN

SERVES 6-8

4 large egg whites
225g (8oz) caster sugar

For the filling
450ml (¾ pint) pouring
    double cream
1 x 410g can pears in natural
    juice, drained and cut
    into long thin strips
6 bulbs stem ginger,
    finely chopped
55g (2oz) dark
    chocolate, melted
icing sugar, for dusting

Preheat the oven to 150°C/Fan 130°C/Gas 2. Line three baking trays with non-stick baking paper and mark each with a 20cm (8in) circle.

Place the egg whites in a large bowl and whisk until stiff. Add the sugar, a teaspoonful at a time, whisking well between each addition, until the mixture is very stiff, stands in peaks, and all the sugar has been added.

Spoon the meringue mixture into a large piping bag fitted with a 1cm (½in) plain nozzle, and pipe the meringue to fill the circles on the baking paper; pipe in circles in a spiral pattern, starting at the centre.

Bake in the preheated oven for about 1–1¼ hours, or until the meringues are crisp and dry and lightly coloured. Allow to cool in the oven and then peel off the baking paper.

Place the cream in a large bowl and lightly whip. Spoon a third into a small bowl (this is for the top layer). Spread half of the remaining cream over one round. Top with half of the pears and ginger. Place the second round on top and spread with the remaining cream. Top with the remaining pears and ginger. Place the final round on top and gently press down. Spread the reserved cream on top and swirl.

Drizzle with the melted chocolate and sprinkle with icing sugar to serve.

TIP
You can make the meringue circles the day before, but don't keep the filled cake for too long.

This is impressive to serve but surprisingly easy to make.

BAKED ALASKA WITH
SERVES 6-8 **ITALIAN MERINGUE**

For the sponge base
2 large eggs
75g (3oz) caster sugar
55g (2oz) self-raising flour

For the filling
1 tablespoon sherry
   (optional)
225g (8oz) strawberries
1 litre (1¾ pints) strawberry
   ice cream

For the Italian meringue
225g (8oz) caster sugar
4 large egg whites
55g (2oz) flaked almonds,
   for sprinkling
icing sugar, to serve
   (optional)

Preheat the oven to 190°C/Fan 170°C/Gas 5. Lightly grease a 23cm (9in) sandwich tin and line the base with non-stick baking paper.

To make the sponge, measure the eggs and sugar into a large bowl and beat with an electric whisk until the mixture is pale and thick enough to just leave a trail when the whisk is lifted. Sift the flour over the surface and gently fold in with a metal spoon. Turn into the prepared tin and tilt the tin to allow the mixture to spread evenly to the sides. Bake in the preheated oven for about 20–25 minutes, until springy to the touch and beginning to shrink from the sides of the tin. Turn out and leave to cool on a wire rack.

Place the cold sponge on an ovenproof serving dish, sprinkle with the sherry, if using, then scatter with the strawberries, leaving a small gap around the edge. Slice the ice cream and arrange it in a dome shape over the strawberries. Place in the freezer.

Preheat the oven to 230°C/Fan 210°C/Gas 8.

To make the Italian meringue, measure the sugar into a stainless steel saucepan. Add 6 tablespoons of water and stir over a low heat until the granules have dissolved. Increase the heat and boil until the syrup reaches 120°C on a sugar thermometer. Remove from the heat and set aside. Place the egg whites in a free-standing mixer and whisk at full speed until stiff. Slowly pour in the syrup, whisking all the time, until thick and glossy.

Take the cake from the freezer and pile the meringue over the top and sides, making sure that it is all covered. Sprinkle over the almonds and bake in the preheated oven for 3–4 minutes, or until well browned. Dust with icing sugar, if using, and serve immediately.

Soufflés like this are not difficult to make, but need a bit of care with the timing.

HOT CHOCOLATE SOUFFLÉS

SERVES 4

115g (4oz) dark chocolate,
  broken into pieces
300ml (½ pint) milk
40g (1½oz) butter
40g (1½oz) plain flour
¼ teaspoon vanilla extract
4 large eggs, separated
55g (2oz) caster sugar
sifted icing sugar, for dusting

TIP

If you are serving a soufflé
for a supper party, make
the sauce base ahead of
time, including the addition
of the yolks and flavouring.
Fold in the whisked egg
whites 40 minutes
before baking.

To make Orange Soufflés,
omit the chocolate and
water and add the finely
grated zest of 2 small
oranges and the juice of
½ orange to the mixture.
Also omit the vanilla extract
and increase the caster
sugar to 75g (3oz).

To make Coffee Soufflés,
omit the chocolate and
water and add 2 tablespoons
strong coffee to the milk;
omit the vanilla extract.

Preheat the oven to 190°C/Fan 170°C/Gas 5 and place a baking tray inside to heat. Grease four 225ml (8fl oz) individual soufflé dishes or a 1.2 litre (2 pint) soufflé dish.

Place the chocolate in a pan with 2 tablespoons water and 2 tablespoons of the milk. Stir over a low heat until the chocolate has melted.

Add the remaining milk and bring to the boil. Remove the pan from the heat.

Melt the butter in a small pan, stir in the flour and cook over a low heat for 2 minutes without browning, stirring continuously. Remove from the heat and stir in the hot chocolate milk. Return to the heat and bring to the boil, stirring until thickened. Add the vanilla extract and leave to cool.

Beat the egg yolks, one at a time, into the cooled chocolate sauce, then sprinkle in the sugar.

Place the egg whites in a large bowl and whisk until they are stiff but not dry. Stir one tablespoon into the mixture, then carefully fold in the remainder.

Pour into the individual soufflé dishes or large soufflé dish and run a teaspoon or your finger around the edge to help it rise and prevent it catching on the edge. Bake on the hot baking tray in the preheated oven for 10 minutes for the individual soufflés or about 40 minutes for the large soufflé.

Dust with icing sugar and serve at once with whipped cream.

This is one of my favourite lemon puddings. I have even baked it ahead of time and reheated it very satisfactorily, in a roasting tin of water for 30 minutes in a moderate oven. The top of the pudding is a spongy mousse while underneath is a sharp lemon sauce.

HOT LEMON SOUFFLÉ PUDDING

SERVES 4–6

75g (3oz) butter, softened
250g (9oz) caster sugar
3 large eggs, separated
75g (3oz) self-raising flour
finely grated zest and juice
    of 2 lemons
450ml (¾ pint) milk

Preheat the oven to 190°C/Fan 170°C/Gas 5. Grease a shallow 1.5 litre (2½ pint) ovenproof dish.

Measure the butter and caster sugar into a bowl. Add the egg yolks and flour, then beat until smooth. Slowly add the lemon zest, juice and milk. Do not worry if the mixture looks curdled at this stage – this is quite normal.

Place the egg whites in a large bowl and whisk until they form soft peaks. Carefully fold the whites into the lemon mixture using a large metal spoon.

Pour the mixture into the prepared ovenproof dish and place in a traybake or roasting tin. Pour in enough boiling water to come halfway up the dish and bake in the preheated oven for about 30 minutes, or until pale golden brown on top.

TIP

Buy thin-skinned lemons that feel heavy for their size. To get maximum juice from them, it helps if the fruit is warm, or at least at room temperature. Before grating the zest, wash and dry the fruit well. Grate the zest on the small-holed side of the grater, and remember to scrape everything off the back of the grater after grating. A pastry brush is a useful tool to do this.

CHAPTER SEVENTEEN

CHEESECAKES

This cheesecake easily serves 8–10, as it is quite sweet and rich and so should be served in small portions. Expect the cheesecake to crack on cooling.

AMERICAN CHOCOLATE RIPPLE CHEESECAKE

SERVES 8-10

For the base
150g (5oz) plain chocolate
    digestive biscuits
55g (2oz) butter

For the cheesecake
150g (5oz) dark chocolate,
    broken into pieces
700g (1½lb) full-fat
    cream cheese
115g (4oz) caster sugar
½ teaspoon vanilla extract
1 large egg

Preheat the oven to 160°C/Fan 140°C/Gas 3. Lightly grease a 20cm (8in) loose-bottomed cake or springform tin.

To make the base, place the biscuits in a plastic bag and crush with a rolling pin. Melt the butter in a medium pan. Remove the pan from the heat and stir in the biscuit crumbs. Press into the prepared tin and leave to set.

To make the cheesecake filling, melt the chocolate gently in a bowl set over a pan of hot water, making sure the base of the bowl doesn't touch the water, stirring occasionally. Cool slightly.

Measure the cream cheese into a large bowl and beat until soft. Add the sugar and beat again until well mixed. Beat in the vanilla extract, then the egg.

Spoon half the cheese mixture on to the biscuit crust, separating the spoonfuls. Add the melted chocolate to the remaining cheese mixture and stir well to mix. Spoon this chocolate mixture in between the plain mixture. Swirl the top with a knife to give a marbled effect.

Bake in the preheated oven for about 1 hour or until the cheesecake becomes puffy around the edges but is still very soft in the centre. Turn off the oven but leave the cheesecake in the oven to cool. Chill well and then loosen the cheesecake from the sides of the tin using a small palette knife.

Serve well chilled.

A sophisticated cheesecake. If you like, you can add a little more brandy to the filling. If ginger is a favourite flavour, the quantity used can be increased as well.

CHOCOLATE, BRANDY AND GINGER CHEESECAKE

SERVES 8

For the base
115g (4oz) ginger biscuits
55g (2oz) butter
30g (1oz) demerara sugar

For the cheesecake
115g (4oz) dark chocolate,
    broken into pieces
3 sheets of platinum
    grade leaf gelatine
2 large eggs, separated
55g (2oz) caster sugar
115g (4oz) full-fat
    cream cheese
150ml (¼ pint) soured cream
4 tablespoons brandy

To decorate
150ml (¼ pint) pouring
    double cream,
    whipped (optional)
chocolate curls (page 402)
2 bulbs stem ginger,
    finely sliced

TIP
There are two sizes of
leaf gelatine available;
we use 11g sheets.

Lightly grease a 20cm (8in) loose-bottomed cake or springform tin.

To make the base, place the biscuits in a plastic bag and crush with a rolling pin. Melt the butter in a medium pan. Remove the pan from the heat and stir in the biscuit crumbs and sugar. Press into the prepared tin and leave to set.

Melt the chocolate gently in a bowl set over a pan of hot water, making sure the base of the bowl doesn't touch the water, stirring occasionally. Allow to cool slightly.

Place the gelatine leaves in a small bowl of cold water and leave to soak.

Beat together the egg yolks, sugar and cream cheese in a large bowl. Add the soured cream and cooled chocolate.

Place the egg whites in a large bowl and whisk until frothy. Fold into the cheese mixture.

Warm the brandy gently in a small pan. Squeeze any water from the gelatine, then add it to the brandy and stir to dissolve. Fold into the cheese mixture.

Pour on to the biscuit base and chill in the fridge to set.

When set, carefully remove the cheesecake from the tin before decorating with whipped cream, if you like, chocolate curls and slices of stem ginger.

An excellent, quick cheesecake that's always popular with my family.
You can vary the fruit topping, depending on what is in season.

EASY LEMON CHEESECAKE

SERVES 8

For the base
175g (6oz) digestive biscuits
75g (3oz) butter
30g (1oz) demerara sugar

For the cheesecake
1 × 397g can full-fat
    condensed milk
250g (9oz) full-fat
    mascarpone cheese
finely grated zest and juice
    of 3 large lemons

For the topping
150ml (¼ pint) pouring
    double cream, whipped
strawberries

You will need a 23cm (9in) loose-bottomed tart tin.

Put the biscuits into a plastic bag and crush with a rolling pin. Melt the butter in a medium pan. Remove the pan from the heat and stir in the biscuit crumbs and sugar. Press evenly over the base and sides of the tin, then leave to set.

To make the cheesecake filling, mix together the condensed milk, mascarpone and lemon zest. Add the lemon juice a little at a time, whisking until the mixture thickens.

Pour the mixture on to the biscuit base and leave to chill in the fridge for 3–4 hours or overnight.

Carefully remove the cheesecake from the tin before decorating with swirls of whipped cream and fresh strawberries.

This is a very quick and easy cheesecake to make. It's delicious to eat, too, as the yoghurt gives the filling a wonderfully fresh flavour.

QUICK CHILLED CHEESECAKE

SERVES 6-8

For the base
175g (6oz) digestive biscuits
75g (3oz) butter
40g (1½oz) demerara sugar

For the cheesecake
225g (8oz) full-fat
    cream cheese
30g (1oz) caster sugar
150ml (¼ pint) double cream
150ml (¼ pint) full-fat
    Greek yoghurt
juice of 1½ lemons

For the topping
175g (6oz) raspberries
    or other soft fruits
1–2 tablespoons
    redcurrant jelly

You will need a 20cm (8in) loose-bottomed cake tin.

Put the biscuits into a plastic bag and crush with a rolling pin. Melt the butter in a medium pan. Remove the pan from the heat and stir in the biscuit crumbs and sugar. Press over the base and sides of the tin, then leave to set.

Measure the cream cheese and sugar into a large bowl or food processor and mix well to blend thoroughly. Add the cream and yoghurt and mix again. Gradually add the lemon juice, whisking all the time. Turn the mixture into the tin on top of the biscuit crust and chill in the fridge overnight to set.

Run a knife round the edge of the biscuit crust to loosen the cheesecake, then push up the base or remove the sides of the tin and slide the cheesecake on to a serving plate.

Arrange the fruit on top of the cheesecake. Heat the redcurrant jelly in a small saucepan until melted, then carefully brush over the fruit. Leave to set. Serve chilled.

Apricot and orange are a lovely flavour combination.This is best served chilled.

APRICOT AND ORANGE CHEESECAKE

SERVES 10

For the base
115g (4oz) digestive
   or oat biscuits
55g (2oz) butter

For the cheesecake
4 sheets of platinum
   grade leaf gelatine
175g (6oz) ready-to-eat
   dried apricots
200ml (7fl oz) freshly
   squeezed orange juice
3 tablespoons clear honey
finely grated zest of
   ½ orange
225g (8oz) full-fat
   cream cheese
150ml (¼ pint) full-fat
   soured cream
2 large eggs, separated
115g (4oz) caster sugar

For the topping
100ml (3½fl oz) pouring
   double cream, whipped
5 small amaretti
   biscuits, crushed
finely grated zest
   of 1 orange

You will need a 23cm (9in) fluted loose-bottomed tin.

—

Place the biscuits in a plastic bag and crush with a rolling pin. Melt the butter in a medium pan. Remove the pan from the heat and stir in the biscuit crumbs. Press into the tin and leave to set.

—

Fill a small bowl with water and add the sheets of gelatine. Leave to soak for 5 minutes.

—

Meanwhile, place the apricots in a pan with the orange juice, bring to the boil and simmer gently for about 10 minutes, or until tender. Turn the apricots and any juice that hasn't been absorbed into a food processor and blend until smooth. Add the honey, orange zest, cream cheese, soured cream and egg yolks and process again.

—

Drain the gelatine and squeeze out any excess water. Return to the bowl and set over a pan of gently simmering water to dissolve. Mix into the apricot mixture.

—

Place the egg whites in a large bowl and whisk until frothy. Add the caster sugar a little at a time, whisking well after each addition. Whisk until all the sugar has been added and the mixture is very stiff.

—

Turn the apricot mixture into the meringue and fold well together. Pour the mixture onto the biscuit crust and chill in the fridge to set.

—

Loosen the edges of the tin and push up the base. Slip the cheesecake on to a serving plate. Mark the cheesecake into 10 wedges, then decorate the top with the whipped cream, amaretti crumbs and orange zest.

A traditional cooked cheesecake. This recipe makes a good large cake, excellent for a party. The centre dips a little on cooling – perfect to hold the fruit!

CONTINENTAL CHEESECAKE

SERVES 12

For the base
175g (6oz) digestive biscuits
75g (3oz) butter
55g (2oz) demerara sugar

For the cheesecake
65g (2½oz) butter, softened
225g (8oz) caster sugar
550g (1¼lb) full-fat curd
    cheese or ricotta
40g (1½oz) plain flour
finely grated zest and
    juice of 2 lemons
4 large eggs, separated
200ml (7fl oz) pouring
    double cream,
    lightly whipped

For the topping
450g (1lb) mixed summer
    fruits (redcurrants,
    blackcurrants,
    blackberries, raspberries
    and strawberries)
caster sugar, to taste
1 level teaspoon arrowroot
150ml (¼ pint) pouring
    double cream, whipped

TIP
Use frozen mixed
summer fruits, if fresh
are unavailable. You
don't have to use all
the fruits suggested
for the topping – choose
your own combinations.

Preheat the oven to 160°C/Fan 140°C/Gas 3. Lightly grease a 25cm (10in) loose-bottomed cake or springform tin and line the base and sides with non-stick baking paper.

Put the biscuits into a plastic bag and crush with a rolling pin. Melt the butter in a medium pan. Remove the pan from the heat and stir in the biscuit crumbs and sugar. Press into the prepared tin and leave to set.

To make the cheesecake filling, measure the butter, sugar, curd cheese or ricotta, flour, lemon zest and juice and egg yolks into a large bowl. Beat until smooth. Fold in the lightly whipped cream.

Place the egg whites in a large bowl and whisk until stiff. Fold the egg whites into the mixture. Pour on to the biscuit crust and bake in the preheated oven for about 1½ hours or until set. Turn off the oven and leave the cheesecake in the oven for a further 1 hour to cool.

Run a knife around the edge of the tin to loosen the cheesecake and push the base up. Remove the baking paper.

To make the topping, cook the redcurrants, blackcurrants and blackberries, if using, in 2 tablespoons of water in a pan and sweeten to taste. When the fruit has softened and released its juices, remove from the heat.

Blend the arrowroot with 2 tablespoons of cold water and add the cooked fruit and liquid from the pan. Return the mixture to the pan, allow to thicken, then leave to cool. Stir the raspberries and strawberries, if using, into the other fruits, then pile on top of the cheesecake, levelling out evenly. Decorate the edge of the cheesecake with piped or spooned whipped cream.

This is a speciality of Florida, where limes grow on the low coral islands – the Keys. My adaptation of the original recipe is very quick to make and delicious!

KEY LIME PIE

SERVES 8

For the base
150g (5oz) ginger biscuits
65g (2½oz) butter
30g (1oz) demerara sugar

For the filling
finely grated zest of
  1 large lime and juice
  of 4 large limes
1 × 397g can full-fat
  condensed milk
450ml (¾ pint)
  double cream

You will need a 20cm (8in) loose-bottomed sandwich tin.

Place the biscuits in a plastic bag and crush with a rolling pin. Melt the butter in a medium pan. Remove the pan from the heat and stir in the biscuit crumbs and sugar. Press over the base and sides of the tin and leave to set.

Measure the lime juice, condensed milk and 300ml (½ pint) of the double cream into a mixing bowl and beat until well blended. Pour onto the prepared crumb crust and gently level the surface. Chill in the fridge for several hours, until set.

Remove the cheesecake from the tin.

Place the remaining cream in a large bowl and whisk until it forms soft peaks. Spread the cream over the pie, then finish with a scattering of grated lime zest. Serve well chilled.

CAKE
DECORATIONS

ALMOND PASTE

You can buy very good ready-made almond paste, but if you do like to make your own, here is the basic recipe to make 675g (1½lb).

225g (8oz) ground almonds
225g (8oz) caster sugar
225g (8oz) icing sugar, sifted
4 large egg yolks or 2 whole large eggs
about 6 drops of almond extract

Mix the ground almonds and sugars together in a large bowl. Add the yolks or whole eggs and almond extract and knead together to form a stiff paste. Do not over-knead as this will make the paste oily. Wrap in non-stick baking paper or a beeswax wrap and store in the fridge for an hour or up to 3 days.

To cover a cake with almond paste

There are two methods to cover a cake with almond paste; which to employ really depends on the type of icing you are going to use. Fondant or ready-to-roll icing is best put over almond paste with rounded edges, using the first method. For royal icing, it is usually better to use the second method as it gives sharper corners to the cake. For both methods, start by standing the cake on a cake board that is 5cm (2in) larger than the size of the cake.

METHOD 1

Lightly dust a work surface with sifted icing sugar, then roll out the almond paste to about 5cm (2in) larger than the top of the cake. Brush the cake all over with warmed apricot jam that has been pushed through a sieve.

—

Carefully lift the almond paste over the cake with the help of rolling pin. Gently level and smooth the top of the paste with the rolling pin, then ease the almond paste down the sides of the cake, smoothing it at the same time.

—

Neatly trim excess almond paste off at the base. Use the excess for making holly leaves and berries; keep it wrapped in clingfilm if not shaping immediately.

Lightly dust a work surface with sifted icing sugar, then roll out one-third of the almond paste to a circle slightly larger than the top of the cake. Using your cake tin base as a guide, cut the almond paste to the exact size.

—

Brush the cake all over with warmed apricot jam that has been pushed through a sieve. Lift the almond paste on to the cake and smooth over gently with a rolling pin. Neaten the edges.

—

Cut a piece of string the height of the cake including the layer of almond paste, and another to fit around the cake. Roll out the remaining almond paste and, using the string as a guide, cut the almond paste to size.

—

Brush a little more jam along the top edge of the strip as a seal, then roll up the strip loosely, place one end against the side of the cake and unroll to cover the sides of the cake completely. Use a small palette knife to smooth over the sides and the joins in the paste.

—

The table on page 400 shows you the quantities of almond paste needed to cover the tops and sides of various sizes of cakes.

ROYAL ICING

You can buy 'instant' royal icing. However, if you do like to make your own, the recipe below makes enough to decorate a 20–23cm (8–9in) round cake.

2 large egg whites
500g (1lb 2oz) icing sugar, sifted
about 4 teaspoons fresh lemon juice

Place the egg whites in a large mixing bowl and whisk lightly with a fork until bubbles begin to form on the surface.

—

Add about half the icing sugar and the lemon juice, and beat well with a wooden spoon for about 10 minutes until brilliant white.

—

Gradually stir in the remaining icing sugar until the correct consistency for piping.

—

Once made, keep the icing covered with a damp cloth to prevent it drying out and use as soon as possible.

HOMEMADE FONDANT ICING

There are some excellent makes of fondant or ready-made icing available. However, if you prefer to make your own, here is the recipe to make 550g (1¼lb).

500g (1lb 2oz) icing sugar
1 generous tablespoon liquid glucose
1 large egg white

Sift the icing sugar into a large mixing bowl, make a well in the centre and add the liquid glucose and egg white.

—

Knead together until the mixture forms a soft ball. Turn out on to a work surface lightly dusted with icing sugar, and knead for about 10 minutes until smooth and brilliant white.

—

Add some sifted icing sugar if the mixture is a bit on the sticky side. Wrap in clingfilm and store in the fridge until required.

To cover a cake with fondant icing
Brush the almond paste with a little sherry, rum or kirsch (this has a sterilising effect and also helps the icing to stick).

—

Roll out the icing on a work surface lightly dusted with icing sugar, to about 5cm (2in) larger than the top of the cake.

—

Lift the icing on to the cake, using a rolling pin for support. Smooth out evenly over the top of the cake with your hands, easing the icing down the sides of the cake.

—

Trim any excess icing from the base of the cake, then finish smoothing with a plastic cake smoother, or carefully with your hands. Leave to dry out at room temperature for about 1 week before decorating.

The table below shows the quantities needed to cover both the sides and top of various sizes of cakes:

Size of tin	Almond Paste	Fondant Icing
15cm (6in) round tin 13cm (5in) square tin	350g (12oz)	350g (12oz)
18cm (7in) round tin 15cm (6in) square tin	450g (1lb)	450g (1lb)
20cm (8in) round tin 18cm (7in) square tin	675g (1½lb)	675g (1½lb)
23cm (9in) round tin 20cm (8in) square tin	750g (1¾lb)	750g (1¾lb)
25cm (10in) round tin 23cm (9in) square tin	900g (2lb)	1kg (2¼lb)
28cm (11in) round tin 25cm (10in) square tin	1kg (2¼lb)	1.2kg (2¾lb)
30cm (12in) round tin 28cm (11in) square tin	1.1kg (2½lb)	1.5kg (3lb)
33cm (13in) round tin 30cm (12in) square tin	1.5kg (3lb)	1.6kg (3½lb)

AMERICAN FROSTING

The 'instant' American Frosting works perfectly well, but if you have a sugar thermometer try this 'proper' version.

450g (1lb) caster sugar
2 large egg whites

Place the sugar in a large, heavy-based pan along with 135ml (4½floz) water and heat gently until the sugar has dissolved. Bring to the boil and boil to 115°C, as registered on a sugar thermometer.

—

Meanwhile, place the egg whites in a large deep bowl and whisk until stiff.

—

Allow the bubbles to settle, then slowly pour the hot syrup on to the egg whites, whisking continuously. When all the sugar has been added, continue whisking until the mixture stands in peaks and just starts to become matt around the edges.

—

Use to sandwich and top the Frosted Walnut Layer Cake (page 56). The icing sets rapidly, so work quickly using a palette knife. Leave to set in a cool place, but not in the fridge.

CRYSTALLISED FLOWERS

You may want to decorate a special cake like the Sponge Christening Cake (page 136) with crystallised flowers. They are very simple to prepare but make a lovely finishing touch.

edible flowers (violets, pansies, japonica, primroses, little roses and polyanthus)
a little beaten egg white
caster sugar, for dusting

Brush the edible flowers with a little beaten egg white.

—

Dust with caster sugar on both sides, then stand them on a wire cake rack in a warm place (over a radiator or in the airing cupboard, for example) and leave until they are crisp and dry, which will take a few hours.

CHOCOLATE DECORATIONS

There are many decorations or finishing touches that you can make with chocolate. They're fun to do and look most impressive.

PERFECT CHOCOLATE CURLS

Place a clean baking tray in the freezer for 15 minutes. Meanwhile, melt white, dark or milk chocolate in a bowl over a pan of simmering water. Pour the melted chocolate onto the back of the cold baking tray and spread out thinly. Leave to set, putting the baking tray back into the freezer for a few minutes if needed. You want it to be completely set but not so hard that it would snap when bent. Hold a sharp knife at a 45-degree angle to the chocolate and either pull towards you or away from you as the chocolate curls around itself. You can adjust the angle and the pressure to have tighter or looser curls. After a few attempts you'll get the hang of it.

CHOCOLATE SHAPES

These can easily be made by melting the chocolate as with chocolate curls, then cutting it into squares or triangles with a sharp knife or cutter. It helps to heat the knife or cutter first. Use a round plain or fluted cutter to stamp out circles.

CHOCOLATE LEAVES

Use a small paintbrush to spread melted chocolate evenly on to the underside of clean, dry leaves. Leave to set and then gently peel the leaf away from the chocolate, not the other way round.

HOW TO TEMPER CHOCOLATE

Tempering chocolate is the process of heating and cooling chocolate, then reheating it again, so that the fat crystals in the cocoa butter stabilise and become shiny and strong. Once tempered, the chocolate will keep its shininess and not become dull. It is perfect for coating cakes and individual chocolates.

Tempering has a reputation for being tricky to do but, in fact, it is achievable at home if you have a thermometer.

There are two main methods of tempering:
1) The traditional, classic method of pouring melted chocolate onto a marble slab and spreading it backwards and forwards until cooled to the desired temperature.
2) The seeding method involves melting two-thirds of the chocolate being used, then adding the remaining one-third of unmelted chocolate and stirring until cooled to the desired temperature.

TEMPERING TEMPERATURES

Whether you want to temper dark, milk or white chocolate, the method is exactly the same. However, the melting temperatures are different.

	Melting Temperature	Cooling Temperature	Reheating Temperature
Dark Chocolate	45–50°C 113–122°F	28–29°C 82–84°F	31–32°C 88–90°F
Milk Chocolate	40–45°C 104–113°F	27–28°C 80–82°F	30–31°C 86–88°F
White Chocolate	40°C 104°F	24–25°C 75–77°F	27–28°C 80–82°F

SEEDING METHOD

MAKES 475G (1LB 1OZ)
475g (1lb 1oz) dark, milk or white
    chocolate drops or in a bar

You will need
1 medium heatproof glass bowl
1 medium saucepan
1 sugar thermometer or digital thermometer
1 rubber spatula

Pour approximately 3cm (1¼in) water into a saucepan and bring to a simmer over a medium-low heat. Once simmering, reduce the heat to its lowest setting.

—

Chop the chocolate (if using a bar) very finely with a large serrated knife or grate the chocolate in a food processor.

—

Tip two-thirds of the chocolate into a heatproof bowl and place over the pan. Make sure the base of the bowl doesn't touch the water, otherwise the chocolate can overheat and burn (known as seizing).

—

Using a rubber spatula, stir the chocolate continuously until it reaches melting temperature (see temperature table). Be careful not to let it go any higher.

—

Carefully remove the bowl from the heat and add the remaining one-third of the chocolate in small amounts, stirring slowly and continuously, until you reach the correct cooling temperature (see temperature table).

—

When the chocolate has reached cooling temperature, place the bowl back over the pan of very gently simmering water and reheat, stirring continuously, until the chocolate reaches the reheating temperature (see temperature table).

—

Carefully remove the bowl from the heat and test for temper by dipping the end of a spoon in the chocolate. If the chocolate has been correctly tempered it will harden evenly and set glossy within 5 minutes.

TIPS TO AVOID FAILURE
If your chocolate tempering doesn't work, you can re-melt and start again from the beginning.

—

Use tempered chocolate immediately, as it only stays in temper for as long as it stays within the reheating temperature range.

—

Leave tempered chocolate to set in a cool place at room temperature. Don't set it in the fridge, as this can cause chocolate to bloom (a white sheen) and lose its shine.

—

Another way to test for temper is to spread a thin layer on a piece of non-stick baking paper, wait for 5 minutes, then try to peel the chocolate from the paper. If you can peel it, and it's not blotchy, it's tempered.

—

Always use an accurate thermometer and keep a close eye on the temperature.

—

Chocolate drops are easier to melt as they are smaller and of uniform size, plus there's no chopping involved.

INDEX

Page numbers in *italic* refer to the illustrations

THANK YOUS

About 33 years ago Lucy Young joined me to be my assistant. One of our first tasks was the TV series *Ultimate Cakes* for the BBC. At the time, we did a book to accompany the series and, about 15 years later, we added more cakes and updated the recipes to make the *Baking Bible*. Now we have modernised it again and added some new up-to-date bakes.

So, thank you Luce for being by my side and masterminding this book. And to Lucinda McCord, who tests the cakes here in our test kitchen – brilliant in every way.

To the lovely Isla Murray for creating all the cakes and bakes for the photographs, what a skill! And to Ant Duncan for the vibrant photos.

To Lizzy Gray for agreeing to give the book another boost and to the very best editor Jo Roberts Miller, who knows each recipe as well as we do!

To Nell Warner at BBC Books and to Emma and Alex at Smith & Gilmour.

Thank you, too, to our book agent Caroline Wood at Felicity Bryan Agency, we are lucky to have you looking after us.

And to my loyal readers – thank you. We hope you enjoy it.

Mary Berry

1

BBC Books, an imprint of Ebury Publishing
20 Vauxhall Bridge Road,
London SW1V 2SA

BBC Books is part of the Penguin Random House group of companies
whose addresses can be found at global.penguinrandomhouse.com

Copyright © Mary Berry 2023

Photography by Ant Duncan
Front cover and photograph on page 9 by Georgia Glynn Smith

Mary Berry has asserted her right to be identified as the author of this
Work in accordance with the Copyright, Designs and Patents Act 1988

First published by BBC Books in 2023

www.penguin.co.uk

A CIP catalogue record for this book is available from the British Library

ISBN 9781785947636

Project Editor and Copyeditor: Jo Roberts-Miller
Food Stylist: Isla Murray
Prop Stylist: Hannah Wilkinson
Design: Smith & Gilmour

Colour origination by Altaimage, London

Printed and bound in China by C&C Offset Printing Co., Ltd

Penguin Random House is committed to a sustainable future
for our business, our readers and our planet. This book is made
from Forest Stewardship Council® certified paper.